Peoples of
the Tundra

Peoples of the Tundra

Northern Siberians in the Post-Communist Transition

John P. Ziker

WAVELAND

PRESS, INC.

Long Grove, Illinois

For information about this book, contact:
    Waveland Press, Inc.
    4180 IL Route 83, Suite 101
    Long Grove, IL 60047-9580
    (847) 634-0081
    info@waveland.com
    www.waveland.com

Cover photo: John Ziker (right) with some of the Dolgan, Nganasan, and Russian inhabitants of Kresty Taimyrskii, at the confluence of the Piasina and Dudypta Rivers, Taimyr Autonomous Region, Krasnoyarskii Krai.

For my daughter, Lena

Contents

Acknowledgements

I am thankful to my many good friends in Ust Avam. This book is dedicated to them for a hopeful and bright future. *Üchügei bultanyy!* (Good hunting!) Special thanks go to Boris and Galina Elogir, Natasha and Zhenya Chuprin, Sveta and Dima Sotnikov, Ilya, Valodya, and Fyodor Bezrukikh, Seva Durakov, Maria, Alla, Boris, and Lyuba Molchanov, and the Manenkov family, who all offered both friendship and logistical support during my research trips. I also thank the Ust Avam Administration for their help and cooperation during my stays. I am grateful for the moral support and academic discussions I have had with my colleagues at the Northern Sector of the Institute of Ethnology and Anthropology (RAN) and Moscow State University, including Dmitri Funk, Viktor Karlov, Nina Meshtyb, and Natalia Novikova. My appreciation goes to the Ethnography Department at Moscow State University and the Institute of Philosophy (RAN), where I had academic affiliations during my field research. The Russian Association of Indigenous Peoples of the North, Siberia, and the Far East (RAIPON), along with the Association of Peoples of Taimyr, helped me immensely during the initial phases of my fieldwork, and for that I am also grateful. I have attended three of RAIPON's national congresses, the latest of which was in April of 2001. They are doing important work and deserve our support. The Agricultural Board of the Taimyr Autonomous Region, the Government Archive of the Taimyr Autonomous Region, and the Territorial Studies Museum in Dudinka were gracious hosts to my research and my work with their archives added to my analysis of change in the regional and community Taimyr economies. During my time in Dudinka, I also spent some time at the Taimyr Center for Folk-Creative Activities and the Boris Molchanov Memorial Museum, regional and city institutions that are continuing to serve the Taimyr's cultural sphere, despite tough budgetary times. I greatly appreciate the hospitality. Dmitri Bogoyavlinskii of the Center for Demography and Human Ecology in Moscow provided the raw data on causes of death in Ust Avam for the 1970–1985 period.

The Wenner-Gren Foundation for Anthropological Research (Richard Carley Hunt Fellowship) and the Kennan Institute of the Woodrow Wilson International Center for Scholars sponsored the preparation of this manuscript. The statements and views expressed herein are those of the author and are not necessarily those of the Woodrow Wilson Center or the Wenner-Gren Foundation. The field research was supported by a grant from the National Science Foundation's Arctic Social Science Program (OPP 9528936), a research fellowship from the International Research & Exchanges Board (IREX), funded by the National Endowment for the Humanities and the U.S. Department of State, Program for Scientific Research in Russia, Eurasia, and Eastern Europe (Title VIII), and two research grants from the American Council of Teachers of Russian (ACTR), funded by the U.S. Department of State, Program for Research and Training on Eastern Europe and the Independent States of the Former Soviet Union (Title VIII). The final editing of the text was conducted while I was a resident postdoctoral fellow at the Max Planck Institute for Social Anthropology, Halle, Germany (2001–2002). My thanks to Chris Hann and the members of the Siberia Project Group.

I thank Igor Krupnik, Peter Collings, Will Palmer, Kerrie Shannon, Blair Ruble, Kathleen Kuehnast, Heather Rice, and Karen Schmidt for commenting on various parts of the manuscript. My doctoral committee at the Department of Anthropology at the University of California, Santa Barbara included Donald Brown, Napoleon Chagnon (chair), David Cleveland, Donald Symons, and Phillip Walker. They were instrumental in my developing a research approach to changing economic systems and people's reaction to these changes. They provided valuable commentary on my dissertation and other publications, parts of which are included in this book. In addition, I greatly appreciate the constructive comments of an anonymous reviewer and Don Rosso at Waveland Press.

Chapter One

Peoples of the Tundra

Since 1991, indigenous peoples in the Arctic region of Siberia have been dealing with the collapse of the Soviet Union and the ensuing disintegration of state companies, which were the main source of employment in their villages. A similar transition has occurred across rural areas of the former Soviet Union and Eastern Europe, but the situation of the Dolgan and Nganasan, for example, is worsened by their remote location in the central Taimyr tundra. In the last half of the twentieth century, these native Siberians were incorporated into the Soviet economy as workers, but they are now practicing a way of life similar in many respects to other hunting and gathering societies in other parts of the world. Hunting, gathering, fishing, and trapping now provide basic needs for families and communities, where ten years ago native hunters made relatively high salaries by Soviet standards, and the stores in native villages were so well stocked that people from the city traveled to shop there. The Dolgan and Nganasan are responding to the post-Soviet transition according to familiar themes in human economic and social organization. How their institutions are being revived tells us something about human nature and the resiliency of tradition.

Many of us in the West know something of the incredible economic difficulties and hardships the people of Russia have gone through since 1991. Soldiers, pensioners, and miners have been paid miserly wages or not paid at all. A recent example in the U.S. news was that of a medical doctor who was paid a month's salary in the form of a truckload of manure. While the majority of Russian citizens are no better off, to put it

1

lightly, in terms of wealth than they were ten years ago, economic, political, and religious freedoms have expanded significantly. In fact, some people in Russia complain that there is too much freedom, particularly in reference to some recently introduced Western social values and rapid accumulation of wealth by the few. Multinational companies have made their mark on the Russian marketplace, especially in the major cities. Foreign religions are spreading in Russia, and state television is interspersed with Western advertisements, along with shows such as *The Simpsons* and *Star Trek*. A job that entails a good day's labor or a state pension is no longer as well-respected and cannot pay the bills, so many have taken to selling things at the pervasive flea markets, bus stops, and kiosks of Russia's cities and towns. But here I tell the story of a people who are on the edge of contemporary Russian society, both economically and geographically. Travel is limited and expensive, so markets are virtually closed to the Dolgan and Nganasan. Thus, they practice what they know best: hunting, fishing, and sharing the catch.

While to some extent the Dolgan and Nganasan are victims of a process they cannot control, they are not leaving their fate to others. The kindness these people show one another, as well as visitors, despite a miserable situation is the surest source of hope for their community's future. There have been pitfalls, and I explore these in some detail: economic depression, substance abuse, and outsiders' speculation of alcohol have adversely affected mortality rates. Their experience, both good and bad, is important for others who might someday end up in an analogous predicament and for those who study societies entering the global market after decades of socialism. How the Dolgan and Nganasan are making it through their particular post-Soviet transition exemplifies human adaptability and human ecology, relevant topics for students of anthropology. For all these reasons, it is important to tell their story. Here I provide a basic ethnography of a native Siberian community as it was in the mid-1990s, describing the most recent of a series of rapid social changes that have affected these people and their ancestors over the last few centuries.

Native People of Taimyr

Located in the central Siberian Arctic, the Taimyr Dolgano-Nenetskii Autonomous Region (*okrug*) is home to approximately 10,000 indigenous people belonging to five native groups, known in the ethnographic literature as the Dolgan, Enets, Evenk, Nenets, and Nganasan (Figures 1.1 and 1.2). The region is approximately twice the area of California (862,100 square km or 332,850 square miles), and the indigenous people live mostly in Taimyr's 17 communities dispersed across the tundra. The increasing re-

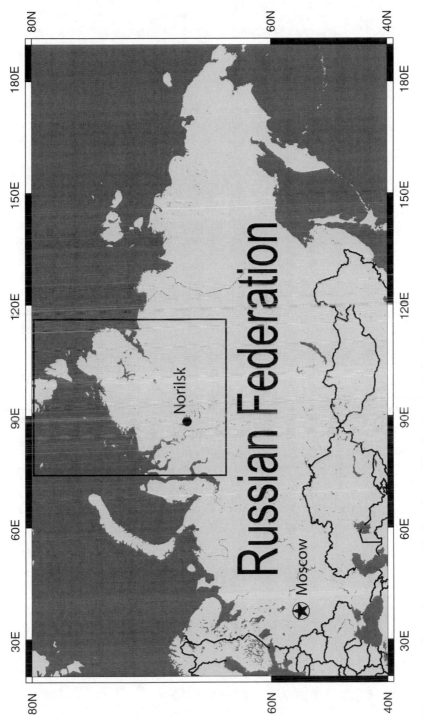

Figure 1.1 The study area and its location within the Russian Federation.

moteness of these communities in the 1990s and how the people are managing it is the focus for this book. My ethnographic research was concentrated in a remote community in the Taimyr Region called Ust Avam.

Two of Russia's native peoples (officially recognized by the Russian government as *malochislennie narody*, or "small-numbering peoples") are represented in Ust Avam: the Dolgan (*tiajono*) and the Nganasan (*nya*). In the 1960s, Soviet ethnographers and the Soviet government began to use the word *Dolgan*—the name of a patrilineal clan—to describe the native people of mixed Yakut, Evenk, and Russian origin living in the Taimyr Peninsula and northwest Yakutia. The term has gained acceptability in Western ethnography, as well as among members of the Dolgan population when they are speaking in Russian. The word *tiajono* is the indigenous word, or ethnonym, that the Dolgan in Ust Avam use to refer to their people. *Tiajono* literally means "people of the tundra" or "people of nature," from the Dolgan word *tia*, or tundra. A number of other terms in the Dolgan language, such as *mastagalar*, or "people of the forest," also are used. These terms

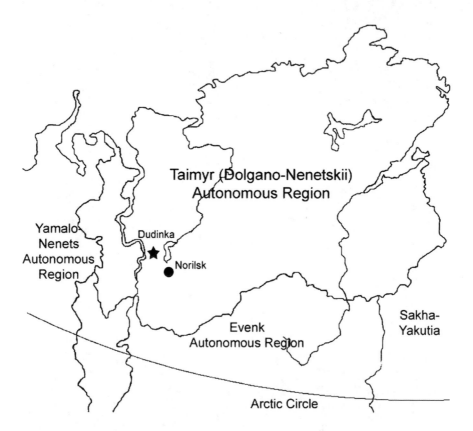

Figure 1.2 Political schematic of north-central Siberia. The Taimyr Autonomous Region and the Evenk Autonomous Region are part of Krasnoyarskii Krai.

represent smaller social groupings, or bands, that existed prior to Soviet modernization in the 1930s. The Dolgan language is similar to Sakha (Yakut), the northernmost branch of the Turkic language family, which spans Eurasia from Turkey to eastern Siberia. The Dolgan population numbers close to 6,000 people. Traditionally, the Dolgan were semi-nomadic reindeer herders, wild-reindeer hunters, fishermen, and trappers (Figure 1.3). This ethnic group has coalesced from local bands over the last two centuries due to migration of indigenous people and government reclassification of ethnicity.

Nganasan is one of six languages in the Samoyedic branch of the Uralic language family. Currently, the majority of the approximately 1,000 Nganasan live alongside the Dolgan in three permanent settlements in Taimyr. Like *Dolgan*, the word *Nganasan* also has a recent origin. In their native language, the Nganasan refer to their ethnic group as *nya*, or "people." The Nganasan traditionally were wild-reindeer hunters, fishermen, and trappers, and they also kept domestic reindeer for transportation (Figure 1.4). It is believed that the ancestors of today's Nganasan were the original inhabitants of the Taimyr Peninsula at the time of contact with Russians in the seventeenth century. After Russian contact was initiated, the Nganasan migrated farther north to avoid colonial representatives, effectively creating a depopulated area in the Kheta River basin and Putorana Mountains, into which the ancestors of the Dolgan moved. The

Figure 1.3 Dolgan hunter Stepan Katyginskii in the forest outside his home in Talnakh, a suburb north of Norilsk. This forest was the home of the Mastagalar.

Figure 1.4 Ekaterina Momde displaying her Nganasan winter parka at their remote fishing and hunting spot on the Dudypta River.

Nganasan are well known in Eurasian ethnography for their shamanist-animist traditions, as they were never converted to Russian Orthodoxy during the colonial period. Some aspects of shamanism still persist in Ust Avam, and these are critically important for identity and cooperation.

Ust Avam's small population is an assortment of ethnicities. While the details of Ust Avam's formation and ethnic composition are discussed later, in summary, the majority of the population descends from the Sakha, Evenk, Dolgan, and Nganasan nations, with a small minority of Russians and people from other former Soviet republics, such as Kyrgyzstan. Despite the mixed ethnic make-up of the community and the difficult economic situation, there was virtually no ethnic violence within the community during the years I studied there. That this is the case in Ust Avam at the same time when ethnic conflict has been a serious problem throughout the former Soviet Union and Yugoslavia presents an important question for students of human behavior.

The Taimyr Autonomous Region is an administrative sub-unit of Krasnoyarskii Krai. *Krai* literally means "edge" or "frontier," which this area was in the seventeenth-century Russian Empire, but in this case it may be translated as "territory." The Taimyr Region's total population is close to 55,000, the majority of whom are ethnically Russians and Ukrainians and live in the region's capital, Dudinka, located on the Yenisei River. Ninety miles to the east of Dudinka is Norilsk (population 169,000), the world's most northerly mining and metallurgical complex. Founded in 1935, Norilsk became a strategically important company town during the Stalin regime. Drawing on its large ore deposits, it currently produces approximately one-third of the world's nickel, along with other valuable metals such as cobalt, gold, silver, platinum, and palladium. Pollution from Norilsk's factories is a problem for the Taimyr Region and for the Arctic as a whole. According to Vladimir Melnichenko, chairman of the Taimyr Committee on Land Use and Environmental Protection, Norilsk Nickel released 24 million tons of waste in 1996, two million tons of which was sulfur dioxide (Melnichenko 1996).

Ust Avam is 400 kilometers northeast of Norilsk by river. Ust Avam's location, on the north side of the Putorana Plateau, has largely spared the community from point-source pollution from the nickel-smelting factories. Still, the fate of Ust Avam has been closely tied to Norilsk. Economic relationships between Ust Avam and Norilsk intensified in the early 1970s when the Avam tundra became the major source of wild-reindeer meat and fish for Norilsk's workers. After the fall of the USSR, Norilsk began to import almost all of its food from abroad. Moving into the global marketplace in the 1990s, Taimyr's food-supplying organizations decreased their dependence on the relatively expensive and complicated food-production system within the Taimyr Region itself. This institutional change has diminished the need for labor in Ust Avam. Analogous stories have developed in indigenous communities across the Russian North and Siberia (e.g., Grant 1995; Fondahl 1997, 1998; Gray 1998; Balzar 1999; Kerttula 2000).

I also conducted research in two other remote communities in the Taimyr Region: Khantaiskoe Ozero and Tukhard. These two communities also represent two native groups each: Evenk and Dolgan in Khantaiskoe Ozero, and Nenets and Enets in Tukhard. Located 200 kilometers to the south of Norilsk, the prevailing winds do carry pollution toward Khantaiskoe Ozero (Lake Khantaiskoe), a community named after the second-deepest lake in Siberia. The lake appears, at first glance, to be a pristine and isolated body of water. At the upper end, the Putorana Mountains rise directly from the shore. However, from the village on the lake's south shore, at times it is possible to smell the sulfur dioxide from Norilsk. Thousands of hectares of reindeer pasture on the north shore of the lake were closed in the 1970s because of airborne heavy-metal contamination. The closure put radical constraints on the reindeer-herding economy of the Khantaiskoe Ozero community, and many were forced to give up their traditional mode of life. In addition, the construction downstream from the lake of the Khantaiskii Hydroelectric Station and Reservoir, which provides electricity to Norilsk, has significantly changed the ecology of Lake Khantaiskoe. The fish species present in the lake are less desirable for sale than those present before the construction of the dam. Khantaiskoe Ozero is in a critical economic position, with few in the community still able to practice reindeer pastoralism and commercial fishing activities limited.

Tukhard is located on the Gydanskii tundra, 75 kilometers west of Dudinka and along the Messoyakha natural-gas pipeline, which supplies Dudinka and Norilsk. As a result of the distance to the Norilsk industrial zone, Tukhard is able to use virtually all of its domestic-reindeer pastures. Over three-quarters of the Tukhard community's households are nomadic pastoralists. Regular helicopter flights bringing workers who service the gas pipeline to the area mean that reindeer herders in Tukhard have much better contact with regional markets than those in either Ust Avam or Khantaiskoe Ozero. Better contact with markets has allowed Tukhard's Nenets and Enets families to convert surplus reindeer meat into cash on a small scale—reindeer herders make deals directly with the gas-pipeline workers. The entire state-owned reindeer herd in Tukhard was distributed to individual families in 1994. Some families entered a reindeer-herding association, called Numpaan, or "rainbow." The rest of the families stayed with the remnant of the state enterprise. When I visited in 1997, there was little difference between the two groups' abilities to market their produce. The mayor of Tukhard, summarizing the situation to me, said, "A radish is no sweeter than a turnip," meaning that neither group was making money.

Additional research was conducted in Taimyr's regional capital, Dudinka, where there is a vibrant native intelligentsia. I got to know some members of the native community in Dudinka and saw how they play a vital role for their relatives and friends in remote villages, for example, by providing a place to stay on occasional trips to the city or while in transit. During Soviet times, villagers regularly sent meat and fish to relatives in the city. This is more difficult now that transportation costs have increased so much, but villagers usually bring as much meat and fish as they can carry. Natives living in the city often yearn for their traditional foods. Dudinka is also home to the regional archives (Gosarkhiv TAO) and the Taimyr Territorial Studies Museum (TOKM). Both of these institutions provided me a place to work and valuable raw data that went into this book.

Hunting and Gathering after the USSR

Hunting and gathering was the dominant mode of production for 99 percent of human evolutionary history. Only relatively recently, in the last 10,000 years, have humans developed more intensive forms of production, such as gardening (horticulture), keeping domestic animals (pastoralism), and intensive agriculture, upon which industrial societies are dependent. In the nineteenth century, both the Dolgan and the Nganasan had mixed hunting, gathering, and pastoral economies. A portion of their products, especially furs, were traded with merchants and given to the czar as tribute. During the period of Soviet administration, from 1930 through 1991, the Dolgan's and Nganasan's domestic economy and traditional social structure were altered significantly, with a rapid transition to a large-scale wage-based economy focused on commercial hunting, fishing, and trapping. Correspondingly, these formerly nomadic people were settled into villages. The Nenets and Enets, on the other hand, were allowed to continue domestic reindeer breeding and maintained a migratory way of life while producing meat for the Soviet economy. All these peoples adapted well to these changes, and their standard of living, as well as educational and professional opportunities, improved for them in the last three decades of Soviet times. With the collapse of the Soviet Union, however, government-managed hunting and fishing enterprises, such as those in Ust Avam, Khantaiskoe Ozero, and Tukhard, have become incapacitated by the withdrawal of central budgetary support. The people there increasingly must rely on their own skills and local relationships in order to survive.

Since 1993, many working-age adults in Ust Avam and other native Siberian communities have become de facto unemployed—they are officially on the job rolls, but receive salaries irregularly or not at all. This status has allowed Ust Avam hunters, for example, to practice household subsistence foraging, occasionally turning in products to the remnants of the state enterprise in hopes of some pay. Allotments of fuel and equipment from the state steadily decreased in the 1990s, but a big, long-term advantage of staying on the job roll was to maintain eligibility for state pensions upon retirement. Ust Avam's official unemployment figures (table 1.1) do not look bad, but they describe a steadily worsening economic situation. Official unemployment figures reflect only those who were laid off or fired and have signed up for benefits. Of the 29 Ust Avam hunters I interviewed in 1997, none had received salaries in the previous year, and 10 had not made any cash at all from hunting. Eleven hunters did make some cash in 1996 through seasonal contract work or by selling to private traders. Their incomes ranged from 480,000 to 12 million rubles, approximately $80 to $2,000. One person received only groceries and supplies. Another person got a liter of 98 percent grain alcohol in exchange for fur pelts. A one-liter bottle cost close to $50 in 1997.

Year	Working-Age Adults	Registered Unemployed	Found Work that Year	Unemployment Rate
1993	375	11	1	0.03
1994	383	19	1	0.05
1995	372	17	0	0.05
1996	376	26	2	0.07

Table 1.1 Official unemployment figures for Ust Avam, 1993–1996. The unemployment rate was calculated as the number of registered unemployed minus the number that found work that year divided by the total number of working-age adults. The Ust Avam village council provided the raw data.

In remote settlements such as Ust Avam, the gradual elimination of capital inputs from the state has resulted in the steady degradation of combustion-powered ground transport and hunting equipment. This equipment cannot be replaced, since people do not have the money to purchase it anew, and the price of snowmobiles, for example, has increased dramatically relative to average salaries in the 1990s (Ziker 1998a: 210). Hunters who had one or two serviceable snowmobiles in the 1992–1994 period are now generally working without them. The degradation of mechanized transport on the local level has resulted in increased hunting on foot. Reindeer-herding activities among the Ust Avam Dolgan and Nganasan were closed down in the 1970s when mechanized transport was introduced to increase hunting efficiency. Whole collective farms and remote stations were closed throughout the Soviet period, and more will be said on this aspect of state administration in chapters to follow. Some Dolgan trappers in the Avam tundra traditionally used dog teams, although the dominant method of transport in the nineteenth and twentieth centuries was the reindeer-driven sleigh. The problem with dog teams is that surplus meat and fish needs to be acquired to feed them, whereas reindeer feed themselves with proper pasturing. These recent infrastructure changes have influenced the mode of production in Ust Avam, decreasing the territorial range within which Dolgan and Nganasan are hunting, fishing, and trapping compared with the Soviet and pre-Soviet periods, as well as altering methods of foraging.

Considering the degradation of equipment and its reduced availability, the costs of searching for prey in terms of time and human energy have increased. Instead of traveling hundreds of kilometers a day to pursue large game in patches where it is located, more hunters focus on resources closer at hand. As a result, a wider range of prey, including such species as Arctic hare and Arctic fox, is being pursued for food than in the Soviet period. Also, the post-Soviet hunting-and-gathering economy has developed in Ust Avam through an expansion of non-market distribution of food. Non-market distribution has been documented in a wide array of hunting-and-gathering societies, and the Dolgan and Nganasan are returning to this practice. No one in the community has been allowed to starve.

Ust Avam is not completely isolated, but nevertheless it is in a state of economic depression. Some people in the community, such as civil-service workers, contract laborers, and pensioners, still receive cash. However, their purchasing power has diminished by an order of magnitude since 1991, and most view their socioeconomic situation as continuing to worsen (Ziker 1998a: 213, Ziker and Shmetterling 1997: 84-85). The commodities produced by native hunters, such as Arctic-fox pelts, have lost considerable value since 1991 (Ziker 1998a: 211). To make matters worse, cash payments have been provided irregularly at best due to transportation delays and alleged managerial and administrative manipulation of accounts. The post-Soviet economy of the rural Taimyr stands in sharp contrast with that of Soviet planning. After years of daily micro-management of the lives of the Dolgan and the Nganasan, Ust Avam residents view the current Russian government policy as *"Zhite, kak khotite"* ("Live as you like") with the freedom to live or to die. They must hunt, fish, gather, and trap for themselves, and their expectations for economic improvements are low. Even so, many people in Ust Avam view their increased reliance upon the domestic mode of production as a temporary situation forced on them by unpredictable political and economic changes occurring in Russia. In the words of a Dolgan hunter, *"Bihigi eredebenebit,"* or, "We are surviving." In making it through this extended depression, the Dolgan and Nganasan are instituting their own traditional safety nets to help one another with food, equipment, and resource management. This process is interesting in light of our shared human history as hunter-gatherers, debates on sustainable resource use, and prospects for long-term human survival.

Connections to the Avam Tundra

Many people ask me questions such as, "Why did you pick far-northern Siberia to conduct your research?" Sometimes, there is a joke about willingly going to Siberia, the traditional province for Russian exile. I originally chose to travel to the Taimyr Region because its sparse, remote population centers looked, on the map, as if they would have given the native people a better opportunity to maintain their traditions through the Soviet era. To some extent this was true, but not in the way I originally thought. Despite the distance from Moscow, Soviet collectivization had had an impact on these people, influencing everything from technology and settlement patterns to social values.

My first trip to the Taimyr Autonomous Region in 1992 would have been impossible without the assistance of the Association of Native Peoples of Taimyr, at that time headed by Nikolai Nikitich Bolshakov. The association hosted my first visit to the region, and Mr. Bolshakov introduced me to indigenous professionals in Dudinka and Norilsk. His thoughts on the future status of the Taimyr's indigenous nations were optimistic. That first visit helped me develop the questions for my doctoral research and gave me a chance to make some good friends, whose story I present here.

In 1992, Mr. Bolshakov introduced me to Boris Nikolaevich Molchanov, the first Dolgan to be named a member of the Union of Artists of the USSR. Over a period of a few weeks, Boris Nikolaevich and I spent hours talking about a variety of topics, such as the situation of Taimyr's native people, what it was that I wanted to learn and study, and how that would figure into everyone's interests. Molchanov had studied at the Krasnoyarsk Art Institute, where he mastered traditional drawing and painting techniques. He started his career with unique representations of Taimyr's environment and native people. Later, he developed a way to illustrate on old reindeer-hide tent coverings, and with that technique he crafted scenes of reindeer-herding life, tundra spirits, and shamans. Boris Nikolaevich and his family led me to their native village, Khantaiskoe Ozero, in August 1992. This trip allowed me to see firsthand the problems facing these people and to talk with the head of the state enterprise in Khantaiskoe Ozero and with indigenous people actually living in a remote settlement. The whole family and I took a boat trip 180 kilometers to the eastern end of the lake, provided by the state enterprise, then stayed for a week at a fish camp with Boris Nikolaevich's sister and her family. It seemed this would be a promising region in which to work, and I was invited back.

In the winter of 1993–94, I went back to Russia and, upon invitation by Nikolai Bolshakov, attended the Second Congress of the Association of Small-Numbering Peoples of the North, Siberia, and the Far East, which took place in Moscow. Afterwards, I traveled to the Taimyr Region. Tragically, Boris Molchanov had passed away that summer, just two months after his fifty-fifth birthday, and I joined his family in their grief. Later, the Center for Folk Creative Activities (Taimyrskii Okruzhnoi Tsenter Narodnogo Tvorchestva), where Boris had his studio, dedicated part of its space to create the Boris Molchanov Memorial Museum, a must-see for anyone visiting Dudinka. Upon my return to Taimyr, Boris had planned to go with me to Ust Avam to visit his cousin, Boris Kononovich Elogir. Boris Molchanov had suggested Ust Avam for my extended ethnographic research, and I wanted to follow up on that suggestion. With the aid of Boris's widow, I received an invitation, and in January 1994 I made my first trip to Ust Avam (Figure 1.5). Boris Elogir, like his cousin, became my good friend. He and his family and relatives helped me with my research and taught me much of what I know about Dolgan culture.

Figure 1.5   The settlement Ust Avam, on the east bank of the Avam River.

Soon after my first arrival in Ust Avam, I went on a one-week trip into the bush to the Elogirs' hunting territory, Elgen. This trip was my first exposure to hunting and trapping in the Avam tundra, the chief concentration for my doctoral research. In looking at these activities over time, I found a way to analyze land use and economic changes as the transition to free-market policy enveloped the Taimyr Region. The immediate goal for that January hunting trip, however, was to check trap lines and prepare bait at Elgen, a hunting territory of more than 175,000 hectares (675 square miles). I traveled with Dima, the son-in-law of Boris Elogir, who was the brigadier at Elgen. The Elogirs constituted a brigade, assigned use rights to Elgen by the government hunting enterprise (*gospromkhoz*) Taimyrskii, centered in Ust Avam. The *gospromkhoz* was still accepting Arctic fox (*Alopex lagopus*) in the winter of 1993–94, and the hunters received compensation for the pelts. Checking the trap lines was part of the brigade's planned assignment, or *naryad*, an economic arrangement with the *gospromkhoz* still in effect from the 1970s and 1980s. In 1994, the hunters were using their allotment of enterprise-supplied gasoline and snowmobiles to fulfill the assignment. The Elgen hunters had opened traps on several trails earlier in the winter, and they had been fairly successful in trapping.

January is a very cold month in the Avam tundra, and the sun does not rise above the horizon until January 17. Twilight lasted for a few short hours when we drove to Elgen. It was during the twilight, around noon, that we took off from Ust Avam on a Russian snowmobile, a Buran, pulling a home-crafted wooden sleigh. I sat most of the way on the sleigh on top of our gear, cinched to the sleigh and covered with a caribou hide, which radiated some heat back to me. We traveled 28 kilometers through larch forest and across frozen lakes, stopping five times along the way to stretch and warm up a bit. I drove the snowmobile for about 15 minutes, after which my right thumb, which had held down the gas lever, went completely numb. With some disbelief about my condition, Dima took off his mitten and showed me the steam coming off his hand. I had never dealt with this kind of cold before. During my fieldwork in the Avam tundra, constantly fighting frostbite in the winter, I tried various arrangements of American, Russian, and native clothing. According to my experience, traditional indigenous moccasins, called *cherchakot* in Dolgan, and parkas and mittens, mastered by local women from animal skins, were superior to anything else. Eventually, I got myself outfitted, but this too was difficult because of my height and shoe size, and new patterns had to be made.

After we arrived at the cabin and unloaded our supplies, Dima showed me how to use a homemade steel-tipped ice pick, or *pishnia*, and I began to punch a hole through the ice on Lake Elgen while he stoked the stove in the cabin. After working for about an hour, I finally broke through the ice, and water welled up into the half-meter-diameter hole. After I carried a few buckets of water into the cabin, Dima showed me how to cover the ice hole with a caribou hide so that it would not freeze too deeply overnight. By

6:00 p.m., tea was ready, and the cabin was warm enough that we could take off our coats. It was minus 35 degrees Celsius (about minus 32 degrees Fahrenheit) outside that day. Eventually, I got better at using a *pishnia* and learned the subtleties of making holes in the ice for fishnets.

Each young adult member of the brigade had his trap lines. A trap line is a snowmobile trail with traps distributed along it. The trap-line trails at Elgen start some distance from the cabin and extend in different directions. They eventually arc back toward the cabin, so the hunter is almost home when he finishes checking traps. The Elgen trap lines were named (e.g., Ivan's trap line, Ivan's second trap line, etc.). We checked one trap line each day on this trip. Two of the trap lines were composed of 10 to 20 traditional deadfall traps, or *pasti*. These deadfalls were passed on from grandfather to grandson, and thus made up an important part of the kinship estate and could provide a deep historical basis for any formal land claims to be made with the regional government, because they were documented in the state-enterprise records. The other, newer trap lines had up to 200 steel leg-hold traps in various configurations—for example, traps positioned on wooden tripods, wooden platforms with pickets on three sides, and converted deadfalls with several leg-hold traps chained up— and these had been set up within the last 15 years.

Dima, who was 29, the same age I was, knew how to maintain both deadfalls and leg-hold traps. During the trip, he commented on, and I observed, the advantages and disadvantages of the different kinds of traps. For example, the steel leg-hold traps were easier to set up and open. The platform- and tripod-type setups were built at the cabin and installed on the trap lines later. When traps are checked, any snow that has drifted on to the trap must be cleaned off, the trap is reset or repositioned, and new bait is added. Ravens had cleaned out most of the traps. The steel traps require a bit of strength to open, and some skill to get the trigger in place, but nothing like the skill required by the deadfalls. The *pasti* have to be constructed *in situ* on the trap line. Heavy trees need to be cut down and dragged to the site. Deadfall traps have a complicated hand-carved trigger setup that takes hours to prepare. If the *pasti* fill up with drifting snow, there is a considerable amount of work required to clean them out and set them back to the ready position.

Despite the greater costs of the deadfalls (i.e., skill and time required for construction and greater time for maintenance), they appeared to be more efficient than the leg-hold traps. Foxes killed in leg-hold traps do not necessarily die instantly (Figure 1.6). In fact, they often live long enough to chew through their legs in order to free themselves from traps; this is one reason the European Community banned the sale of fur caught in this manner in 1991 (EEC 3254/91). During this one-week trip in January 1994, we found four chewed-through legs in leg-hold traps and only one whole fox. Of the three foxes trapped in *pasti*, all were in good condition, appearing to have died more or less instantly.

Figure 1.6 An Arctic fox caught in a leg-hold trap (on a platform with pickets) but still alive, demonstrating a limitation of the modern technology.

The contrast between traditional and modern traps is great, especially when viewed in terms of costs and benefits. The steel traps, like most other modern equipment, were supplied free of charge to hunters working for the *gospromkhoz*. The enterprise supplied large numbers of these traps to the brigades in an attempt to increase overall production. The replacement of traditional technology penetrated many aspects of life in Ust Avam during the 1970s and 1980s, from clothing to transportation to housing. With the breakup of the socialist economy, however, the native population and experts were divided on what to expect. The Russian government, under pressure from native political groups and ethnographers, favored protecting "traditional" methods and territory. President Boris Yeltsin issued a decree in April 1992 allowing native Siberians to claim ancestral hunting, fishing, and reindeer-herding lands (Yeltsin 1992). With this decree, a new form of property was created: family/clan or communal holdings. This topic came up during my first trip to Elgen.

> *January 12, 1994.* This evening Dima told me that someone came and told them that they could rent the land and establish a family/clan holding. All the capital, including the cabin, traps, and snowmobiles, would remain with them, free of charge. The problem would be with supplies like gas, diesel fuel, and bullets. They could try and conclude deals with military pilots that fly in these parts, exchanging meat and fish for supplies. But deals like that are uncertain.
>
> *Excerpt from the author's journal*

The question of establishing family/clan holdings is one that I would come upon over and over again during the initial phases of my research. What was a clan in this context, and did this have any relationship to the anthropological use of the term? Were family/clan holdings a form of private property or a type of reservation? In order to answer these questions, I planned to look at a number of factors, including work patterns, social and economic relationships, and the process of establishing the holdings. In this book, I describe these and other important variables associated with changes in land use and other local economic strategies used to deal with the collapse of the Soviet Union. Chapter 6 specifically covers family/clan holdings and the reasons for their formation in the Taimyr Region.

Methods

During my fieldwork in Ust Avam, which took place over twelve months from 1994 through 1997, I utilized a series of techniques to document changing ecological, economic, and political relationships. The information I collected was to be used to check the expectations of the models of social change I brought into the field. The Russian ethnographers A. A. Pika and V. V. Prokhorov (1994) proposed that the transition to capitalism in the Russian north should supplement traditional aspects of the northern native mixed economy with modern implements and information. The result should be a revitalization of northern indigenous ethnicity, which would represent a greater level of empowerment than has been observed historically in this part of the world and in other places where indigenous populations have been incorporated into the world system (Bodley 1990, Wallerstein 2000, Weatherford 1988, Wolf 1982). My question was whether contemporary family/clan holdings could be held up as examples of neotraditionalism. On the other hand, what were the implications for the vast majority of native households in the Taimyr Region that did not claim hunting territory as a family/clan holding?

Pertti Pelto (1987) proposed a different sort of model for north-Eurasian development based on the experience of the Finnish Saami. In Pelto's model, mechanized transport replaced animal- and human-driven transport among the Saami. As a result, people became dependent on non-local energy sources, industry, and politics, and this replacement led to socioeconomic differentiation of families into rich and poor. Replacement of animal-driven transport had already occurred among native Siberians under socialism. While the effect was greater in Ust Avam, the Tukhard reindeer herders were also allotted snowmobiles in the 1980s and early 1990s, and some activities, such as round-ups, were made easier. While socioeconomic differentiation was limited for native Siberians because the socialist system did not allow for outright accumulation of wealth, a kind of social differentiation did occur when many migrated to cities, where there were more opportunities for education and non-traditional careers. Under capitalism, family/clan holdings could represent entrepreneurial activity and increased socioeconomic differentiation, following Pelto's snowmobile-revolution model.

As it turned out, I needed a new model to describe changes occurring among the Taimyr Region's native population, so I came up with an alternative based on my preliminary work in Ust Avam. The key concept in my model is a decrease in dependency on the larger economy, the reverse of the snowmobile revolution. In Ust Avam, people have been forced to become less dependent on the Russian and global economies due to decreasing access to government and services. Reliance on the local subsistence economy and sharing networks has been the result, with reduced exchanges in the larger economy. Following discussions with Ust Avam hunters and their families, I call this alternative the survival-economy model.

In order to test the applicability of these models, my ethnographic research compared households that maintain use rights to state-enterprise hunting land with those that have taken a family/clan holding. The research employed ethnographic methods such as participant observation and informal, unstructured interviews to get an idea of the history of the population and its resource-use patterns. Participant observation, one of the hallmarks of cultural anthropology, allows the researcher to get a better understanding of life in another society by learning and participating in the activities of that society. As a technique for extended fieldwork, participant observation also helps build rapport with the community and establish perspective on social processes. For example, I participated in more than 100 hunting-and-gathering trips from 1994 through 1997 (Figure 1.7). These trips lasted from less than a day to several weeks, and I was able to document the time spent on various productive activities, the inputs (such as equipment, fuel, and labor), the outputs, and the location and distance traveled. These data allow an analysis of predictability and efficiency for a series of foraging tasks, as well as an analysis of what sector of the economy—cash or subsistence—the catch was intended for.

I also used informal, unstructured interviews, generally at the beginning of my research, in order to outline Ust Avam's history and land-tenure traditions. Later, I used socio-demographic methods and structured interviews to understand the social structure of the community and its population dynamics. There were 673 individuals (167 households) registered to live in Ust Avam and the surrounding tundra. The administration of Ust Avam defined a household as a group of individuals living together in one apartment. I conducted a complete community census in 1997, interviewing 79 adults, in a random sample of the households. The questions in these structured interviews were based on the prominent themes generated out of the unstructured interviews.

I approached the problem of social change in the Siberian Arctic from a social and ecological perspective. At the foundation of Dolgan and Nganasan society are human-to-land relationships. Renewable natural resources such as plants, fish, and animals have been, and still are, particularly important for the Dolgan and Nganasan. I was interested in production techniques and the use of renewable resources, and how and why these had changed since the breakup of the Soviet Union. Interviews with hunters who had worked for the *gospromkhoz* also focused on production information for the Soviet period, views on relationships to the land, and opinions about post-Soviet changes in local land tenure (Ziker 1998b, 2001).

Within the larger community of Ust Avam, my inquiry was focused on the changing importance of the market and sharing economies. Included in the structured interviews was a series of questions about economic change, family land-use history, sharing patterns, incomes, and consumption requirements. Regarding economic change, I asked participants in formal interviews their opinions on the relative importance of different types of economic conduct before and after the fall of the USSR. These economic patterns are widely discussed within sociocultural anthropology, and therefore, I hoped they would provide a good basis for comparison and evaluation of the models of social change: one-way transfers of resources (generalized reciprocity), food and labor exchange (balanced reciprocity), barter, and cash purchases, as well as antagonistic exchange, such as borrowing and never returning (negative reciprocity). The results strongly suggested that barter had increased, especially with outsiders, while cash purchases had decreased, and there were mixed opinions on the other economic forms (Ziker 1998a). Participants were also interviewed about income, expenses, and sources of capital equipment and spare parts prior to and after the breakup of the Soviet Union. This information was used to evaluate the alternative models of social and economic change discussed above.

Figure 1.7   Yegor Elogir and John Ziker at a hunting camp, May 1996.

On another level of analysis, I was interested in changing relationships between the local community and the larger economy and to what extent these changes were due to some kind of grass-roots action or top-down decision making. With regard to land use, interviews focused on reasons for establishing family/clan holdings versus reasons for remaining in the state enterprise. In addition to extended ethnographic research in Ust Avam, archival and statistical data made available by various offices of the Taimyr regional government, the archive of the Taimyr Region, and the Regional Studies Museum were also used to describe changes in land use and property (Ziker 1999, 1998a, 1998b).

Outline

Since the fall of communism in Russia, but especially since 1993, the value of goods produced by the Dolgan, Nganasan, and other native populations of the region has fallen drastically, while the costs of non-local goods and services have skyrocketed. Economic development, something that seemed within grasp at the end of the 1980s, has become a faint dream in Ust Avam. The opposite has actually occurred. The economy has fragmented, and people have been trying simply to survive. As a result, activities that once brought cash into local households are now generally limited to providing domestic subsistence.

The central economic activities in the Avam tundra, as locals lovingly refer to it, are wild-reindeer (caribou) hunting, fishing, and trapping. With a return to subsistence production, ecological variables are becoming more important, and these are discussed in chapter 2. A wide variety of terrestrial mammals, birds, and fish are utilized by the hunters/fishermen/trappers of the Avam tundra. Most of these provide food and other important materials. The ecology/economy link can be seen in production, distribution, and consumption patterns. Many in Ust Avam are also schoolteachers, artists, and workers. But cash income is somewhat irregular, depending on increasingly limited helicopter flights to the village, and cash is quite often shared among and between families. Chapter 2 begins by describing the geography and climate of the Avam tundra, as well as the species of animals and plants the Dolgan and Nganasan use. Then, hunting seasons and techniques, food sharing and preparation, and exchange patterns with the larger society are described. Distribution of bush food and products within the local community and between local hunters and the urban organizations reflects a dual economy. The subsistence, or informal, economy and the formal economy operate simultaneously, but with different purposes. Chapter 2 provides examples of both economies and, within these, considerations of profit and risk. Anthropologists have long debated the importance of profit and risk for elemental economic organization. Polanyi (1957) placed the market system and entrepreneurial motivations firmly in recent human history. Social institutions that mediate risk likely have a much deeper history and may be related to ecological factors, such as resource patchiness and environmental uncertainty (e.g., Cashdan 1989, Alkire 1965). This chapter looks at these factors in the local economy of the Avam community.

Ust Avam, like most rural native populations in Siberia, has gone through several periods of transition. Chapter 3 describes three major eras in the history of Taimyr's native populations in terms of collaboration with and resistance to colonization. The first period was the czarist subjugation of Taimyr and the subsequent development of government and merchant trade. This period connected the indigenous people to the global economy as producers of fine furs. The Russian government recognized the importance of the indigenous people with ostensible autonomy as subject nations under the Russian Empire. The Communist Revolution in 1917 began the next major phase of native Siberian history, which covers the institution of Soviet rule and the rise of government enterprises. The Dolgan and Nganasan resisted the transition to communism when the Soviet government established its authority in the region in 1930. There was a rebellion in 1932, during which both natives and Communist Party operatives were killed. When I first traveled to Taimyr in 1992, I heard the official version of the revolt—that it was caused by wealthy renegade reindeer herders. Throughout my research, I uncovered more details and was eventually lucky enough to meet and interview a firsthand observer. Before the intense development efforts by the Soviet government in the 1970s, families in both Nganasan and Dolgan groups depended on herds of domestic reindeer as they lived semi-nomadically on adjacent home territories stretching across the Taimyr Peninsula. From the 1930s through the 1960s, however, the initial Soviet cultural stations were "closed down" and indigenous families were forcibly moved to new and larger settlements. The third period is the post-Communist political and economic transformation, with increasing isolation of native villages and the collapse of government enterprises. The process of social change in the first two eras coincided with initial periods of conflict and subsequent development of institutions. In the most recent period of transition since the fall of communism, there has been little or no conflict and also virtually no development.

The settlement process had many trade-offs. For example, during the later part of the socialist period (1970s–1980s), education and employment opportunities for native people allowed some to become nationally recognized writers, artists, and politicians. The majority lived comfortably by Soviet standards. However, dormitory education, television, and other lifestyle changes resulted in the loss of native languages and other traditions (Karlov 1991, Sokolova 1990, Pika and Prokhorov 1988). By 1980, the state had completely phased out reindeer herding in Ust Avam and other villages in the central Taimyr Region. Once people settled into centralized settlements, commercial caribou hunting, fishing, and trapping became the main state-sponsored industry. The loss of reindeer herding and traditional land tenure in the 1970s affected native traditions, but the economy was growing at that time, so there was local support for these changes.

The communities of Tukhard and Khantaiskoe Ozero maintained reindeer herds throughout the Soviet period. While the situation in these settlements is similar to that in Ust Avam—inactivity in the labor force, alcohol abuse, and loss of traditional language—reindeer-herding families have been able to survive, living semi-independently from the industrial world. Nevertheless, without good salaries, many families are dropping out of reindeer herding, and the herds that remain have diminished by fifty percent since the early 1990s.

With the more recent breakdown of the Russian economy, the situation is considerably worse than in the 1970s, and this is described in chapter 4. Ust Avam requires outside support in the form of fuel, heavy equipment, and transportation. The Russian government can no longer afford to give this support in the manner in which the Soviet Union could, and the 1980s are now remembered as a golden age. Depression has become a factor, as has the concentrated availability of alcohol. Scarce salaries and pensions are often spent on alcohol, which is consumed among friends and relatives almost immediately. While alcohol provides a quick fix in that it helps people forget about their miserable economic situation, binge drinking creates additional problems, since it leaves people with little money for staples. Even worse, children are sometimes orphaned—alcohol-related deaths have become an increasing problem in Ust Avam since 1991 (chapter 4).

Despite major changes, people in Ust Avam are maintaining certain aspects of their traditional social organization and worldview in the context of the unpredictable Russian economy. Chapter 5 summarizes the current indigenous views of the cosmos, nature, and surrounding peoples and the author's experiences with shamans. Shamans have been important in local indigenous social life for as long as historical records have been kept on native Siberian peoples. Shamans provided social services such as healing, initiating, and identifying enemies. They adjudicated disputes, blessed new dwellings, and were involved in births, marriages, and deaths. Shamans entertained, passed on traditional stories, and kept people in spiritual balance. Today, the people of Ust Avam maintain some aspects of indigenous Dolgan and Nganasan shamanism in their post-Soviet cosmological philosophy and worldview, and these are particularly important for land tenure, interfamilial cooperation, and identity.

Chapter 6 is dedicated to the topic of land use in the Avam tundra. The chapter reviews two processes that inform property relations among the Dolgan and Nganasan. The first process focuses on recent large-scale political and economic change and how these changes affect land use and land claims. The second process is the internal, community-level social organization and dynamics that influence land tenure. Factors on both levels have led to the focus on subsistence production with little need for formal land claims. Numerous native and tribal peoples around the world are dealing with increasing involvement in the world economy. In contrast, since the fall of the USSR in 1991, communities like Ust Avam have become more isolated, and production of commodities has significantly diminished. The collapse of government support and the decline of outside goods and services make production of large surpluses of caribou meat, fish, and fur unprofitable. Similarly, private ownership of hunting territory would not confer financial benefits as one might expect. Rather, some land surrounding Ust Avam has reverted to communal use, and informal negotiations among Ust Avam hunters determine who goes where to hunt in the communal hunting territory. Since most people end up sharing some portion of what they catch, formal title to the land would provide little or no advantage. Dealing with the regional authorities poses a whole new set of problems. The result is that people relate to property in a variety of ways, and there are a number of social, political, and economic factors that go into decisions about how humans use the land and its resources.

Faced with globalization, northern native peoples will not disappear. Rather, they will adapt to new circumstances, while maintaining traditions to whatever extent they can. Compared to the current industrial technologies of nonrenewable-resource use, the Dolgan and Nganasan use these ecologically fragile lands and resources in a way that is viable for the long term. Their more ecologically sustainable approach is influenced by the local demographics and social structure, economic strategies oriented to reducing risk, and indigenous ecological understandings. Chapter 7 summarizes my conclusions on the importance of this work in terms of hunter-gatherer studies, globalization and social change, circumpolar political processes, and post-Soviet reform.

Chapter Two

Making a Living
Ecology and Economy

Anthropologists typically examine economies in terms of production, distribution, and consumption systems, or how goods are made, allocated, and used. In Ust Avam, maximization of hunting returns, encouraged during the Soviet period, is no longer a practical goal for hunters. Rather, minimizing risks associated with domestic subsistence has become the preeminent concern within families and community. The Dolgan and Nganasan have extensive knowledge of the tundra and its plants, animals, geography, and climate, and their experience helps them make a living in a place where survival is inextricably tied to the vagaries of the weather and the reproductive cycles and migrations of other organisms. Thus, hunting seasons and techniques in Ust Avam are important for understanding productive strategies, such as cooperative and individual foraging. Food distribution and consumption strategies have also developed in Ust Avam to serve as a social safety net that helps make up for variation in production and provides for those that can no longer provide for themselves.

Geography

Surrounding Ust Avam and extending east across the Taimyr lowlands is the most northerly forest in the world. The primary tree that grows there is Daur's larch, similar to North American tamarack, which obtains diameters of up to 40 centimeters and heights of up to 10 meters. In Dolgan, the forest is called the *Ary-Mas*, or sparse forest, because larch trees lose their needles in the fall. It has been important for human survival in this region for thousands of years, and there is evidence that it extended farther north during the Taimyr's Mesolithic, or Middle Stone Age, the time period to which the earliest evidence of human activity has been found (Pitul'ko 1999a). Tundra and taiga are found in the Putorana Mountains in the southern Taimyr Region. These southern biomes are important wintering grounds for Taimyr's reindeer. North of the Ary-Mas, tundra predominates today. Considered Arctic desert, the northern half of the Taimyr Peninsula, beginning with the Burranga Mountains, has little vegetation except for lichens and mosses. The northern zones are important summer feeding and calving grounds for the largest herd of wild reindeer in the world, currently estimated at close to 1,000,000 head.

There are thousands of lakes, four major river systems, and uncounted streams in the Taimyr Region. The Yenisei River, one of Siberia's biggest rivers, dominates the western Taimyr lowlands. Its headwaters are located in the Sayan Mountains in south Siberia. A considerable number of Taimyr's lakes and rivers drain into the Yenisei River. The Yenisei River empties into the Yenisei Gulf, and eventually flows to the Kara Sea and Arctic Ocean.

The three other major river systems are of regional origin. The Piasina River and its tributaries are located in the central longitudes of the Taimyr Peninsula. Originating in the Putorana Mountains near Norilsk, the Piasina River flows north to the Arctic Ocean. The Avam River, which also flows north out of the Putorana, joins the Dudypta River, which is an eastern tributary of the Piasina system. The Avam and Dudypta Rivers are the main waterways through the Avam tundra, the area typically utilized by the Dolgan and Nganasan in Ust Avam. In the eastern part of the Taimyr Region, there are two other large river systems: the Khatanga River, which runs northeast from the Putorana Mountains to the Laptev Sea; and in the north-central Taimyr, Lake Taimyr and the Upper Taimyr River drain north to the Arctic Ocean.

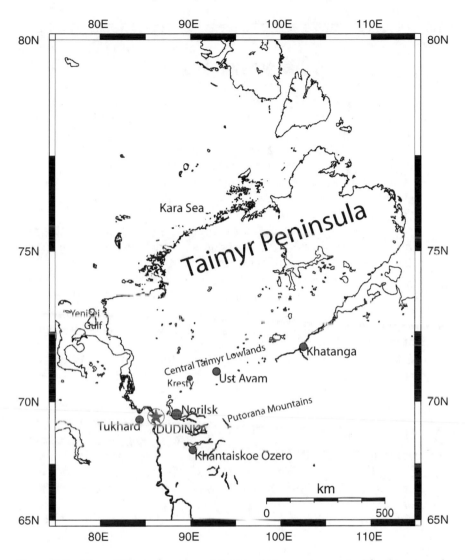

Figure 2.1 Map of the study area and the population centers visited for this research.

🎵🎵

Climate and Fauna

Taimyr experiences striking seasonal changes. The polar day and polar night (the seasons when the sun doesn't set or rise, respectively) are longer as one goes farther north (table 2.1). Winter temperatures reach –50 degrees Celsius at Ust Avam. Blizzards are common through April, and massive snowdrifts form. In treeless areas, the snow is often blown clean due to incessant winds and lake ice can obtain a thickness of 2 meters. At the end of January, the polar night gives way and the sun begins to emerge above the horizon.

Rapidly increasing daylight hours characterize the spring months, but temperatures remain below freezing. The snowmelt usually comes to a close at the end of June, the height of the polar day. During the melt-off there is a period of high water when the river ice breaks up, flows downriver, and creates temporary dams. During the high-water period, fish migrate upstream and people can travel by boat to hard-to-access areas. On the larger lakes the ice breaks up more slowly and, in some years, ice on some lakes does not break up at all, according to Ust Avam residents.

The Arctic day also lasts two months. From the second half of May until the end of July the sun does not set. The tundra and forest-tundra vegetation is green during July and the first half of August. Many species of wildflowers bloom at that time. The growing season is in effect for five or six weeks. During the second half of August, air temperatures approach freezing again. Fall is short, as wind and rainstorms quickly strip the trees and bush of their colorful foliage. At the end of September or beginning of October, the rivers and lakes begin to freeze.

Despite its harsh climate, Taimyr is rich with fauna. Taimyr's wild reindeer (*Rangifer tarandus sibiricus*) population is the largest in the world, as already mentioned. Wild reindeer are basically the same animal as the North American caribou. For simplicity's sake, I will use the term caribou for

Daylight (Season)	Dates	Number of Days
Polar Day (Spring, Summer)	May 19 – July 25	68
White Nights (Summer)	July 26 – August 17	23
Light Nights (Fall)	August 18 – September 16	30
Dark Nights (Winter)	September 17 – November 30	73
Polar Night (Winter)	December 1 – January 13	45
Dark Nights (Winter)	January 14 – March 27	73
Light Nights (Winter)	March 28 – April 26	30
White Nights (Winter)	April 27 – May 18	23

Table 2.1   Seasons, dates, and duration of seasons at Dudinka.

the wild animals and reindeer for the domesticated herds. Reindeer are actually herded, hitched to sleds, and driven with reins and prods. In Russian, caribou are simply called wild northern deer (*dikii severnii olen'*), and the Dolgan and Nganasan usually simplify this to *dikie* (wild ones) when speaking Russian, or alternatively, use the word *karibu*—a Russianized version of caribou. There are, in fact, several caribou groups in the region. Ust Avam hunters pointed out to me obvious morphological differences between the northern and southern herds as they migrated through the area. The southern population is bigger, has a longer muzzle, and is more darkly colored.

Taimyr's lakes and rivers are populated by a number of fish families (e.g., sturgeon, whitefish, trout, pike, and burbot). Fish are a vital source of food for the region's native people and urban population. Migratory birds fly north to reproduce in the Taimyr Region. Geese, ducks, loons, storks, as well as many predatory species, such as peregrine falcons, come into sight at the beginning of June. The World Wildlife Foundation supports an international project to study and protect nesting grounds in several areas of the Taimyr Region, since birds from all over Eurasia fly there in the summer to reproduce. Native families traditionally utilized some of these migratory species, such as geese, for food but their impact on the birds' numbers has likely been minimal when compared to the disruption of wintering grounds and wetlands from development in southern latitudes. There has been a noticeable decline in some varieties, which are now considered threatened or endangered species, such as the lesser white-fronted goose and the red-breasted goose. Rock ptarmigans are year-round inhabitants of the Taimyr Region and are also a food source, especially in the spring when other prey is not available.

Berries and mushrooms grow in the tundra, and both are collected for food. Berry species include red whortleberry (low-bush cranberry), cloudberry, blueberry, crowberry, dog's rose, and red currant. Mushroom varieties include *mokhovik*, *myslyata*, *podberezovik*, and *siroyezhki*. Although there are good and bad years for mushrooms and berries, there is a good amount of effort put forward to collect them, and they provide a nice change of pace from meat, fish, and fowl.

In Taimyr's forest zone moose are rarely encountered at present. Khariton Laptev, a member of the Northern Sea Expedition in the late eighteenth century, found moose regularly in the southern Taimyr lowlands (Troitskii 1987:14). Since moose are rare, the Dolgan and Nganasan hunt them only when absolutely necessary—there is social pressure amongst Ust Avam hunters against killing rare animals. On the slopes of the Putorana Mountains isolated populations of mountain snow sheep (*Ovis canadensis*) live. The Russian government protects these mountain sheep, and Ust Avam hunters do not hunt them. Musk oxen were reintroduced from Canada and Alaska in the 1970s. In 1974, Canadian Prime Minister Pierre Trudeau gave 10 young musk oxen as a present to the Soviet Union. An additional 20 were purchased in Alaska in 1975. Now, the herd numbers over 1,000, and Ust Avam hunters have spotted solitary males along the Piasina and Dudypta Rivers, several hundred kilometers from the Lower Bikada reserve where the animals were released. Hunting musk oxen is not locally condoned.

The main non-human predators are Arctic fox, polar and brown bear, wolverine, and tundra wolf. Lynx are present in the region but are extremely rare. Arctic hare, lemming, and mice are widely encountered in the area. A wide variety of terrestrial mammals, birds, and fish are utilized by the hunters/fishermen/trappers of the Avam tundra. Below, I list the common name and scientific name of these prey types. Most of these species are utilized as food. Some of them, such as wolverine, wolf, and ermine, are utilized for their pelt only. Utilization of prey is discussed in more detail below.

Terrestrial Mammals
Arctic Fox (*Alopex lagopus*)
Arctic Hare (*Lepus timidus*)
Ermine (*Mustela erminea*)
Grey Wolf (*Canis lupis*)
Moose (*Alces alces*)
Red Fox (*Vulpes vulpes*)
Siberian Brown Bear
    (*Ursus arctos*)
Wild Reindeer
    (*Rangifer tarandus sibiricus*)
Wolverine (*Gulo gulo*)

Birds
Bean Goose (*Anser fabalis*)
Grey Duck (*Melanitta nigra*)
Lesser White-fronted Goose
    (*Anser erythropus*)
Red-breasted Goose
    (*Branta ruficollis*)
Rock Ptarmigan
    (*Lagopus lagopus*)
Ruff (*Philomachus pugnax*)
White-fronted Goose
    (*Anser albifrons*)

Fish
Burbot (*Lota lota*)
Chir (*Coregonus nasus*)
Golets (*Salvelimus dryagini*)
Kharius-beliak (*Thymallus arcticus*)
Muksun (*Coregonus muksun*)
Nel'ma (*Stenodus leucichthys*)
Omul' (*Coregonus autumnalis*)
Peliad' (*Coregonus pelyad*)
Pike (*Esox lucius*)
Riapushka (*Coregonus sardinella*)
Sig (*Coregonus lavaretus pidschian*)
Sterliad' (*Acipenser ruthenis ruthenis*)
Sturgeon (*Acipenser baeri*)
Taimen (*Hucho taimen*)
Valek (*Coregonus spp.*)

Hunting Seasons

Foraging is important as Dolgan and Nganasan families depend on game and fish for nearly every meal. The term "foraging" is used here more or less synonymously with hunting and gathering, a mode of production thought of as typical in band-living human societies (Ingold 1995). The emphasis on country food is strong in Ust Avam, as well as with hunters and families out on the tundra. Local meat and fish provide at least one type of entrée for almost every meal based on my analysis of 1,150 meals with the Dolgan and Nganasan. Use of imported, canned, or fresh-frozen protein in Ust Avam diminished from 4.4 percent in 1994–95 to 0.4 percent during 1996–97. It is not just a question of calories and nutrients, although foraged foods are generally more nutritious than store-bought foods. Bush food imparts pride and satisfaction to hunter, cook, and end user that store foods do not.

> My estimate is that we consume three whole caribou per month for our family of four. That does not count the meat we give away. We eat meat or fish three meals a day. Last year, the caribou migrated away quickly and I shot only enough for us until New Year. After the New Year, I fished and trapped with snares. I caught rabbit, partridge, and arctic fox. There was always meat on the table.
>
> *Valery, Ust Avam, 1996*

The annual climatic cycle and the hunting activities that go along with it are implicitly recognized in the names of the months in both the Dolgan and Nganasan languages. The Nganasan have two "years," a summer year with four months and a winter year with eight months. These are summarized in table 2.2 (following Popov 1966). The names of the Nganasan months are associated with major subsistence seasons or episodes in the seasonal cycle.

The Dolgan month names also reflect ecological shifts throughout the year. Table 2.3 gives their English translations. One Dolgan month name, April, makes direct reference to domestic reindeer—the milking month. Domestic reindeer provided the means of transportation and wealth among the Dolgan. The Nganasan, on the other hand, traditionally were hunter-gatherers that adopted reindeer herding in the nineteenth and twentieth centuries, and they make no reference to domestic reindeer in the names of their months.

Name	Activity	Time of Year
(Summer Year)		
First Fawns Month	caribou hunt, ptarmigan netting	May/June
Fish Appearance Month	fowl netting and shooting, fish netting reindeer calving, summer gear preparation	June/July
Goose Molting Month	tundra caribou hunt, goose netting	July/August
Gosling Month	tundra caribou hunt, goose hunt	August/September
(Winter Year)		
Big Month	caribou hunt with reindeer decoys caribou hunt at water crossings	September/October
Autumn Month	caribou hunt, Arctic fox trapping	October/November
Hornless [Deer] Month	fishing season ends, caribou hunt	November/December
Dark Month	firewood gathering, Arctic fox trapping	December/January
Sunrise Month	firewood gathering, Arctic fox trapping	January/February
Frosted [Trees] Month	firewood gathering, Arctic fox trapping	February/March
Blackening [of Trees]	caribou hunt, Arctic fox trapping, repair	March/April
Cold Month	caribou hunt, ptarmigan netting, Arctic fox trapping	April/May

Table 2.2   The Nganasan calendar.

English Translation	Dolgan	Month
Sun Comes Up Month	Kün Taksar Yia	January
Chimney Pipe Month	Üöles Yia	February
Face Warms Up Month	Hyrai Hylyiar Yia	March
Reindeer Milking Month	Taba Emiidir Yia	April
Fawning Begins Month	Tugut Törüür Yia	May
Ice Flow Month	Kömüöl Yia	June
Mosquito Spill-Out Month	Kumaar Tüher Yia	July
Gadfly Month	Yrgatka Yia	August
Muddy [Water] Month	Bulkaahyn Yia	September
Ice Freezes Month	Buus Toŋor Yia	October
Sun Drops Month	Kün Tüher Yia	November
Dark Winter Month	Karaŋa Kyhyn Yia	December
Dark Time	Karaŋa Kem	December (first half)
Mouse Goes Time	Kutuiak Kaamar Keme	December (second half)

Table 2.3   The Dolgan calendar.

᚛᚛

Hunt Types

Based on the tasks of some 120 hunting and fishing trips for which I have records, as well as informal interviews with Ust Avam hunters, I defined the hunt types that are listed below. For example, caribou were hunted nine months of the year, using three kinds of hunting techniques. The technique used depended on the conditions of the tundra at a particular time of year. Fishing techniques also varied depending on climatic condition and the species available at a given time.

Travel, Incidental Hunting

When traveling in the tundra, either on snowmobile, boat, or foot, most hunters of the Avam tundra carry a loaded rifle or shotgun. At some times of year, such as in June and October, brown bear migrate (north and south respectively), following the caribou migration. Carrying a firearm is required for protection. In addition, it is likely that a hunter could come across caribou while traveling. Carrying a loaded firearm, the hunter is ready to pursue the caribou right when they are encountered. The Dolgan do not normally pursue bear for food, as they are considered sacred animals and referred to by the euphemism *emiaksin*, or old woman. If a bear has to be killed because it is harassing a campsite, it will be mourned like a relative. Economically, a bear represents a potentially large source of protein and fat, and the fact that the Dolgan do not usually pursue bear for food is interesting. More will be said on the significance of the taboo on bear hunting in chapter 5. The Nganasan also have a spiritual relationship with the bear—they end their shamanic seances with the bear dance. There are a number of factors that potentially explain the relationship with bear, including the ancestral taboo, the fact that bear are dangerous animals and there are plenty of not-so-dangerous caribou to hunt, and the possibility that the bear are infected with trichinosis. Trichinosis is a parasite that can infect humans and other meat-eating mammals. While it is effectively eliminated with proper cooking, bear meat and fat are rarely consumed in Ust Avam.

Early Fall (and Late Spring) On-Water Caribou Hunt (with or without Fishing)

Caribou are hunted as they cross rivers during their northern and southern migrations. Actually, one might say that there are two on-water hunts because the degree of organization is different. There is the state-hunting-enterprise (*gospromkhoz*) on-water hunt, mainly on the Piasina and upper Dudypta Rivers, and the subsistence on-water hunt, mainly on the lower Dudypta and Avam Rivers, near Ust Avam. This description focuses on the subsistence on-water hunt, since few Ust Avam hunters participated in the *gospromkhoz* on-water hunt in 1997. The two hunts are similar, except the *gospromkhoz* hunt is conducted on a larger scale, and the hunters are usually non-indigenous city-dwellers, flown in for the occasion.

Ust Avam hunters take positions on high banks or on the roofs of hunting cabins overlooking the river. There, they wait with binoculars to spot migrating groups of caribou preparing to cross. When the lead animals are approximately halfway across the river, the hunters run down to a boat, start the motor, and race to head off the herd. The boats are typically 15-foot aluminum-hull rowboats equipped with 15- to 30-horsepower outboard motors. A hunter at the bow shoots at the animals, usually with a 12-gauge shotgun. Sometimes fishnets are installed in the river near the lookout post and kept there for the duration of the hunt. Fishing provides food for the hunters while they are waiting for caribou to cross the river.

During the on-water hunts that I observed in 1997 from two to 12 animals were killed. Before motors and shotguns were available, Dolgan and Nganasan hunters used canoes and spears, and even fewer animals were likely to be killed. On the wider Piasina River, reportedly, the *gospromkhoz* used two boats, and virtually all the animals crossing the river at that time were killed—sometimes up to 100.

Since the temperature is still above freezing during the on-water hunt, it is important to butcher the animals quickly. If the animals are not processed right away, seagulls and ravens can attack the carcass, and natural processes of decomposition can reduce the meat's quality. In the subsistence hunt, the caribou, which float in the water due to their hollow hair, are gathered, tied to the boat, and taken to shore. The hunters drag them onto the beach and begin butchering right there. Minimally, the internal organs are removed and the blood is drained (and often drunk). When transportation is a problem or there is no place to store the meat, the hides are removed and the meat is cut into ten or so major sections, placed on a rack to dry, and packed in large flour bags. Subsistence hunters keep many parts of the caribou that the non-native *gospromkhoz* hunters throw away: the heads, lower stomachs, and bone marrow (*chanko*) from the lower parts of the legs. The *chanko* and internal organs, such as the heart, liver, and kidneys, may be eaten on the spot.

In the *gospromkhoz* on-water hunt, particularly during its height in the 1970s and 1980s, special butchering installations were used. The floating caribou were caught and placed on a conveyer that transported them to the butchering building. Heads and hides were often thrown away—the decaying accumulations of these parts can still be seen today not far from many of the installations. The meat was stored in large underground ice chambers dug into the riverbank until barges or helicopters came to transport the meat to the city. In 1997, there was one hunting brigade in the

Avam subdivision that shot caribou for the *gospromkhoz* during the fall on-water hunt. And while most of the hunters were non-natives from Norilsk, the *gospromkhoz* was in such a state of disorganization that they had not yet transported the caribou from fall 1996—these were being stored in two underground ice chambers. They shot approximately 800 caribou during the fall 1997 on-water hunt at a spot on the upper Dudypta River.

Fall (and Winter) On-Land Caribou Hunt (with or without Fishing)

In the fall after the rivers freeze, usually by the beginning of October, caribou are hunted on foot or with snowmobiles. Again, the Avam hunters take positions on elevated locations throughout the tundra and wait for caribou to migrate through their area. Caribou tend to take certain paths, and some hunters are able to observe these migration routes from their cabin or from wooden towers (*maiak*) built by Soviet geographers for surveys. After a small herd has moved through, they might chase it on snowmobile, stopping to shoot with a rifle when the animals cross in front. Sometimes, the hunters position themselves downwind on the migration path and hunt the animals on foot, later using a snowmobile to transport the meat. In the late winter, snowmobiles are used exclusively, since the hunters must travel over 100 kilometers to the south to hunt. Fishnets are installed on lakes after they freeze in the fall. Caribou hunting does not preclude checking fishnets, as necessary. When it is warmer, especially in the early fall, fishnets need to be checked every day or every other day, or else the fish begin to rot. Usually, this is the period just before the caribou begin to migrate.

The fall on-land caribou hunt was historically the major source of income for a number of Ust Avam hunting brigades. During the socialist period, a brigade with three hunters typically had a goal of 150 caribou and the meat was of considerably higher quality than meat produced during the summer on-water hunt because of higher fat content and less spoilage. In the winter of 1996–97, the *gospromkhoz* accepted the caribou from several hunting brigades. One brigade turned in 90 caribou (two helicopter loads), the largest number. In addition to the meat turned in to the *gospromkhoz*, the fall on-land caribou hunt generates the majority of the meat needed for consumption in the settlement throughout the winter. During the 1990s, *gospromkhoz* hunters kept a significant portion of the caribou they shot for their own consumption and to give away to relatives and other people. For example, the brigade that turned in 90 caribou during the winter of 1996–97 kept 40 caribou for themselves.

Summer On-Land Caribou Hunt (with or without Fishing)

In the summer, a few caribou forage individually or in small herds in the forest-tundra transition zone. Hunters with cabins or shelters in this ecological zone go out to their spots on foot and hunt caribou as needed for subsistence. In the summer of 1997, I participated in one such hunt, which produced one adult and one year-old deer, which we butchered and packed into 50-kilogram plastic flour bags, which we then carried on our shoulders several kilometers back to the boat.

Spring Goose Hunt

Spring goose season is the most exciting hunt for the Avam tundra population (figure 2.2.). Boys as young as ten years old participate in this hunt, which signals the end of the leanest time of the year, April and May. Hunters spread out from the settlement, usually on foot, but sometimes with snowmobiles or on boats after the ice breaks. In 1997, the river ice broke up two and a half weeks earlier than normal, so boats were used. Positions are agreed upon prior to the opening of the season. The hunters construct blinds, digging into the snow or building them up with brush. Hunters wear white sheets or some other camouflaged clothing (*maskhalat*) and set up decoys cut out of particleboard or plywood and painted black or brown. They wait for a flock of geese to approach for landing before shooting with shotguns. The geese shot are used for family subsistence.

Summer Goose Hunt

In the summer, geese molt and cannot fly. Some hunters who have cabins north of the tree line walk the tundra and shoot a few geese with shotguns. These geese are used for subsistence only and are sometimes stored for use during the fall in small underground ice chambers that the people have dug under a shed near their house or cabin.

Figure 2.2 A successful spring goose hunt,
May 1996.

Open-Water Net-Fishing (Upriver and Downriver Migrating Whitefish)

After the ice breaks up and flows in early June, and until the river freezes over in late September, nets are used on the open water to catch fish. Several species of whitefish migrate upriver after the ice flow and downriver prior to the freeze. Large-cell nets (50- to 60-millimeter cells) are used to catch chir, muksun, and the rare nelma on the Avam and Dudypta Rivers. Smaller-cell nets (30- to 40-millimeter cells) are used to catch sig and peliad. Sometimes the younger chir, known locally as *pod-chirka*, literally "under-chir," muksun, pike, and burbot get into these nets. Nets are generally one to two meters high by 25 to 50 meters long. The nets are kept afloat with a variety of objects, including old hunks of styrofoam, old ketchup bottles, and commercial and homemade floats. The nets are anchored to the river bottom with rocks or bricks tied to bottom corners with cord. The net is kept perpendicular with 15-centimeter-diameter iron rings, tied at regular intervals at the bottom of the net. The fishermen make these iron rings in the village from single-strand 5-millimeter-diameter iron wire spun onto homemade cranks and cut with a wedge and hammer. Prior to the availability of this metal—there is a big pile of it in Ust Avam—fishermen used rocks tied on with the root of a tundra bush.

Many fishermen weave their own nets with nylon line, either purchased or previously provided by the *gospromkhoz*. Some of the nets used for summer fishing were provided by the *gospromkhoz* during the socialist period and written off the balance sheet after one season's use. The nets remained the personal property of the fishermen. These nets are ubiquitously twisted nylon of various colors and thickness. Recently, some individuals (mostly non-native residents) have purchased clear nylon fish line and they make their nets from this material. They must still tie floats and weights to the net. These clear nets work better for some species, such as sig and peliad. Pike tend to tear up the clear nets when caught, so these nets require significant daily repairs and are usually used only for one open-water season. The heavier twisted nylon nets usually require repairs after a season's use, and adult and elderly men are often seen reweaving nets after fishing season.

Nets are usually carried on boats to the location for installation. The nets are installed at an angle to or perpendicular to the shore, usually close to one side or the other. In some instances, a small tributary can be completely netted off for the duration of one- to three-day hunting excursions. During the summer, fishnets need to be checked daily. The fish tend to go bad after two days, or seagulls and eagles see the fish caught in the nets and attempt to eat them.

On open water, it usually requires two people to check fishnets using an aluminum boat, or one person using a *vetka*, the traditional wooden canoe. On aluminum boats, one person rows the boat, and the other sits on the nose of the boat, pulling it up and checking for fish. On a *vetka*, the fisherman can pull the boat along the net as it is checked.

Burbot Fishing

Burbot (*Lota lota*) is a freshwater fish that resembles, and is related to, the cod. Burbot is a bottom feeder. The burbot are caught with bait and hooks (figure 2.3.). The bait usually comprises sections of peliad or the small tugunki. Up to 25 hooks are attached to a single line (*peremiot*) weighted with bricks. Instead of hooks, long, thin, carved pieces of caribou bone are sometimes used. The *peremiot* is installed in rivers or lakes and checked like fishnets. Young children are significant producers of burbot. They usually tie one hook to a line and fish from the shore or pick holes in the ice after the freeze. There is a deficit of hooks in the village, and children regularly ask for hooks from their elders and visitors.

Figure 2.3 Burbot fishing on the Avam River. The burbot is beaten on the head so that the hook can be removed. It is acceptable to hit the head of the burbot only if it is caught from a river. The Dolgan state that a burbot must not be beaten if caught in a lake since the fish do not migrate and the lake must be honored.

Ice Fishing with Nets (Installing, Checking, and Removing Nets as Needed)

Winter-ice fishnets are usually installed soon after the freeze in October, at first on the river near the village, then, as soon as the water freezes enough to drive a snowmobile across, on lakes in the common-use territory surrounding the village and on the more distant hunting territories. Ice fishing with nets is difficult. The nets must be installed under the ice and checked regularly. The ice holes freeze over quickly, and by the end of winter the ice reaches a thickness of two meters.

In addition to the nets (with weights, anchors, and floats), the equipment needed to install nets under the ice includes an ice pick (*pishnia*), ice-straining shovel, long-board, and a long cord. Several test holes are picked with the *pishnia*, and the depth is measured with a long cord tied to a brick or rock. Ice thickens downward into the water as winter progresses, and the nets must be placed deep enough so that the ice does not freeze into the top of the net. If it freezes into the ice, a net is usually unsalvageable.

Preferably, nets are installed when the ice is thin. After determining the best location for the net, a line is tied to one end of long carved board, or *etungak*. The *etungak* is fed into the water, the end with the attached line is last. The last one-half meter is forced under the ice with an underhand pitch. The far end of the *etungak* is located by looking through the ice, and a hole is picked at that spot. The *etungak* is pushed along under the ice in the direction that the net is supposed to be installed; then another hole is picked through ice. This process is repeated until the desired length is obtained. Then, the *etungak* is taken out of the water. The net is attached to the end of the line and pulled through the water to the far hole. Usually, a series of four or eight 25-meter nets is installed in this way, either in a straight line or a T-formation. A line attached to each of the top corners of the net is tied to a trimmed branch, or in some cases a thick wire attached to a board. The board or branch is stuck on to the edge of the ice hole with wet snow, and a sizeable portion of it projects out of the ice. The branch or board projecting out of the ice is used to locate the ice hole and net after the water in the ice hole freezes and snow drifts onto it.

Nets under the ice need to be checked at least every two or three days in the early winter, and once a week or so later in the winter (figure 2.4.). After snow is cleared off the old ice hole and the surrounding 30 to 50 centimeters with a shovel, an ice pick is used to chip ice out of the ice hole. Care has to be taken not to break the branch or wire holding the net. This is difficult with the homemade *pishnia*, which is usually has a two-meter-long handle and a steel, lead-filled point. The ice hole is widened at the bottom, so that the net does not freeze to the ice while it is being checked and fish do not fall out of the net as it is pulled out of the hole. Ice holes at both ends of a net must be cleared before checking for fish. The far end of the net is untied from the branch or wire and attached to the long line, or *pro-*

Figure 2.4 Boris Elogir with a portion of the fish caught on Lake Elgen after one day, October 1996. He and I installed nets under the ice the previous afternoon.

gon. The near end of the net is pulled, a length of the net is checked, and the float is placed on snow at the perimeter of the ice hole with the rest of the net hanging in the water. The floats are arranged around the opening of the hole so that when the net is pulled back under the ice each section of the net falls into the water in the proper order. The net is pulled back into position with the *progon* and tied back to the small branch, board, or wire.

Spring Thin-Ice Fishing

In April and May, the ice-fishing season is over. The only source of fresh fish then is in the upper drainage of the Avam River. Each year at that time, the thin-ice fishing technique is used to obtain small sig, peliad, and harius. Hunters/fishermen must travel up to 100 kilometers to the upper drainage of the Avam River in the foothills of the Putorana Plateau, where there is a steep grade. Because of the grade, there are spots in the rivers that do not freeze all winter long—a surprising phenomenon with such a cold climate. There are deeper portions of the river where young fish (up to 25 centimeters long) spend the winter. As winter progresses, the water gradually drains away and the river becomes shallower. Ice that forms on these pools collapses under the weight of snow and then melts in the running water. Thin ice is formed this way throughout the winter.

For thin-ice fishing, fishermen choose portions of the river where the ice is about three centimeters thick and directly on top of the water. They pick a few holes in the ice and determine whether there are any fish in the pool they have chosen. If there are fish, the fishermen install nets with small 25-millimeter cells. Next, they cut young larch trees with an ax and make poles by shaving the branches and bark. In a row, the fishermen walk up and down the ice over the pool and slap the poles on the ice. Having installed several nets across the pool, they effectively scare the fish into the nets. The fishermen check the net after several passes down the thin-ice-covered pool and repeat the process throughout the day. After a full sleigh-load is obtained, the hunters do not return to that pool to fish for at least one year.

Seine *(Nevod)* Fishing

Fishing with a U-shaped seine (*nevod*) is fairly simple, but labor-intensive. One person rows a boat, another person feeds the seine into the water, and at least two more are waiting on shore to pull the seine. The fishermen arrange the *nevod* on the nose of the boat, on top of a black ventilation sleeve or tarp, so that it does not get stuck on the boat edge. The *nevod* has 1.5-meter-high walls. Iron rings are attached to the bottom, and styrofoam floats are attached to the top, as with other nets. The *nevods* I saw were put together from several different kinds of net, but they all had very small cells (10 mm and 15 mm). In the middle of the *nevod* is a 2-meter-long pouch (*karman*) where the fish collect as the *nevod* is pulled to shore. On both ends of the *nevod,* 25 meters or so of nylon cord are attached. Several meters before the *karman* falls into the water, the fishermen start turning the boat. The *karman* is in the middle and at the farthest point from the shore. Four people are required pull the *nevod* in to shore. They have to be careful to pull at the same rate and to pull the lower end of the *nevod* closer to the water than the upper end. When the *karman* gets close to shore, everyone runs with the *nevod*, so that it comes out quickly and the fish do not have a chance to swim away. After picking all the fish out of the net, washing them in a bucket, and bagging them, the fishermen take the *nevod* out again, a short distance downstream.

Several different species and sizes of fish are caught with this method. The main small fish is the tugunok, about the size of a small sardine. I also observed baby valek, sig, and peliad about the same size. Sometimes larger fish are caught. Fishing returns with this method varied from a half-bucket (1.5 kg) to a full bag (40 kg) in 1997. Fishermen reported to me that they caught up to a full rowboat in two or three throws with this method 30 years ago, but returns vary significantly from year to year depending on water levels and other environmental factors.

Arctic Fox Trapping

As described above, Arctic fox trapping is equipment- and labor-intensive. Trap lines must be set up and maintained. It is not uncommon for there to be 300 steel leg-hold traps on one trap line. Bait must be prepared. In the fall, during the caribou hunts, hunters who plan to conduct Arctic fox trapping later in the season make piles of the portions of the caribou not kept for consumption or exchange with the *gospromkhoz*. These portions usually include the lungs and esophagus, as well as the large stomach and intestines. Later in the winter, these piles are uncovered, broken up, and the frozen chunks cut up with an ax in a large, flat-bottomed wooden bin.

Trap lines must be checked every few days. Travel is usually conducted on snowmobile, but more hunters are going on foot or by skis in recent years. Prior to 1971, trappers traveled their trap line by reindeer team and sleigh, or dog team among the non-reindeer herding and sedentary Doŋgot Dolgan. After a fox is taken from the trap (usually dead), the animal is thawed out and the hide is carefully removed. Trappers attempt to keep everything, including the claws, nose, lips, and ears, attached to the hide. The fat is then removed from the hide by hand and with rags. No scraper or knife is used for removing the fat. The hide is worth more if all the parts are present. The removal of the hide and fat and placement of the skin on a stretcher is time-consuming. Sometimes, the retired fathers or mothers of hunters do the tanning. The whole process can take up to an hour for an experienced trapper.

Collecting

There is little equipment required for berry and mushroom collecting. Small plastic buckets (12 to 15 liters) are usually used. The collectors, usually women and children, leave the village on foot in August and search the surrounding tundra for a variety of mushrooms and berries. According to my informants who cite "Russian biologists," there are no poisonous mushrooms in the Avam tundra. All but the smallest and slimiest are gathered. There are several varieties of berries that are relished (cloudberry, blueberry, crowberry, low-bush cranberry, and very rarely red currant and a kind of raspberry). The mushroom and berry harvest is closely dependent on the weather, as cold and dry summers do not favor mushrooms and berries. Elder residents of Ust Avam who I interviewed told me that in the past they did not eat mushrooms, which were considered reindeer food before the Russians "taught them how to eat mushrooms."

Residents of Ust Avam also collect green onion sprouts soon after the ice breaks. Big onion patches are far from the village, so travel by boat is required for picking large quantities. Some people may pick and eat green onion while they are taking a stroll or fishing. In other cases a hunter and younger male and female relatives may plan and make a special onion-picking trip. The onion is eaten fresh. My attempts at drying the onion for future use in soup were not successful—the dried onion had no flavor. A number of other plants are collected generally for medicinal purposes, but this is not a very widespread activity in the community. For example, tea made from *bagul'nik* (*Ledum palustre*), a short, strong-smelling evergreen bush that grows in swampy areas, is used as an expectorant.

Firewood Collecting

There are three types of trees collected for firewood in the Avam tundra: deadfall (often created in the spring ice-flow), live trees, and ancient trees (washed out of the permafrost). Hunters and other villagers transport firewood by foot, boat, and snowmobile. Prior to 1971, when the *gospromkhoz* began shipments of coal to the village, firewood brigades were formed in the fall, and logs were transported to the village by tractor. Before settlement in Ust Avam, each family took care of its own firewood needs daily. The *baloks* and *chums* did not require much wood to heat, and large *talnik* bush could be used. Today, large apartments require a significant amount of fuel to heat them throughout the winter. Firewood is now used mainly as kindling. Coal shipments to the village have been diminishing, however, and each family received only five tons during the summer of 1997. To the extent that coal shipments decrease, more firewood will be required for Ust Avam.

On walks through the tundra during the summer, men usually gather dead trees and make teepee-shaped piles. Otherwise, deadfall would be frozen into the ground and covered with snow. At hunting cabins, deadfall is collected or trees are cut with gasoline-powered saws. The trees are carried on sleighs pulled by the hunters on foot or by snowmobiles.

In the late summer, deadfall along the Avam River is collected and transported to the village by boat. Live trees are rarely cut down presently. In the winter and spring, a hunter may occasionally go into the tundra and cut down larch trees for firewood, but care is taken to choose unhealthy-looking trees. The logs are then transported to the hunting camp, apartment, or cabin by the sleigh load. In the tundra north of the village, there are many lakes in deep depressions. Ancient trees commonly wash out of the shoreline. Hunters often collect these ancient trees and transport them by snowmobile to their cabin.

Other (Ptarmigan/Hare Hunting and Snaring)

Throughout the winter, hunters use snares to catch Arctic hare and ptarmigan. Hunters usually travel on skis from the village to snare lines they have set up on the communal hunting territory surrounding the village. I have no observations of snaring, but I know of several hunters that use this method, as well as a few people that do not have snowmobiles.

Throughout the winter, but especially in the spring (April/May) when there are no other food resources, some hunters go out in the tundra with snowmobiles, or on skis, to hunt ptarmigan. The hunters carry Toz 5.62-millimeter rifles for this purpose. The Toz is similar to a .22 caliber rifle.

Maintenance

While not direct hunting, much time during hunting excursions is dedicated to maintenance of hunting equipment. This occurs sporadically during longer hunting trips or regularly in preparation for returning to the village. The analysis of productivity below discounts the time dedicated to maintenance prior to returning to the village. It includes maintenance time immediately prior to or during hunting excursions.

To contrast the month names of the traditional calendars, I developed a calendar of foraging activities observed during my fieldwork (table 2.4). This calendar shows the distribution of the hunt types defined above based on my observations, and it compares favorably with the traditional calendars shown above.

Month	Foraging Activities
January	Arctic fox trapping, ice fishing with nets, incidental hunting
February	none observed
March	none observed
April	thin-ice fishing, incidental hunting, ice fishing with nets
May	ice fishing with nets, on-land caribou hunt, goose hunting
June	goose hunting, water fishing with nets, on-water caribou hunt
July	open water fishing with nets
August	seine fishing, mushroom and berry collecting, on-water caribou hunt
September	seine fishing, water fishing with nets, on-water caribou hunt, firewood
October	water fishing with nets, ice fishing with nets, burbot fishing, on-land caribou hunting
November	none observed
December	ice fishing with nets

Table 2.4   Productive activities by month (Ust Avam, 1993 through 1997).

Division of Labor

Who actually procures the various kinds of locally obtained foods? And who handles the complex butchering, processing, and storage of these hunted and gathered foods in Ust Avam? These are questions that bring into play social contexts and gender relations in Ust Avam's local economy. Adult men are the main actors in most of the hunt types listed above. Men are generally the people who own and maintain hunting, fishing, and trapping equipment, and they are the ones who go into the tundra most often to procure necessary raw materials and food. Women, young boys, and young girls are included in production too—mostly in plant collecting and burbot fishing. Elderly men are also involved to a smaller extent. They are generally limited to open-water fishing on the river immediately adjacent to the village, and they also help out with tanning Arctic fox pelts. Everyone that produces some food, even if it is only a few small fish, obtains some degree of self-satisfaction and pride, especially when the food is brought home or brought out for special occasions, such as cloudberry preserves served at New Year's dinner.

Women play a very important role in the processing and distribution of locally procured foods, as well as food preparation and fashioning clothes from caribou hides and the pelts of fur-bearing animals. Without clothes made from animal furs, it would be difficult to hunt and travel in the Avam tundra for most of the winter. Men generally do the rough butchery of caribou—taking out the internal organs and cutting the animal into manageable, 10- to 20-kilogram pieces, such as hindquarters, rump, sides of ribs, vertebrae, head, etc. Sometimes men only take out the internal organs and women do the rest of the butchery, including the remainder of the rough butchery and the finer butchery. Finer butchery is required for cooking, i.e., cutting sides of ribs into individual ribs for soup, or turning a rump into ground meat. When men do the cooking, as is the case on hunting excursions, I noted differences in the foods consumed—men eat more raw meat and fewer menu items—largely due to the avoidance of fine butchery. Without women doing the food preparation, the Dolgan and Nganasan diet would be fairly monotonous. Women do most of the preparation of hides for clothing, including scraping, softening, piecing together, and sewing. Traditional clothes are fairly intricate, and the outer layers usually have beaded designs or colored sections of fur, cloth, or hides. These can take weeks to prepare.

Women's food distribution is conducted on two levels. First, after the adult and adolescent men in the household bring home large portions of caribou or bags of fish, the woman of the house decides what to use, how much to store, and how much to distribute to relatives and friends. Sec-

Figure 2.5 Galina Elogir sews beads on felt to master a traditional Dolgan belt for a dress parka.

ondarily, after receiving meat or fish from relatives or friends, women may redistribute a portion of this food to other relatives and friends that are in need. This sort of "free" distribution of meat is fairly typical of hunting-and-gathering societies. As discussed in more detail below, locally procured foods are transferred from producing households to non-producing households fairly regularly in Ust Avam.

Production Harvests and Efficiency

In order to understand Ust Avam hunters' decisions about what, when, and how much to hunt, it is helpful to review an important anthropological debate on the nature of human economies, the "formalist vs. substantivist" debate. The American college student is familiar, at least intuitively, with basic principles relevant to the U.S. economy, such as the role of price in supply and demand. In an ideal economic model, when prices are lowered consumer demand increases. Producers, however, will produce more and increase supply at higher prices. There are a number of formal principles, such as supply and demand and the profit motive, that are fundamental to industrial economies, like that of the United States. Such assumptions were argued to be universal in human societies, and this was the focus of the formalist position in the 1950s and 1960s. The substantivists argued that one needs to understand a society's culture in order to make sense of certain economic traditions, especially those that had high apparent costs, such as a Kwakiutl potlatch. One underlying assumption that everyone seems to agree upon now is that humans are rational actors that strive to maximize their satisfaction, or utility, considering many variables and conditions.

Rather than focus on human abilities to calculate value, economic anthropologists have more recently focused on actual systems of production, distribution, and consumption, and the cultural milieu under which values, morals, and customs are established (Jochim 1976, Wilk 1996, Halperin 1994). Anthropologists have discovered that among traditional hunting-and-gathering peoples, economic values are embedded in traditions that focus on subsistence requirements and economic leveling. The same is true for peasant societies. Subsistence needs are met with relative ease in most documented foraging societies, and households tend not to accumulate large surpluses.

Since hunter-gatherer peoples are usually mobile, surplus can be a burden. In this case, producing more of something provides smaller and smaller benefits for each additional unit of labor. This effect is called diminishing marginal value. Human abilities to calculate economic utility likely include expectations about marginal-value effects. As mentioned above, anthropologists have long observed that the meat from big-game kills in hunting-and-gathering societies tends to be shared widely within local bands and communities. One possible reason is the relatively low value of extra portions (Blurton Jones 1987; Peterson 1993).

During the socialist period, this was clearly not the case for Ust Avam, as hunters were encouraged to maximize production of foraged foods that were turned in to the state enterprise. Individual hunters were handsomely rewarded with monetary incentives, awards, and vacation packages, and hunting brigades vied with one another in "socialist competitions" to produce the most. Since the socialist period, state production incentives disappeared along with most capital inputs to communities like Ust Avam. Now, with the goal of providing for one's family and helping those in the community that cannot help themselves, relatively little surplus is being produced, and what surplus there is often goes to those in the community that have no meat or fish. Economic anthropologist Marshall Sahlins (1972) characterized the domestic mode of production for hunting-and-gathering societies as one of "underproduction." Current conditions in Ust Avam provide little benefit to do work beyond family subsistence needs plus what is needed for sharing, so one could say Ust Avam's economy is underproducing (i.e., producing just what it needs). Entrepreneurial activity is now virtually impossible in Ust Avam, and hunters spend much less time in productive activities, an irony considering the free-market reforms following the collapse of the Soviet Union.

Why is it that a reliance on subsistence has been emphasized in Ust Avam, and not massive migration to the urban centers? The answer lies in part in the unpredictability of the larger market economy and Ust Avam's minimal exposure to it. In contrast, I found that subsistence hunting and fishing is a highly predictable activity. Tables 2.5 and 2.6 summarize the data for 118 foraging excursions and 10 foraging tasks for which efficiency data were collected.

Table 2.5 provides information on 11 of the foraging tasks defined above, giving the number of observations of each type of foraging task and the proportion that were successful. Successful foraging excursions were those during which any food item was produced. Based on these data, the

Task	n	Success Rate (%)
On-water caribou hunt	8	100
Ice-crust fishing	2	100
Seine fishing	3	100
Berry/mushroom hunting	6	100
Open-water net fishing	12	83.3
Ice fishing with nets	37	75.7
Goose hunt	4	75
Burbot fishing with hooks	10	70
On-land caribou hunt	10	60
Arctic-fox trapping	7	28.6
Travel, incidental hunting	19	5.3

Table 2.5   The predictability of foraging (Ust Avam, 1993 through 1997).

Task	Harvest (kg/h-hr)	Product
On-land caribou hunt	6.1	caribou
Ice fishing with nets	4.3	fish
Ice-crust fishing	3.23	fish
On-water caribou hunt	2.86	caribou
	0.07	fish
Open-water net fishing	2.13	fish
Seine fishing	2.06	fish
Burbot fishing with hooks	1.91	fish
Travel/incidental hunting	0.92	caribou
Berry/mushroom collecting	0.13	berry/mushrooms
	0.84	caribou
Goose hunt	0.11	goose
	0.13	fish
	0.01	ruff

Table 2.6   Harvest per unit production time (Ust Avam, 1993 through 1997).

majority of foraging tasks in Ust Avam have a high success rate. The chances that a hunter will return from a hunting excursion empty-handed are relatively low, except for Arctic-fox trapping. The productivity of Arctic fox varies greatly from year to year, depending on the rodent population. Even travel through the tundra provides some small food returns.

Table 2.6 provides harvest data for ten food-producing tasks and ranks the tasks in order of efficiency. The harvest figures are provided in units of kilograms per hunter-hour. I recorded the quantity of each species obtained in the foraging excursions I observed, as well as the time required and the number of participants. Average weights for each species were used to generate the harvest data (table 2.6). The on-land caribou hunt, with a relatively low success rate (60%), as shown in table 2.5, is the most efficient task, producing more than 6 kilograms of meat per hunter-hour. This particular task is one of the most important for Ust Avam, since it occurs in the late fall and provides the community with meat for most of the winter.

The information in tables 2.5 and 2.6 demonstrates the stability provided to households involved in subsistence hunting and fishing in Ust Avam. While they are no longer being paid regularly to produce meat and fish for the state, the hunters are providing for their families and others in the community, procuring a wide variety of resources at various efficiencies. The formal economy provides no such predictability.

Food Distribution and Sharing

When the ruble devalued greatly in 1992 1995, transportation costs to Ust Avam and other remote settlements increased dramatically relative to salaries and pensions. There are no roads to Ust Avam (figure 2.5), so consumer supplies and prices have been affected by deregulation of transportation. In addition, the volume and quality of groceries, generally carbohydrates, and consumer goods, such as clothing, have diminished as old reserves were used up. For example, during my first visit in 1994, there were a number of types of dried bulk grains, dried potatoes and onions, and pasta for sale in the community's store. After privatization, the cost of air travel and shipping increased significantly, reducing the average villager's ability to travel and to send large or heavy packages to the urban centers. Few people in remote settlements can now afford a visit to the city, so it is difficult for the Dolgan and Nganasan in Ust Avam to make money by selling or bartering traditional products in urban markets, unlike rural communities in more connected parts of the former Soviet Union. Given that the formal economy has become relatively expensive, people in Ust Avam are surviving by sharing products that are produced locally according to informal traditional rules.

Figure 2.5   A truck drives on the Yenisei River, not far from Dudinka. Trucks rarely make it all the way to Ust Avam.

Among many hunting-and-gathering peoples, the ethic of meat sharing is argued to be part of hunters' reciprocal relationship with the prey species (Hallowell 1960, Fienup-Riordan 1990, Bird-David 1992, Nuttall 1992). From this perspective, animals are considered non-human persons that must be treated properly. Part of the proper treatment of the animal is to give some of it away to other people in the community. In Ust Avam, it is said that food sharing contributes to good future hunting. The animal is perceived to be giving itself up to the hunter and will only continue to do so if it is cared for by means of ritual and sharing. This theme is brought up again in chapters 5 and 6, where cosmological understandings of Dolgan and Nganasan land and resource use are discussed in more detail. Typical answers to my queries about food sharing reflect its spiritual and social significance.

> If I get a caribou, I am obliged to give away some of the meat. I mean if I did not give some away, the hunt does not happen. It is that kind of nature. We share, if we catch game.
>
> *Sergei, Ust Avam, 1997*

> I only have the ribs left from the caribou I killed on Saturday. Most of it I gave away. It's a big sin if you don't give meat away. You will not have any luck hunting, if you don't give meat away. Some people come two or three times a winter for meat. My brother and father feed themselves. Sometimes I go to them or they come to me, if we had an unlucky hunt. I think this is the same as it was before 1991. Old women and men are the most often to ask for food. I give it to them without a word.
>
> *Valery, Ust Avam, 1996*

This ethic of sharing, widespread among native peoples, means that certain individuals supply resources through kinship and friendship networks, often in a sustained one-way flow. Since there is no immediate observable material benefit to good hunters that consistently give food away, there is reason to look at social factors that favor food transfer. Kinship relationships, high social visibility and commitment, and informal social control often are linked with hunter-gatherer systems of distribution, and these conditions are present in Ust Avam's informal sharing economy.

In the Avam tundra, I asked 79 heads of households about the source of their meat and fish in order to determine protein distribution patterns using my structured survey. Locally hunted and fished protein comprise the bulk of that consumed in Ust Avam. In 1,150 meals that I recorded, 96 percent came from locally hunted sources. The ratio of protein dishes to meals was close to 1:1 for the winter months and 0.8:1 for the summer months. For Arctic populations generally, daily intake of calories in the form of protein is important. The Ust Avam community is no exception.

Many households do not include active hunters or fishermen. Table 2.7 summarizes responses to the question on source of meat and fish for 79 households interviewed in 1997. Close to half (48%) of informants answered that their main source of meat and fish was their own hunting and fishing activities in the tundra (coded "hunting"). Of the 38 respondents who answered "hunting," 35 were men and three were women. "Offspring" were the source of protein for one male and four female respondents. Five women answered that their "spouses" were the main

Sources of Meat and Fish	Respondents	
	n	%
Hunting	38	48.1
Offspring	5	6.3
Spouse	5	6.3
Purchase	4	5.1
Other Relatives	3	3.8
Mixed Sources (n = 24)		
(a) Purchases and gifts from kin or friends	6	7.6
(b) Gifts from relatives and friends	4	5.1
(c) Hunting plus purchases from *gospromkhoz* or hunters	4	5.1
(d) Fishing, but purchases of meat	4	5.1
(e) Gifts from consanguineal or affinal relatives	2	2.5
(f) Hunting, gifts, or purchases	1	1.3
(g) Hunting, purchases of fish	1	1.3
(h) Hunting, but fish from relatives	1	1.3
(i) Gift from relatives and social security	1	1.3
TOTAL	79	100

Table 2.7 Responses to the question on source of meat and fish, 79 Household Sample, 1997.

source of protein. Two women and two men answered that most of their local protein was "purchased" from the *gospromkhoz* or directly from hunters. "Other relatives" were the main source for one man and two women. Of those respondents describing single sources of protein, subsistence hunting was the most important, especially since it is likely that "offspring," "spouses," and "other relatives" gained most of their protein through "hunting." Of the respondents who did not hunt or have a member of the immediate family who hunts, "offspring" and "other relatives" provided protein through regular gifts. "Purchasing" appears to be a supplemental strategy.

Twenty-four respondents (30.4%) gave multiple answers to the question of where they get their meat and fish (coded "mixed sources"). Of these 24, seven were men and 17 were women. Six of the seven men included "hunting" and "purchasing." Of the 17 women, only four noted "hunting." Twelve women included "relatives," and 10 women included "purchasing." Again, with mixed sources the data indicate a heavy reliance on subsistence hunting and sharing with relatives. "Purchasing" meat and fish from the *gospromkhoz* or directly from hunters was an option for 20 (25.3%) of the respondents (four single-source responses plus 16 mixed-source responses). Most of the mixed-source responses listed purchasing as a supplementary strategy.

Where families get their meat and fish is only part of the local protein distribution picture. The vast majority (93.7%) of the 79 individuals taking part in the survey gave away meat and fish. Table 2.8 provides rank-order answers to the question, "To whom do you give meat and fish?" Many of the 79 heads of households interviewed provided multiple answers to this question. The most common answer was "relatives" (consanguineal and/or affinal kin). Some people mentioned specific relatives, while others simply stated "relatives." When interviewees mentioned two categories of people to whom they gave meat and fish, the category mentioned second most often was "friends."

Order Mentioned Recipients of Meat and/or Fish	1st	2nd	3rd	4th
Relatives (*rodnia*)	49	6	0	0
Friends	5	13	1	0
Affinal Kin	3	0	0	0
Neighbors	2	3	0	0
Pensioners, Single Mothers	7	8	2	1
Other People Who Ask	8	7	6	0
Outsiders	0	2	0	0
No One	5	0	0	0

Table 2.8 Rank-ordering of responses by 79 heads of households to the question, "To whom do you give meat and fish?"

How much do hunting and fishing households give away relative to their own needs? Put another way, how much meat and fish are they investing in the local social system? This was very hard to determine through direct observation. The bulk of meat and fish distribution took place behind closed doors or at inopportune times for observation, such as at the helicopter pad. My direct observations being limited, I asked the 79 heads of households during interviews, "How much meat and fish do you require for yourselves, and beyond that how much do you share with other households?" Most informants could not distinguish between these amounts and stated the total amount they required for a year or season. Some stated that it is a sin to count such things. Twelve people gave relative estimates of their own caribou consumption and distribution for the winter (nine months), seven gave estimates on fish, and two gave estimates on fowl.

Five of the twelve who estimated winter caribou requirements indicated they gave away as much as they used themselves, from two to twenty caribou carcasses. One informant stated that the family consumed more than they gave away—forty versus ten caribou carcasses for the winter. The remaining six household heads stated that they consumed less than what they gave away. Four households gave away double what they consumed, one gave away triple, and another gave away quadruple their own consumption!

The results with fish are similar. Three household heads estimated they consumed less than they give away. Two informants estimated similar quantities consumed and given away. One family estimated that they consumed more than they gave away. The estimates ranged from one to twenty bags consumed and from four to fifteen bags given away in one winter (1 bag = 40 kg).

While these data are provisional, it is clear that, at least for some families, significant portions of the meat and fish obtained are given to other families in the community. Most of this food appears to go to affinal and consanguineal relatives, according to the survey. Friends and neighbors also receive meat and fish, as well as pensioners, single mothers, invalids, and "other people who ask." The result is that it is rare that any household goes without protein, the major meal component. The tradition of sharing meat and fish has a long history among the Dolgan and Nganasan, but the tradition may be of greater importance today than it was during the Soviet period.

> In the camp there would be three to five families. If someone killed a caribou they would split it among all the families. This distribution occurred especially for the first kill. After that everyone started to hunt. If someone was unlucky we helped out. People still give meat if I ask. Some people give meat, some do not—it depends on their soul.
>
> *Yuri, Ust Avam, 1996*

> Meat is given simply so, to relatives, distant relatives, or to trustworthy working people. There is no expectation of a return in labor or goods.

> The person that has a snowmobile brings water for friends, relatives, etc.
> At Khantaiskoe, when I was bringing water, I would make eight trips.
> People would say, "Zhenya bring us water. We wish you a good wife."
>
> *Zhenya, Ust Avam, 1995*

Since meat and fish are transferred from primary producers to those in need, it was unexpected that some of the respondents who did not hunt or fish stated that they gave meat and fish away to other families. As shown in table 2.7, thirty respondents (38%) answered that their main source of meat and fish was either purchased or given by friends, relatives, and other people. Twenty-seven of these people (90%) said that they gave meat and fish to relatives, friends, single mothers, pensioners, affines, and "other people who ask." What kind of benefit do they gain by giving away meat and fish if they themselves have a limited quantity of it? Researchers have identified a number of advantages (Woodburn 1982, Cashdan 1989, Hill and Kaplan 1993, Blurton Jones 1987, Hawkes 1993, Peterson 1993, Bliege Bird and Bird 1997, Winterhalder 1997, Gurven et al. 2000). One widely accepted hypothesis is that meat sharing reduces the risk of people not having enough food over an extended period of time. For exchange to work as a buffering mechanism in this way, present abundance is converted into a future obligation (Halstead and O'Shea 1989: 4).

For certain households, such as one with four invalid pensioners or a single mother with nine young children, the buffering hypothesis does not make sense, since the receiving household has limited ability to fulfill its return obligation. To the contrary, I have documented a sustained, one-way flow of meat and fish from hunting to non-hunting households. According to informants in both households, this flow has been maintained for two generations.

The buffering hypothesis appears to apply, however, in the case of two non-hunting households sharing meat at various times, such as might be the case with single pensioners. The receiving households can reciprocate when they have meat or fish themselves; their sources of meat and fish are likely to be different than the giving household, since everyone has their own set of relatives, friends, and neighbors, and both households are likely to have the ability to fulfill their obligation at different times. The buffering hypothesis also appears to work for non-related, casual hunting partners and their households. During one point in time, hunter A has meat and gives some to hunter B, who does not have meat. They go hunting or fishing together sometimes, but not always. At another point in time, hunter A does not have meat but hunter B does, and hunter B gives some meat to hunter A. I have documented this kind of exchange for two such hunters and their households.

Sharing may be motivationally closer to Marshall Sahlins' (1972) concept of *generalized* reciprocity than to the concept of *balanced* reciprocity. When someone gives meat and fish in a bag, it is said that the receiver should return the bag with something in it. The value of the thing returned is not significant. It can be matches, cigarettes, or some homemade fry bread, for example. This type of return is symbolic of future cooperation, a characteristic of generalized reciprocity. The value of the thing returned or the timing of the return is not what is important, but rather the exchange itself.

I did not document any signs of heightened status for successful hunting households in their equipment, household appliances, or domicile. In fact, some of the more successful hunters lived in the worst houses and could not sell meat or fish if their lives depended on it. Several hunters complained to me about how people had money for alcohol, but not for meat and fish.

Without a cash market for locally produced meat and fish, information about who has it is important. The *gospromkhoz's* staff hunters, as well as sports hunters and fishermen, are often observed returning to the village carrying large burlap bags with butchered caribou or fish. Fairly accurate estimates of the amount brought into the village are made. "So-and-so brought six bags in this morning," was a common type of conversation opener. This subsistence information spreads rapidly. When someone needs meat or fish, they usually know which house to go to to ask for meat and fish. If the hunter/fisher has a surplus of meat or fish and someone really needs some, he or she usually gives it. Successful hunters/fishers could be accused of being stingy or greedy if they do not share their catch. The charge of being greedy would carry some cost, and charges made as rumors must be dispelled, even if the accusation is unfounded. These conditions are similar to those in other groups of hunter-gatherers where economic leveling is institutionalized (e.g., !Kung "insulting the meat" [Lee 1993]; and Mardudjara foodstuffs exchange [Tonkinson 1978]). Hiding or securing meat and fish in Ust Avam certainly carries a cost. Building a secure shed or underground ice-chamber is difficult and impossible to hide. Preserving meat and fish in the village also carries a cost; as smoking or drying is done outside, it is like an advertisement of surplus.

Food Consumption

The availability of non-local foods, such as flour, sugar, canned foods, and vegetables, varies both geographically and temporally for indigenous communities in the Taimyr Region. Imported carbohydrates have been present in the diets of northern Siberian peoples for at least two centuries, but their relative importance in the diet has varied considerably through time and from place to place. Variation in access to imported carbohydrates reflects the organization and efficiency of trade networks and government subsidies. The merchant trade of the 1800s was fairly inefficient in north central Siberia, and supplies of imported carbohydrates were sporadic at best.

> Imported goods, such as flour, tea and sugar were probably used by all
> the [circumpolar peoples] even in the 19th century, but the amount of
> such goods in the daily diet can hardly have been large. Islavin (1847,
> 33 f.) reports the diet of the Samoyeds, for instance, consisted of
> bread, reindeer meat, fresh and dried fish, wild birds and berries. The
> consumption of bread was so small, however, that it did not make
> much difference whether it was included with reindeer meat and fish
> or not. (Eidlitz 1969:3)

The Russian government has supplied flour and grain to northern Siberians for almost two centuries. In 1822, Count M. M. Speranskii, a progressive activist and governor of Siberia, set up "bread-reserve" stores in
the Turukhansk district, which included the Taimyr Peninsula (Troitskii
1987: 63) and other northern districts of Siberia (Okladnikov 1968: 458).
The stores sold flour and grain at government-controlled prices for cash or
in exchange for fur-bearing animal pelts. There were at least three stores
built in the territory of the Dolgan and Nganasan (Karachintsev 1892: 1–
3). The bread-reserve system was part of series of reforms in Siberia that
were meant to improve the governance and regulate taxation for the indigenous population (Okladnikov 1968: 462; Forsyth 1992: 156). The
stores reportedly saved some groups from starvation in the nineteenth
century, providing an alternative to trade with private merchants. But it
has been reported that the people running the stores tended to abuse their
power by charging natives more than they were supposed to (Forsyth
1992: 160). The bread-reserve store in Khatanga operated until the late
1920s, when it was nationalized by the Soviets under *Gostorg*, the government trade organization (Troitskii 1987: 63).

Owing to their scarcity and high cost, imported carbohydrates played
an important symbolic role in the diets of indigenous people living in northern Siberia during the pre-Soviet and early Soviet periods. The following
excerpt from an interview with Aksenya ("Oksye") Bezrukikh, in which she
describes her wedding feast, suggests this symbolic significance.

> As I got ready to get married, they first killed the wedding reindeer.
> Father killed two reindeer and Grisha [her future father-in-law] killed
> two reindeer. In all there were four reindeer. It was such a wedding.
> They boiled the meat separately for the bride and groom in a different
> *chum* [teepee]. From the reindeer, they began to make food. It all went
> for food. Nothing was left. There were two full kettles of meat, the
> heads and all. Nothing was left. They made *amaha* [pemmican]. They
> made *alady* [pancakes]. There was Russian food, sugar, and candy
> called "Monponseiya". All the Russian food was the reserve of my
> grandmother and her husband. There was Soviet power at that time.

By far, the bulk of Oksye's wedding food consisted of reindeer meat.
When she left for her new husband's camp, her family sent her with eight
reindeer, each one loaded with two bags of dried reindeer meat and dried
fish. The inclusion of imported carbohydrates symbolized the wealth in-

volved in her wedding, a point mentioned in several sections of her description of the marriage. Describing the "Russian food" as the reserve of her grandmother, Oksye underscored the relative value of carbohydrates at that time to a reindeer-herding people with minimal storage capacity.

After World War II through the 1960s, collectives in the Taimyr Region were combined into larger units (*sovkhoz*), and permanent settlements were constructed. Over 80 collectives in Taimyr were formed into 17 state enterprises by 1971. At the time of *sovkhoz* formation, Aksenya's band was dispersed to a number of locations including Ust Avam. Each state enterprise had a corresponding settlement with permanent housing, schools, clinics, and stores. During the 1970s and 1980s, the regional trade organization TORO (Taimyr Wholesale Retail Organization) supplied food, mainly carbohydrate foods such as flour, grain, canned fruits and vegetables, sugar, and candy, by barge to Ust Avam and other settlements. People living in the villages generally had access to these goods. Hunters in the Avam tundra also received similar goods from the state enterprise, or purchased them from the store to take out to their cabins on snowmobiles for the season.

Since the end of the Soviet Union, the supply of consumer goods to the Russian North has been privatized and decentralized. While the Russian government continued to subsidize the transport of basic foodstuffs to remote indigenous communities, the amount and variety of what is supplied has been reduced. Access to carbohydrates has diminished. The situation was bad enough that, in 1998, helicopters from the Ministry of Extreme Situations were used to supply sugar and flour to Ust Avam, a fabulously expensive means of transportation for a government unable to meet its budgeted expenditures. Helicopters cost the equivalent of $1200 an hour in 1997, and it is a four hour round-trip to Ust Avam from the nearest heliport. A letter received in December 1998 from a friend in Ust Avam underscores this reduced availability of carbohydrates: "Changes in the settlement are still not exactly understandable. They are flying in sugar and flour on MI-6 helicopters but there is not enough for everyone." This change in availability of non-local foods has put renewed emphasis on locally produced foods, such as reindeer meat, fish, fowl, and tundra plants.

In the Taimyr Region, sub-zero storage is possible outdoors for six months of the year, and even longer underground. Chambers are dug into the permafrost, coated with water that freezes on the walls, and sealed with a number of insulated doorways. Some of these freezers, built by the state enterprise for storage of caribou meat, hold up to 200 tons. Some households have small underground freezers that hold much smaller amounts—up to several hundred kilograms. Long-term freezer storage of fresh meat and fish is not desirable however, because the foods dry out, lose taste, or go bad due to poor sanitary conditions. Various indigenous preservation techniques, such as drying and salting, are used to store meat and fish for the rest of the year. These techniques are described below. Another way food quality is kept high is by hunting and fishing throughout the year, concentrated around the major migration periods.

I derived the following food preparation techniques from five Dolgan informants in Ust Avam. In May 1997, I asked several individuals to list native food items using the free-listing technique described in Weller and Romney (1988). A core number of items were repeated in each of the lists; two individuals listed over 30 dishes, while the other three listed less than 15. These listed items were divided into eight categories based on degree of preparation. Direct observation and participation in Nganasan and Nenets meals revealed similar variation in degree of food preparation.

Raw *(hagudai)*

The most common items eaten *hagudai* are: the flesh and liver of chir (*Coregonus nasus*), a two-plus-kilogram freshwater whitefish; and various soft organs from caribou, such as kidney, liver, heart, and brain. Chir often has thick fat deposits on its underside and in its intestines and this makes it, and other types of fat whitefish, the most desirable for *hagudai*. The intestinal fat is often separated and melted in a water bath to make oil; fish oil is used as a vitamin supplement and for cooking. Usually, *hagudai* items are eaten immediately after the kill or catch. The fish or meat is scaled or cut into individual portions. The person then uses his or her own knife to cut the item into bite-sized portions, often using his or her teeth to hold one end of the item while cutting. Certain portions of *hagudai* fish are not consumed when eating. Whitefish *hagudai* is usually prepared from fillets. The backbone and ribs are not wasted, however; they are chopped up with an ax and also eaten raw. The dish is called *doktoro*. If *doktoro* is not prepared, the remaining pieces (head, backbone, and ribs) are usually boiled for soup.

Raw Frozen *(kyspyt)*

Both meat and, more commonly, fish are eaten *kyspyt*. *Kyspyt balyk*, or raw frozen fish, is prepared two ways (*stroganina* and *rubanina*) depending on the time of year and storage temperature. *Stroganina*, from the Russian verb *strogat'* or "carve," requires that the fish be solidly frozen. The fish is scaled and warmed a little in a fire, stove, or warm water for a few moments, then the skin is peeled off with a knife and eaten. The flesh of the frozen fish is then carved into thin shavings, often dipped in salt and pepper, and consumed before it defrosts. Rarely, meat is prepared as *stroganina*. More commonly, caribou liver and kidney are consumed *kyspyt*. *Rubanina*, from the Russian verb *rubit'*, meaning "hew," is usually prepared in warmer weather when the fish is not completely frozen or a frozen fish would melt too quickly. After the fish is scaled, it is cut into three- to four-centimeter sections. Each person gets a section and uses his or her own knife to cut smaller pieces before it all melts.

Raw Salted *(tustak)*

Fish can be prepared with the use of salt, *tustak balyk*. Each person has his or her own style when it comes to salting fish. Large and medium-sized fish are often gutted, butterfly-cut, and salted. Then they are rolled into burlap bags and stored in a cool, dry place for a day. The excess salt is brushed off and the fish can be either hung to dry (*vyalit'*) or consumed right away, usually cut into sushi-sized pieces and eaten with bread. *Kolodka* is prepared with smaller fish, usually small whitefish. Fish are rinsed, but not scaled or gutted. They are placed in layers and salted in either a wooden barrel or large aluminum tray. The salt draws liquid from the fish and creates salty brine in which the fish remain until consumption.

Shish Kebab *(ölü)*

Usually prepared on foraging trips, *ölü* requires only a sharpened stick and a fire. The stick is poked through entire small fish or pieces of caribou meat, liver, kidney, and heart, and placed into the fire. Often *ölü* is cooked medium rare, or *hüriigii*.

Boiled *(busput or kös)*

Meat and fish are boiled, pulled out of the water, cooled off, sliced, and eaten. This is called boiled meat (*busput et*) or boiled fish (*busput balyk*). Two main types of soup prepared are *min*, or consommé, and *butugehs* (soup with flour added to thicken the stock). Depending on availability, some kind of industrially prepared pasta, potato, or other dried vegetable is added to *min*. Soup is usually prepared with fish, caribou, or goose.

Fried *(zharitalybit)*

Since frying requires fat or oil, the use of this technique depended on the fat of animals or fish. During the Soviet era, with larger supplies of vegetable oil, lard, and butter, it became quite common. The most traditional form of fried meat is *kerdi et*, or cut meat. *Kerdi et* is prepared from the soft cuts of meat, heart, liver, kidney, and tongue, and is usually fried with caribou fat, either intestinal or surface. Sometimes a boiled grain such as buckwheat or rice, boiled potatoes, or pasta is added to the pan after the meat is fried. *Kerdi et* is usually sautéed until well-done. Another popular fried meat dish is fried cutlets, or *et kutlehttar*. As with the Dolgan word "to fry," zharitalybit, the word for cutlets is also of Russian origin, possibly indicating the relatively recent adoption of this preparation technique. Preparation of cutlets requires a meat grinder, which was not widely available before the 1917 revolution. Fish is fried in a familiar manner. After cleaning and cutting into sections, the fish is immersed in flour and fried in vegetable oil or fish oil.

Dried *(kopyt)* or Smoked *(kurbut)*

Reindeer meat and fish can be dried or smoked, with or without salt, to preserve the food for some time. Large whitefish are scaled, fillets are prepared, and the flesh is cut every two centimeters or so, without cutting through to the skin. These fillets are then hung in a *chum* (a conical-pole tent with caribou skin cover) where a small fire produces smoke, and flies and mosquitoes do not venture. If the weather is dry, the fillets are brought out to dry in the sun during the day; the result is called *yukola*. The dried flesh and skin are eaten, often with tea. Meat is similarly prepared, cut into long slices and hung in a *chum* outside, or from the ceiling of some apartments. When partially dry, the meat can be cut up into small pieces and set out in the sun to dry completely. This is called *ehlükteh*, or popularly, *semochki* (Russian for "sunflower seeds") and is traditionally prepared for the winter. In the spring and early fall, flies are not very numerous in the tundra, and meat and fish is dried outside without spoilage.

Rendered Fat *(busput heh)*

Fat surrounding a caribou's intestines, as well as fat from the outer layer of the meat, is rendered (melted) and cooled to produce blocks. Caribou bone marrow is also boiled and cooled to produce *ongok hehteh*, which is used like butter for bread. Internal and external caribou fat is used for frying, as well as in preparation of a traditional dish, *amaha*. For *amaha*, boiled meat is dried and pounded or, after drying, is put through a

Figure 2.6 Lightly smoked whitefish, *yukola*, is dried in the sun on specialized racks, hunting spot Zapornaia, July 1997.

meat grinder and pounded a bit. Rendered fat is melted and poured over the meat powder in a large bowl. The mixture is cooled off, and it congeals to a solid. The solid bar, *amaha*, is then sliced or broken off and eaten. Fish is prepared similarly with rendered fish fat. This is called *barka*. Rendered fish fat is also used to prepare fry bread of various types, although currently vegetable oil from the store is more commonly used.

*   *   *

When these preparation techniques are grouped according to a binary classification, "raw" and "cooked," the relative importance of raw protein in the diet of the Dolgan and Nganasan can be estimated. With this goal, raw preparation categories include *hagudai*, *tustak*, *rubanina*, and *stroganina*. The cooked categories include *amaha*, *ölü*, *busput*, *zharitalybit*, and *min* and *butugehs*. I created an "other" food preparation category that includes meals with no flesh-food dish. "Other" meals were almost exclusively tea- and coffee-drinking episodes with consumption of baked goods, open-faced cheese sandwiches, or bread and butter.

There were some interesting gender differences in food preparation techniques. The techniques described above were analyzed for seasonal biases among males and females in all locations: cities, such as Dudinka; villages, such as Ust Avam; and tundra camps and cabins. For 1,150 meals that

Figure 2.7 *Kopytky*, or the lower extremities of the reindeer leg, are being thawed so that the marrow can be rendered and the bones boiled to make meat jello (*kholodets*). Also, the hide (*kamus*) from this section of the leg is tanned and used for construction of boots. In the foreground, there is a basin with several small whitefish being warmed for *busput balyk*.

I observed and participated in, males used the *stroganina* and *hagudai* preparation techniques more often than females. Females used fried and soup preparation techniques significantly more often than males. The drymeat, boiled/broiled, *rubanina*, and sandwich preparation techniques were used approximately the same among males and females in all locations.

The gender differences are likely due to the disrupted settlement pattern in Ust Avam, where most of the observations in this sample were made. For communities like Ust Avam, having lost their domestic reindeer during the transition from collectives to state enterprises, men that were employed as hunters or fishermen began to spend more time alone in the tundra. Children were sent to boarding schools for most of the year, and women and the elderly remained in the villages or moved to the city. A similar process of segregation of men and women occurred in many subarctic Indian hunting communities in Canada and Alaska when services were centralized after World War II. Both men and women in Ust Avam stated that the raw-frozen consumption techniques were used more often when they lived in the tundra. That men used these techniques more often is at least partially related to the fact that men spent more time on the tundra. The raw preparation techniques—except for the raw-frozen sectioning, which is most common during a short period in the spring—are most widely practiced in the tundra and among bachelors in the settlement. Among Tukhard's reindeer-herding families and other communities where women live out in the tundra, women eat raw meat and fish almost as often as men, and more often than women living in settlements and the urban centers. Consuming raw-flesh foods appears to be most important nutritionally where calorie requirements are highest and there are few high-carbohydrate foods such as vegetables and grains.

While cooking is evidenced in all human societies (Brown 1991), ecological, nutritional, and cultural contexts create variation in its use across human populations. Eating raw flesh is not necessarily relegated to nature or the primitive (Levi-Strauss 1969a). Early anthropologists explained the consumption of raw flesh foods among Arctic peoples as a result of difficulties in fuel procurement (Bogoras 1904, Høygaard 1941) or scarcity of fuel (Murdock 1887)—a rather ethnocentric interpretation. There are clear nutritional and medical advantages to eating raw meat and fish under ecological conditions such as those in the Arctic. Raw flesh foods contain important nutrients not found in cooked flesh foods. Early Arctic explorers that did not eat raw flesh foods often got scurvy and many died from the disease (Stefansson 1927). Stefansson (1927: 2–3) reported that Arctic explorers that adopted the native tradition of eating fresh uncooked meat and fish did not develop scurvy. A few members of Stefansson's expedition, subsisting mainly on groceries and dried beef, developed scurvy within a few months and were later cured in several days with a diet of raw musk-ox meat.

The importance of raw flesh foods for nutritional health was also documented in Thomas' (1927) medical anthropological study of health and diet among Eskimos in Greenland. The Greenlandic populations showed no scurvy, rickets, or unusual prevalence of vascular disease in populations that ate fresh, uncooked meat, fish, and fowl. In contrast, among the natives of Labrador, who had been in contact with civilization for a longer period of time and had adopted imported foods and cooking methods, both scurvy and rickets were "almost universal" (Thomas 1927: 17). Consumption of raw protein is the indigenous tradition among native people in the Taimyr Region, as well as among other circumpolar peoples (Eidlitz 1969). Some cooking techniques, like pan-frying, and foods such as mushrooms, now in use in the Siberian Arctic were borrowed from people representing the former colonial power.

Hunting and fishing in Ust Avam provides essential nutrients to the Dolgan and Nganasan who live there. Meals that include raw meat and fish are often treated as small celebrations. There are at least two types of satisfaction that go into eating a raw meat or fish. One is the satiation of hunger in a way that cooked meat and fish do not. This feeling is qualitative, but real nonetheless, according to my experience. Another form of satisfaction is the perpetuation of tradition. The traditions of *kyspyt balyk* and *hagudai* are cornerstones of native lifestyle and identity. For example, I often visited a particular family, whose members became some of my best friends in Ust Avam. Most of their meals included *hagudai* meat or fish, and visitors were invited to eat if they arrived in time.

Figure 2.8 In the 1970s, the *gospromkhoz* in Taimyr began to use diesel-powered tugboats and barges, as well as small freighters, to supply Ust Avam. Since these vessels have a deeper draft, they were not able to travel up the Avam River to the old settlement of Novorybnoe, a reason cited for the settlement's closure.

Borya and I went over to Pedr's in the morning. Ilzhya cut up a small-
ish frozen whitefish (*podchir*). We ate *rubanina* (frozen chunks). Ladi
woke up a bit later and joined us. Vasya came over just as we finished
up. He also wanted some but we already had munched all of it.

May 29, 1997, author's journal entry

Thus, people in Ust Avam appear to take nutrients into consideration
when choosing what to eat. Rather than maximizing one factor, such as
calories or vitamins, the data suggest that a number of nutritional, social,
and ecological variables are considered to be important. For all three sections of Ust Avam's economy (production, distribution, and consumption),
there is evidence of the importance of ecology and reduction of risk
through diversification of strategies. These have become more important
for family and community survival in the post-Communist transition.

Chapter Three

The Loud Years
Resistance and Collaboration

As human societies become larger, kinship cooperation and high community visibility become less important, and new, often formal, mechanisms for social interaction are invented and implemented. Formal social control implies that some people within society are putting the rules into practice, and this results in social hierarchies where the benefits of cooperation become unequally distributed (Durkheim 1933, Berreman 1981, Beteille 1986). Inequality and the process of social differentiation are compounded when a colonial power takes control of an indigenous people (Wolf 1982, Bodley 1990). Physical or ideological coercion is beneficial to some individuals, but costly to those being coerced (van den Berghe 1979, Gramsci 1985). For example, the initial Russian colonization of Siberia, including the Taimyr Region, began with economic exploitation and political control, which were beneficial to the colonizers and detrimental to the indigenous population. Because of these inequalities, it is often the case that the people being colonized put up some kind of resistance, ranging in intensity from individual deception to organized conflict. Nevertheless, the advantages dealt out to certain individuals by the colonial power often provide a basis for collaboration, eventually weakening the resistance. In Siberia over time, cooperative activities built through progressive policies, intermarriage, and mixing of traditions benefited the native people. Similarly, during the Soviet period, phases of conflict and cooperation led to

63

the integration of the Taimyr native peoples into the planned economy and the Communist Party's political sphere.

Social inequality, brought about through empire building, colonial expansion, and more recently, globalization, is a multilinear process. Multilinearity means social organization may take on different characteristics depending on location and history. For example, with the breakdown of formal institutions in the post-Soviet period, informal local solidarity has again become important for individual and community survival in remote areas such as Ust Avam. In contrast, the development of the global economy has affected urban locations and places with access to goods and services. This dichotomy represents a fragmentation of Russian society, an important topic for academics and policymakers alike.

Prehistoric Human Occupation of the Taimyr Peninsula

How cooperative or antagonistic inter-ethnic group relations were at specific prehistoric periods is an important topic of investigation in archaeology, having implications for our understanding of contemporary human sociality. Prehistorically, there were numerous migrations on the Taimyr Peninsula on both the local and population scales, providing a backdrop for a history of blending of material culture and language. This blending could have occurred through peaceful borrowing of traditions from neighboring groups, although the history of conquest and migration in southern Siberia may indicate a more nefarious past, with technologically advanced populations coming north and assimilating preexisting populations. Southern Siberia has a history of pastoral conquest and empire building dating back to the Bronze Age (Herodotus IV, Sinor 1990). This military expansion may have forced some populations to migrate north and across the tundra and taiga, and thus it seems likely that mixing of peoples and traditions through direct or indirect violence was the rule in northern Eurasia.

The earliest evidence of human activity on the Taimyr Peninsula was discovered in 1967 near the Volochanka River, not far from Ust Avam (Khlobystin 1972). Objects from that site date to 7,000 years before present and are similar in type—including microblades and composite tools—to other east Siberian Mesolithic, or Middle Stone Age, sites (Khlobystin and Gracheva 1973, Pitul'ko 2001). At that time, the climate in Taimyr was warmer than today; forests grew several hundred kilometers north of their present northern boundary. These ancient trees continue to wash out of the permafrost, allowing Ust Avam hunters to dry them and use them for firewood sometimes. From 6,000 to 3,000 years before present, it is likely that the people living on the Taimyr Peninsula were related to or maintained some kind of affinity with east Siberian hunting peoples (Khlobystin 1982, 1984). The earliest evidence of the use of iron, from sites along the Piasina River, dates to 2,500 years before present where a unique ceramic type developed that may represent a synthesis of eastern and western Siberian traditions (Khlobystin and Gracheva 1993).

The early inhabitants of Taimyr most likely lived by following herds of caribou on their annual north-south migration. For example, the Oleny Brook site just south of Lake Taimyr is located on a caribou migration route near the summer calving grounds. Pitul'ko (1996) found bone and antler knife-handles, spear and arrow heads, fragments of barbed bone fish spears, a harness swivel block, and decorated bone fragments, as well as thin-walled and thick-walled ceramics. One artifact analyzed by radiocarbon dating is 1,880 +/–75 years old (Pitul'ko 1999b). Faunal remains at Oleny Brook included caribou bones, fish bones and scales, and bones of goose, duck, and rock ptarmigan. Taimyr historians propose that these early inhabitants were paleo-Siberian hunter-gatherers, possibly related to the ancestors of the present-day Nganasan, Yukagir, Chukchi, and Siberian Eskimo (Troitskii 1987).

The prehistory of the peoples of the Taimyr Peninsula demonstrates cultural connections to other areas of Siberia, and likely to North America as well. In the historical period, similarities in reindeer-herding technology and religion, including shamanism, just to mention two kinds of traditions, are widely distributed among the native peoples of northern Europe and Asia. Just how these connections originated and were maintained is still open to debate. With Russian expansion into Siberia, however, there is historical documentation of the processes of conflict and cooperation that influenced the social, political, and economic organization of indigenous Siberian peoples.

Russian Expansion

Beginning in the twelfth century, Russian armies moved northeast from Novgorod into the lands west of the Ural Mountains (Bakhrushin 1959). There they subdued the local Finno-Ugric-speaking peoples and took tribute mainly in the form of furs (Fisher 1943). Tribute, although not invented by Russians, became an integral part of Russian imperial expansion and relations with the indigenous Siberian peoples, symbolizing Russian protection from militarily hostile neighbors.

In the fifteenth and sixteenth centuries, Moscow became stronger, and in 1552 Ivan IV's (Ivan the Terrible) armies conquered the Kazan' Tartar khanate. The Tartars were successors to a series of horse-mounted, nomadic warrior peoples that conquered the steppes during the Iron Age (Khazanov 1984, Sinor 1990). These nomadic tribes extracted surplus agricultural production from sedentary groups and controlled trade networks from the Greek Black Sea colonies to China (Herodotus IV). The steppe nomads and the reindeer herders and hunters of the taiga and mountain regions were also involved in some kind of exchange, most probably tribute to the ruling nomads. Found in burial mounds across Eurasia, the Scythian "animal-style" artwork attests to these networks of exchange (Bashilov 1989, Vainshtein 1991). The Tartars ruled an area from Romania (Stahl 1980) to eastern Siberia (Forsyth 1992).

With the defeat of the Kazan' Tartars, Russia reversed over two centuries of eastern domination and opened the door to its own conquest of the Tartars' former subjects and beyond (Bakhrushin 1959). Russian explorers moved toward the northern part of Siberia from the Ural Mountains beginning in the sixteenth century. They found virtually untapped fur-bearing resources in the northern forests, as well as native populations that were relatively peaceful in comparison to the Tartar-Mongols in the south. The czar's forces, capitalizing on preexisting indigenous antagonisms, moved across Siberia during the seventeenth century, but the nomadic groups in the north proved difficult to master (Forsyth 1992: 58–60, 77, 90, 148–150; Osherenko and Golovnev 1999).

Ten to fifteen years after the first explorers, who were usually fur trappers, entered the region, the czar's musketeers *(streletskie otriady)*—a special military corps instituted by Ivan the Terrible—followed to claim the land in the czar's name. These troops took tribute from native Siberian people as recognition of the Russian czar's sovereignty and collected a 10 percent tax from Russian fur trappers that had already penetrated the region. Because of the tax required by the czar, trappers did not hurry to inform the government of new fur-trapping lands, and since they held discoveries in secret there is no exact date for the first Russian occupation of Taimyr. By the 1570s, the imperial government ordered the building of Mangazei, a small wooden fortress that soon turned into a city and the center of Russian expansion into the Siberian Arctic.

The most important resource exported from Siberia after the Russian conquest was sable pelts. During the sixteenth and seventeenth centuries, the fur trade accounted for 10 to 15 percent of the total income of the state (Fisher 1943: 118–120, Bakhrushin 1959: 11). The czar attempted to monopolize the fur trade by using the military to collect tribute. Sable remained a major export commodity until the eighteenth century, when Canadian fur entered European and Asian markets (Fisher 1943).

In the first part of the seventeenth century, Russian explorers attracted by the sable followed the Kotui River to the Kheta and Khatanga Rivers in the eastern part of the Taimyr Peninsula, called Piasida at that time. Controlling the Kheta and Khatanga Rivers, Russian fur trappers built winter cabins on high banks, usually at the river confluences. Many rivers and campsites in the Taimyr Region got Russian names during this period: Zhdanikha, Boyarka, Romanikha, Novaya, Nizhnyaya, and Balakhna (Troitskii 1987: 35). Russian hunters came from Mangazei through Turukhansk, located on the Yenisei River, later to become a famous outpost for government exiles. Most Russians trapped for two to three years in the Piasida then returned to Russia with furs. It was from such fur traders that seventeenth-century Dutch and English merchants, searching for a river route to China through Russia, first heard about the resources and inhabitants of the Yenisei, Piasina, and Khatanga Rivers (Alekseev 1932: 207–228; 236–266).

In addition to the anecdotal sources, the best source of information on the first Russian expansion into the Taimyr comes from the Mangazei tribute books. Furs collected in tribute were strictly controlled. If even one fur registered in the tribute book got lost, the guilty party faced a jail sentence. Thus, Russian scholars consider the tribute books to be a better source of information than annals and other documents of that period. Siberian ethnographer B. O. Dolgikh used information from surviving copies of the Mangazei tribute books to reconstruct the tribal and clan structure of seventeenth-century Siberia (Dolgikh 1960), as well as to support his interpretation of the origin of the Dolgan nationality (Dolgikh 1963). Unfortunately, the originals were lost when the Mangazei archive was burned in the 1908 anarchist revolt in Turukhansk.

Tribute, or *yasak* (from the Turkish *yasa* or law), was an obligatory offering designated by law for Siberian native people. Tribute was required immediately after pledging loyalty to the czar. Valuable fur was the usual form of tribute payment, which comprised an important portion of the state's export income. Tribute-giving people in the Piasida paid from two to five sable furs per person per year. Able-bodied men from the ages of 16 to 50 were obliged to give tribute. Sable could be replaced with Arctic fox at the rate of ten to one!

Following the Kheta and Khatanga river basins from Mangazei, Russian cossacks subdued the Samoyedic-speaking populations in the eastern Taimyr Peninsula. These people were the Vadei Ngnanasans, called Tavo or Tavgi by early Russian explorers. From the Tavgi, the Russians heard of the Piasida Samodii, later called the Avai or Avam Samoyed, living in the Yenisei and Piasina River basins. Russian fur trappers and tribute collectors traveled back west to the rivers of the Piasina system on wooden rowboats that were carried through a series of small lakes and swamps called the Taganari *volok* between the Avam and Volochanka Rivers. The name Volochanka comes from the Russian verb *volochit'*—to portage.

Tribute collectors had trouble collecting from the nomadic tribes of the Piasida, and they tried to profit for themselves while collecting for the czar. In addition to the "legal" tribute collected by the czar's representatives and cossack infantry, independent bands of tribute collectors, private entrepreneurs, and Russian colonial government officials often took tribute for themselves. Some native groups ended up giving payment under duress several times a year; smaller bands were ruined in this manner and resistance to tribute collectors was prevalent (Forsyth 1992: 45). Table 3.1 shows the tribute collected for 1629 (Petrova n.d.: 9). The "clans" giving tribute were generally small, probably representing extended family

Collection Point	Clan	Number of Souls	Tribute
Khatangskoe winter-cabin, Khatanga River	Kisloi Shapki	11	21 sables
	Vyrui	12	24 sables
	Tyrendii Tyagorov	33	72 sables
	Tyrendii Khyrov	6	12 sables
	Savita	17	36 sables
	Syruyev	20	48 sables
	Parasiyev	16	16 sables
	Bykutin	7	14 sables
	Selyakin	4	9 sables
	Mundukun	1	2 sables
Yeseiskoe winter-cabin, Lake Yesei	Tydirsin	7	14 sables
	Sakeev	10	20 sables
	Khoruyev	2	4 sables
Piasidskoe winter-cabin, Piasina River	Piasidskii	2	4 sables
	Savitskoi	3	6 sables
	Terabeyev	1	2 sables
	Topeev	1	2 sables

Table 3.1 Tribute collections in the Taimyr Region for 1629.

camps. The largest had 33 working-aged men (souls). Also, note that tribute was recorded in terms of sables only. Presently there is no sable hunted on the Khatanga or Piasina Rivers.

The coercive nature of the Russian conquest was exemplified by the method used to facilitate tribute. The collectors took hostages, called *amanat*, from each clan and held them under guard until tribute was fully paid (Forsyth 1992: 45, 76–78, 89–91). These harsh tactics along with forced overhunting led to protest and armed conflict with the czar's troops. In 1666, the Tavgi Samoyed (Nganasan) attacked a caravan carrying the year's tribute collection and destroyed the Khetsk tribute winter post. After 1666, the tribute books mention the Avam winter post, which was apparently the successor of the Khetsk tribute house (Troitskii 1987: 37). In 1683, a garrison of the Yesei tribute winter post was destroyed.

Throughout the seventeenth century, tribute significantly decreased, and collectors were ordered to give out symbolic payment in the czar's name in exchange for tribute. For example, they gave flour, beads, copper pots, knives, and wool felt in hopes of increasing the number of pelts received and attracting collaborators. The taking of tribute in some respects began to resemble a form of barter at this point. Local residents brought the intended number of furs and, in exchange, got tin and beads (Petrova n.d.: 11). More generous gifts were given out the first time the tribe came under Russian rule. Later, the czar's representatives tried to get as many furs as they could while giving out as few presents as possible.

Usually, the tribute payers did not enter the cossacks' winter cabin, where the tribute collectors and the *amanat* sat. The exchange was conducted through the window. Similarly, exchange with Russian merchants was conducted with great care. The merchant and client did not approach one another. The article being exchanged for trade goods was tossed to the merchant. The trade good was taken quickly, and weapons were not dropped from either person's hands (Petrova n.d.: 11–12).

Formation of the Dolgan Nationality

At the end of the seventeenth century, Yakut and Evenk bands from central and southern Siberia began to move into the Khatanga River valley. Evenk groups herding in the northern forests were often in debt to Yakut traders, according to imperial Russian records, and "unpaid debts were hung on every *chum*" (Karachintsev 1892: 3). *Chum* is the Russian word that refers to the conical poled tents or teepees of many native Siberian groups. These Yakut and Evenk came from the lower Anabar River and from the upper Vilyui River in southern Siberia, where they had hidden from greedy tribute collectors in Yakutia (Troitskii 1987: 15). What is called the Dolgan nationality today is built up from these descendants of these Yakut and Evenk populations, along with intermarried Russians and individuals from Samoyedic-speaking bands (Dolgikh 1963: 125; Anderson 1998b: 77–105, 2000: 81–96).

Soon after the first Yakut immigration at the beginning of the eighteenth century, the Russian Orthodox Church built a church in Khatanga to serve the Russian community and convert the "wandering" tribes (Troitskii 1987: 49). There were approximately 50 Russians in the Khatanga area at that time, and they founded the Zatundrinskoye Peasant Society of the Avam parish. The name Zatundra, meaning "beyond the tundra," came from Russian residents of the lower Yenisei River, who had to cross an unforested stretch of tundra to reach the Ary-Mas region. In the first decade of the eighteenth century, Russian missionaries began mass conversions of the Yakut and Evenk people to Christianity. The Tavgi Samoyed (Nganasan) did not submit to conversion *en masse*. This is the time when the Dolgan nation began to be registered in the czar's tribute books. Often people that converted took the family name of their godfather, usually Russian tribute collectors, accompanying cossacks from Turukhansk, or Russian merchants. As a result, today the Dolgan generally have Russian family names such as Chuprin, Sotnikov, Portnyagin, Barkhatov, Kirgizov, and Laptukhov.

After conversion to Christianity, intermarriage of Yakuts, Evenks, and Russian Zatundra peasants became more common (Dolgikh 1963: 125). In 1896, orthodox Dolgan in the Dolgano-Tungus *uprava* (county) numbered 139 men and 139 women, and in the Yeniseisko-Zhigano-Tungus *uprava*, they numbered 299 men and 394 women (TOKM 01–21, 17: 1). It was generally Russian men that took native wives, and the children of mixed marriages learned the language of the mother. Thus, the Turkic Yakut language became the *lingua franca* for the southern and eastern half of the Taimyr Peninsula with admixtures of Evenk and Russian vocabulary. The people of the northern and western half of Taimyr generally kept their Samoyedic Nganasan, Enets, and Nenets languages.

There was some mixing of traditions other than language. Russians borrowed local native traditional clothing and the custom of consuming raw and fresh-frozen fish to prevent scurvy. Native people borrowed some hunting methods, fishing techniques, dog-sleigh transport, instruments, and housing style from Russian trappers.

> Each winter post has a closed-in yard where hay is stored, a raised storage room, sauna, and doghouse. Firewood and snow for water are also stored there. For Arctic fox trapping, traps, called *kulemy, pasti*, and *klialtsy*, are set. The trap line starts directly from the cabin. The number of lines depends on the number of workers. Workers are paid every third animal—the owner gets two. At the distance that one can travel one day on a dog sled, smaller cabins are built where a person can get warmed up and feed the dogs. Furs are left in the smaller cabins. To check one trap line the hunter takes 6 to 8 days. On the return trip the hunter checks the traps again and gathers the furs. (Troitskii 1987: 56)

The tribute-taking representatives of the czar and Russian fur trappers were only part of the influence on the indigenous populations of the region. Russian merchants, also generally from Turukhansk, engaged in exchange with the native population. In 1822, Count M. M. Speranskii, the progressive activist and governor of Siberia, opened "bread-reserve" stores in the Turukhansk district and other northern districts of Siberia (Okladnikov 1968: 458). The stores sold flour and grain at government-controlled prices for cash or exchange for fur, and there were at least three stores built in the Taimyr Zatundra (Karachintsev 1892: 1–3).

Underlying this supposedly philanthropic and paternalistically cooperative policy, the people that guarded and served in bread-reserve stores, picked from educated cossacks of Turukhansk, appointed for several years at a time, and located more than a thousand kilometers from their boss, often acted to maximize profits for themselves. In addition to acting as salesmen, they served administrative and police functions, wore military dress, and received a portion of grain for their disposal. The system of bread-reserve stores was a loss to the Siberian administration. Despite the misuse of power by the salesmen, the stores saved some groups from starvation in the nineteenth century by providing an alternative to speculative private merchants. The Khatanga store operated until the 1920s, when it was switched over to the government trade organization, *Gostorg*.

Independent merchant families worked in Taimyr until 1928, when they were ordered out of the region. In 1923, Victor Koreshkov visited the four Dudinka merchant families and described them in his memoirs (TOKM Fund A). One merchant, Pusse, was considered an old-timer with a large extended household. Several young native women worked for him keeping house, tanning animal hides, and sewing simple dresses and shirts for sale. Pusse's sons supposedly had sexual liaisons with these native women, but when they became pregnant, the children were not recognized by their Russian fathers. The women were either returned to their own families, or the children were kept for labor—an example of Russian and native populations assimilating into the Dolgan nationality.

Pusse's sons made *baloks* or house sleighs, and sold them to the native population. Their main source of income, however, was from exchange of trade goods and alcohol for fur. The Russian merchants of Dudinka morally outraged Koreshkov, and his descriptions of the exploitative practices of the Dudinka merchants were later used in regional literature touting the advances of socialism.

Generally, Russian merchants used native indebtedness to secure labor services. According to my oldest informant in Ust Avam, her parent's family, husband's family, and mother's sister's husband all worked for different merchants. Previously, these heads of households must have paid debts to merchants in the form of reindeer, and the families herded the merchants' reindeer along with their own. The winter trade caravans along the Dudinka-Khatanga winter road utilized the merchants' reindeer and native labor to transport trade goods east and furs west. Thus, in addition to herding reindeer, trapping, and fishing, some Dolgan were traditionally involved with Russians through long-distance exchanges. There was a range of characteristic social relationships in historic Piasida, from coercive tribute to cooperative exchange, that led to the formation of the Dolgan people.

The Communist Revolution and the Formation of the Regional Government

The Russian civil war created havoc, and the Siberian natives suffered both at the hands of the White Guard (czarist) and the Red (bolshevik) armies (Forsyth 1992: 248, 257). The northern regions, both west of the Ural Mountains and in Siberia, were under the control of White Army commander Kolchak until 1919 (Uvachan 1971: 87). The White Army maintained a stronghold in Dudinka, but it too fell to the Red Army in 1920 (Forsyth 1992: 248). Many native people were pressed into service at that time. Others had to slaughter their reindeer to survive during and after the war. Traditionally, reindeer were slaughtered only in quite exceptional cases among the Nganasan (Popov 1966: 63). Redoubling pressure on the traditional way of life, those people who lost their deer became dependent on relatives with large herds. This process exacerbated indigenous socioeconomic differentiation that the Communist Party was later to criticize and attack.

Attitudes and actions intended to improve the situation for the native peoples of Siberia often made it easier for the new Russian governments to influence them. For example, the Russian Provisional Government abolished tribute collection after the February 1917 Revolution, and the Soviets distributed grain and medicine, canceled debts to merchants left over from the czarist period, and prohibited the sale of alcohol in Siberia from 1923 through 1925 (Forsyth 1992: 242–243). The November 1917 Declaration of Rights of the Peoples of Russia proclaimed all ethnic groups free and equal, able to pursue their future as they determined (Sergeyev 1964: 487; Uvachan 1971: 116). These actions facilitated some native people's initial support of Soviet power.

As the new Soviet regime began to stabilize in the early 1920s, more and more people in Turukhanskii Krai joined the Communist Party. These individuals, less than 100 total, lived in Turukhansk and Dudinka. In 1922, native people in the Zatundra, including Dolgan, Nganasan, Evenk, and Yakut, gathered and elected King Barkhatov as their representative to the Third Congress of Soviets of Yenisei Gubernia. Barkhatov announced to the congress that his constituents had sent him to find out whether the Communists were to be their friends or enemies. He obviously made friends, and the congress appointed him to the Yenisei *gubispolkom*, or provincial executive committee (Uvachan 1971: 119–120).

The 1917 Declaration of Rights had little effect on existing social inequalities in Siberia, and the Communist Party, the Central Executive Committee, and its ministries began to develop a nationality policy that would incorporate Siberian peoples into the supposedly egalitarian national economy (Sergeyev 1964: 487). The first attempts at bringing Soviet power to the northern native peoples were made by the People's Commissar of Nationalities and its Department of National Minorities. The department had a wide agenda including protection of indigenous people from exploitation and extinction; regulation of hunting and fishing territories, reindeer-herding pastures, traditional trades, and fur-bearing animals; improvement of the indigenous economic situation; and coordination of indigenous participation in socialist construction, considering their unique northern living conditions (Uvachan 1971: 110). At the same time, the new Soviet government was not ignorant of the vast mineral resources of the north. Lenin gave orders to mine graphite for export of electrodes in 1920 (ibid.: 105), and beginning in 1921, the northern sea route committee organized geological expeditions into Turukhanskii Krai (ibid.).

In December of 1922, the Fourth Congress of Soviets of Yenisei Gubernia recommended administrative-territorial reapportionment to speed up native integration into the socialist state (Uvachan 1971: 121). The congress was most likely acting on recommendations of the provincial executive committee (*gubispolkom*) and its territorial commission, which had already discussed the idea of separating off Turukhanskii Krai, the future Krasnoyarskii Krai, as an independent administrative unit in November 1922 (Uvachan 1971: 129).

On January 31, 1923, the Yenisei *gubispolkom* accepted a resolution separating Turukhanskii Krai from the rest of the province. On February 7, 1923 the Yenisei *gubispolkom* confirmed two documents—"Edict about management of Turukhansk indigenous tribes" and "Edict about Northern inspectors of Turukhanskii Krai"—that determined the relationship between the national government and local native groups for the next few years. The first edict determined that the administrative organs for the nomadic indigenous tribes would be clan soviets (councils), the highest organ of power for native groups. The new clan soviets, successors to the clan administrations set up by the Speranskii reforms, were to be elected legislative bodies with a chairman, two members, and assistants (Uvachan 1971: 363). Clan soviet acts and orders, in agreement with the Soviet constitution and laws and orders of central and local powers, were to be obligatory for the native populations they administered. This type of top-down decision making was characteristic of the Soviet period.

The territorial commission created four land-inspection regions in Turukhanskii Krai to facilitate the transition to clan soviet administration (table 3.2). Anderson (1998a: 76–77) suggests that the land inspectors practiced a form of intelligence-gathering to identify "points where mobile hunters and herders would return in order to trade, fish, or encounter friends and relatives," and thus to improve control over these peoples.

As a result of trips into the tundra by these inspectors, 20 clan soviets and the Tazovsk indigenous executive committee were created by the first half of 1924. In the Khatanga Zatundrenskii territory, which included the Avam tundra, several clan soviets appeared. These included the Avamskii Tungusskii and Avamskii Samoyedskii, Boganidskii Tungusskii, Zatundrenskii Yakutskii, Dolgano-Yesseiskii, Zatundrenskii Krest'yanskii, and Vadeevskii Samoyedskii—the ancestors of the Dolgan and the Nganasan in the central Taimyr lowlands.

In 1924, the All-Russia Central Executive Committee (VTsIK) created the Committee of the North. The committee was created to further hasten the incorporation of indigenous Siberian people into "socialist construction." It was responsible for establishing cultural "bases" or stations (medical and veterinary stations, shops, and boarding schools that allowed only Russian as the language of instruction) throughout Siberia (Sergeyev 1964: 491, Forsyth 1989: 80). In the Taimyr Region these bases were constructed along the Dudinka-Khatanga tract at points identified by the land inspector.

The Soviet government's intervention in the daily affairs of Siberia's aboriginal groups became even more intrusive in 1926, as it formulated and began implementation of policies outlawing "primitive customs." The

Russian Communist Party viewed many of the indigenous traditions, such as mutual aid, caring for the elderly, and "sharing the spoils," as relics of primitive communism, a barrier to socialist development. Clan retribution, blood money, bride price, arranged marriage, and shamanism also made tribal social organization "inferior" (Ivanov et al. 1964: 733, 787; Forsyth 1992: 244; Sergeyev 1964: 498). Despite the Party's measures, many peo-

Land Inspection Region	Location	Native Population	Inspector's Residence	Inspector
Tazovskii	West of the Yenisei River including the Taz River area	Obdorskii, Tazovskii, Beregovii Yurak (Nenets), Bishenskii and Timsko-Karakonskii Ostyako-Samoyed (Enets), Chapogirskii and Pankagir-skii Tungus (Evenk)	Tazovskay chapel	F. E. Golovachev
Zatundrenskii	East of the Yenisei River to the confluence of the Kureika, Kotui, and Kheta Rivers	Ostyako-Samoyed, Dolgan, Zatundrenskii peasant, Samoyed-Tavgii (Ngana-san); Tungus, and Yakut groups	Dudinka-Khatanga tract	F. I. Klimentyev
Ilimpiiskii	Nikhnii Tunguskii River basin	Tungus and Yakut	Monastyrskoye	E. S. Saveliev
Southern	Shoreline of Yenisei, Sym, Yelogui, and Podkamen-naya Tunguska river basins	Yeniseitsy, Elogyiskii Ostyako-Samoyed, Symskii and Podkamenno-Tungusskii Tungus	Podkamennaya Tunguska	I. D. Potapov

Table 3.2   Land Inspection Regions in Turukhanskii Krai, 1923.

ple continued to practice customs such as shamanism in private (Milovsky 1992). Also in 1926, the VTsIK adopted a "temporary directive" that called for the re-election of soviets at traditional clan gathering places and institution of regional native congresses and party executive committees (Sergeyev 1964: 492). Moscow, through its new administrative structures, aimed to transform the aboriginal Siberians into workers for the modern socialist state.

On December 10, 1930, the VTsIK created the Taimyr National (Dolgano-Nenetskii) Region, along with 15 other national regions throughout Siberia (Uvachan 1971: 375). Local administrations sanctioned under the 1926 "temporary directive" for northern native communities were to be replaced. Using the standards for election of soviets as specified in the Soviet constitution, kulaks (rich property owners), shamans (religious specialists), or former kings (native representatives of the czar) could not serve on the clan soviets and regional native congresses. Thus, the new national regions were to speed up the allegedly egalitarian and agnostic socialist movement.

The Soviet of People's Commissars began economic projects to incorporate native Siberians as early as 1920. The people's commissars sanctioned cooperative trade with indigenous populations, and several cooperative and government trade organizations operated under a November 14, 1920 decree on "practical measures for supply of the hunting/trapping population with groceries and hunting instruments" (Uvachan 1971: 104). The cooperatives opened trading posts, called *factoria*, at established meeting places along the Dudinka-Khatanga road and other major travel routes such as the Yenisei River. Under the 1920 measure, cooperatives were to supply groceries and trade goods at stable prices in order to contend with speculative merchants and private entrepreneurs.

At the end of the New Economic Policy in 1927, private enterprise was outlawed altogether in the north, and the Soviet of People's Commissars created the state-owned "Integral" Corporation to serve regions of the far north settled by indigenous tribes (Uvachan 1971: 161). Beginning in 1928, two trade organizations served the Taimyr's rural population, "*Taimyrintegralsoyuz*" (Taimyr Integral Union) and "*Vostsibpushnina*" (East Siberian Furs) with 47 stores (Stetsyuk et al. 1990: 3). The Integral Corporation provided trade goods and hunting and fishing implements, and took in commodities produced by the native people, a pattern repeated on a larger scale during the USSR. The Integral Corporation continued to set up stores across Taimyr until 1937, when there were 69 trading posts.

In addition to stores, *Taimyrintegralsoyuz* supported "simple comradeship units" (*tovarishchestvo*) sometimes referred to as "simple production units" or PPO, in which native people received significant subsidies for hunting, fishing, and trapping implements. The simple comradeship units were to play a role in preparing the native population for production in larger-scale collective farms, since party operatives were already in place to implement the transition. For example, working for the territorial land inspector, one agent finessed his way into a position as secretary of the district executive committee that oversaw clan soviets and, later, as manager of the Integral store in Volochanka, assisted in regional collectivization of local native groups (TOKM 4696(1): 5).

Collectivization, Rebellion, and Repression

Initiated in 1929, Stalin's program of collectivization affected the native peoples of Siberia in a number of ways. Collectivization of Russian peasants in southern Siberia and European Russia resulted in the forced deportation of thousands of non-natives to northern Siberia, where they depended on the indigenous people for survival (Forsyth 1989: 79–80). By the early 1930s, Communist Party operatives began collectivization of reindeer herders using subsidized trade goods and the idea of class conflict, effectively excluding heads of families from the decision-making process. Both the Nganasan and Dolgan of the Taimyr Region resisted collectivization until the late 1930s. The newly created Taimyr regional administration conducted a "war" against single-family economic units, and many of them were counted as *kulaky*, or rich peasants. These so-called kulaks led a resistance movement in response to collectivization policies, and many were later arrested and executed. The insurrection eventually included populations in the Avam and Khatanga districts of the Taimyr region, as well as the Yesei (Ilimipii) district of Yakutia. Russian military regiments used bloodshed to quell the uprising.

The debacle started in December 1931, when the regional administration decided to create a soviet reindeer-herding farm in the Volochanka district. The reindeer were to be purchased from rich Dolgans and Nganasans in the area, but not with cash. The appointed director of the state farm was to make payments through the preexisting Volochanka cooperative in the following manner: 40 percent government bonds; 40 percent I.O.U.s from the Siberia territory executive committee; and 20 percent money and trade goods through the cooperative (TOKM 4696(1): 2). With eighty percent of the compensation in the form of territorial bonds and I.O.U.'s, the Dolgan and Nganasan did not view this development positively. In addition to the pressure to "sell" private reindeer to the developing state farm, in 1931, the Volochanka boarding school was founded and its first teacher arrived. District executive committee administrators conducted "agitation" among the native population to turn their children in for education.

In a 1932 top-secret letter to Moscow, the staff of the Taimyr executive committee hinted at upcoming conflicts with the native population (TOKM 01–21/5a: 7). The letter claimed that kulaks in the backward indigenous soviets were opposing all their activities, especially after recent elections. According to the letter, particularly difficult were the Avam, Taimyr, Vadeev, and Laptosolyansk native soviets. The Avam, Taimyr, and Vadeev nomadic soviets were generally Nganasan, and the Laptosolyansk consisted of 66 Nenets households (TOKM 01–21/5b). The insurrection appears to have started with these groups and spread to the Dolgans. Collectivization and other activities managed by the regional executive committee united these disparate populations. Matters became desperate after authorized representatives of the district executive committee came to give fur assignments to the native households. Some native soviets supported the resistance, and at least one chairman refused to fulfill his duties. The top-secret letter claimed that the most backward soviet, Taimyr, where almost no one spoke Russian, was supporting the kulaks through "kinship law of the elders." Obviously, collectivization was not going well there, and an ethnocentric attitude toward native customs only worsened the conflict.

The native resistance made four demands during the regional party conference and regional congress of soviets at the end of January 1932 (Stetsyuk et al. 1990: 4): 1) Do not victimize the kulaks (no assignments and no fines for not fulfilling assignments); 2) Free the population from trapping for one year; 3) Free the population from payment of taxes; 4) Free the population from freight transport. After these demands were made in public, households from different nomadic soviets in the Khatanga and Avam tundra began to gather at the Taimyr soviet; similar demands were made at native soviets across the region.

In response to these demands, the Taimyr executive committee sent twelve more agents into the tundra to ensure fur production and purchase of reindeer. They also gave an order to bring kulaks refusing to fulfill assignments to court. They sent a letter to all native soviets declaring that those individuals refusing to oppose kulaks would be appropriately punished and district soviets were ordered to increase "class awareness." The regional executive committee further planned to conduct expulsions of native soviet chairs supporting kulaks and to force kulaks to fulfill fur assignments. Individuals arrested were to be sent to Igarka, south on the Yenisei River, since there were no facilities for incarceration or guarding in Dudinka.

At the beginning of April, an assembly took place at Barkhatov station, not far from the territory of the Taimyr clan soviet, northeast of Ust Avam. The results of that meeting were sent as a telegram to Moscow (TOKM 01–21/5a: 4). The meeting included representatives from the Zhigano-Dolgano-Tungus, Dolgano-Yakut, Yakut, Dolgano-Krest'yane, and Samoyed-Dolgan clan soviets, and three separate Samoyed (Nenets and Enets) soviets. The assembly asserted their brotherhood with the Russian working class and their aspiration for equal freedoms. The telegram, addressed to the All-Russia Executive Committee, requested an independent commission to investigate the actions of the Taimyr regional executive committee. In the spring of 1932, at station Mironovskii, another assembly voted to disband the collective farm and return to individual family ownership of the herds. This action was not well received by the regional executive committee.

On April 22, 1932, a Russian military regiment from Dudinka opened fire on a meeting of native people in the Avam tundra. The regiment's instructions were to "bring the population to immediate responsibility, collect everyone, and force them. In case of resistance, level the ground with machine-gun fire" (TOKM 01–21/5a: 2). Men representing the native resistance then began to take Gostorg and Integral freight trains, which carried fur and other raw material into the tundra. The following quote is an excerpt from "The Loud Year," a story about this rebellion, told to me by Aksinya "Oksye" Bezrukikh, who was a firsthand observer. Her family worked for Gostorg, so her perspective is more supportive of Soviet power than one at first might imagine:

> They came in with guns and many bullets. They had many bullets on their chests. "If you do not assist us, you will never leave this spot," the bandits threatened. Mukulai told Anufry, my husband, to agree with the bandits for his own safety. Anufry left, and I was alone with my child, still in the bassinet. I had Kristina and a new child then. I fell asleep with them.
>
> They conducted the meeting. They brought in the old man, Kristafor Porotov. In that meeting they said, "We are taking all your reindeer, because they belong to the *Gostorg*. If you have private reindeer, ride only on them." That's how they conducted the meeting. We sat on three sleighs, and left.
>
> The next day there was no raw material left [furs they were taking to Dudinka]. It was all taken to Volochanka. After that, we argished to the north.
>
> Then we argished, and arrived at a camp. There were a lot of people, and some sort of meeting. But we were late for the meeting. It was a jovial environment. Girls were being given away as brides. Deer were being harnessed. Some men were eating those deer, not knowing whose they were. How could they be such *atamans* [cossack soldiers]? One neighbor took someone's *aku*, hand-fed doe, and slaughtered it immediately. How could this be? People went around telling this story. Killing another person's deer? And that's how these people lived before our *argish* arrived.
>
> When we came, we made peace with this other group. Later, a regiment (*otriad*) came from above. There was Maxim, Kaltara, and my *kuitue* [categorical son-in-law]. Only Gregory was not there. Why would he come, the old man? Why the *otriad* brought them, I did not understand. They came on the best deer, and along with them there were a bunch of Russian soldiers from Norilsk.
>
> In these houses, the shooting began, when they met with the Russians. The Nganasan and Dolgan bandits fought against the Russians. There was not much shooting, however, and there were no deaths. The bandits ran away; they left the shot up baloks.

We collected the empty houses. All our stuff was in there, along with freight sleighs. We got the houses together in one area. Everyone else ran away. These were empty houses. There were 10 or 20 houses. Our side guarded these houses, and waited for these people.

The bandits killed a lot of people, party workers, *komsomol* workers. There was a place, Dolgany maybe, where one party worker was killed and *komsomolsty*. The bandits wanted to crush Soviet power and instill their own. Onocho, a relative, came visiting. Their grandfather asked him how he could think of fighting Soviet power with his bare hands. Their grandfather said, "You will not win over that power. One airplane will come and get you all." Onocho replied, "The war is starting from us. It is from Khatanga and Yakutia, and it is the time to fight."

After the initial military action native leaders began to send telegrams to the regional executive committee in Dudinka and the Committee of the North in Moscow and to make written announcements to the population (TOKM 01–21/5a: 1). The individuals writing the statements were literate and most likely chairs of local clan soviets or collective farms. Anisim Popov, for example, was the chair of the Kosareva collective farm at Zhdanikha of the Khantaga nomadic soviet and signed one telegram (TOKM 4696(1): 6). These leaders were variously termed bandits or anti-Soviet agents in the correspondence of the regional executive community at that time.

After the Communist Revolution of 1917, the semi-nomadic settlement pattern of Taimyr's native population changed very little, but relationships with the larger economy became more involved. The new government canceled debts to merchants, and merchant reindeer herds were used for government trade. Perhaps these actions facilitated initial indigenous support of Soviet rule. With administrative and economic changes initiated in 1930, however, native leaders began a written campaign against the regional representatives of Soviet power. The campaign was framed in ethnic, not political, terms. The indigenous leaders were not critical of the "center of Soviet power," but of the regional Russian administration's inhumane and malicious implementation of that power. Taimyr's native resistance took Russian hostages, but military intervention quickly squelched the movement (TOKM 01–21/5a: 3).

After the 1932 rebellion, the regional executive committee, through its district committees, began to purchase reindeer from native households for the collective and state farms. By 1937, approximately 25 percent of the region's reindeer belonged to collective farms (Stetsyuk et al., 1990: 6). Many so-called kulaks along with shamans and former kings were arrested and executed in the late 1930s, and their reindeer also were transferred to collective farms (TOKM GIK 111, GIK 112, GIK 288, GIK 465). Although arrested as kulaks, kings, and shamans, these individuals were likely executed as revenge for their support of the 1932 insurrection and to put an end to any thoughts of native independence. My friends in Ust Avam have suggested that native kulaks were generally community elders.

Indeed, based on a database put together by the Taimyr Regional-Studies Museum (TOKM NSKF), the average age of those arrested in the Dudinka and Avam districts was 49 years.

The regional executive committee tacitly approved of the repression that went along with enforced collectivization in Taimyr. Individuals were arrested at stations along the Dudinka-Khatanga road, brought to Dudinka, and executed by representatives of the NKVD (predecessor of the KGB), generally in Dudinka. The Regional Soviet of Workers' Deputies, even with its native representatives, was in no position to oppose the activities of the NKVD either.

Despite the resistance shown in 1932, by the onset of World War II most of the Siberian native peoples had become members of collective farms. As members of a collective farm, many reindeer-herding families continued their semi-nomadic lifestyle, riding to the stations to turn in goods, buy supplies, and visit with friends and relatives. Nonetheless, they spent most of the year herding, hunting, or at fish-camps along the major rivers.

Life in the collective farm was difficult, to put it mildly, and World War II put severe restrictions on availability of imported food and consumer goods. Workers were paid miserly wages, calculated by the workday. The value of one workday was figured at the end of the fiscal year, after all profits and expenses were balanced. Profits were then divided among workers by the workdays they contributed. Collective farm members received monthly advances for groceries. This system left most members further in debt and dependency on the collective. In the 1955 work book of one collective farm worker, I found listed the official workdays and tasks: fur trapping, reindeer herding, 45 workdays, 29/4/55; moved freight to Dolgany, 1 ton, 10 workdays, 29/4/55; turned in caribou meat 35 kg, 4.2 workdays, 14/5/55; turned in caribou meat 265 kg, 31 workdays, 27/6/55; cut boards, 700 meters, 15.75 workdays, 28/7/55. By this time, the native adults in the Taimyr tundra were workers in a hierarchically organized political economy.

By 1938, there were five collectives in the Avam tundra. Two of these were centered in the foothills of the Putorana Mountains, kolkhoz Kalinin at Dolgany and kolkhoz Soviet Arctic at Medvezhii Yar. The other three collectives, Pura at Pura, Malenkov at Old Avam, and Eight Congress at Letovya, were located on the Dudypta and Piasina Rivers. The reindeer herds, at this time mainly the property of the collective, were used to transport goods back and forth from Dudinka to Khatanga. The Avam tundra collectives controlled the portion of the trail from the Piasina River to Letovya and Volochanka, and there were a number of additional stations along the trail. The community of Ust Avam began to take its present form in the late 1950s, when the government began to close stations along the Dudinka-Khatanga reindeer trail. When the government closed these stations, it concentrated social services, such as education and medical care,

Figure 3.1   In Ust Avam, there is no running water. The *gospromkhoz* brought this horse to the settlement to carry water. The *gospromkhoz* employed a number of individuals in non-hunting jobs, such as horse caretaker, tractor driver, electrician, and janitor.

along with the local administration, to three new locations: Novorybnoe, on the middle Avam River; Old Avam, at the confluence of the Avam and Dudypta Rivers; and Kresty, at the confluence of the Dudypta and Piasina Rivers. After several phases of collective farm consolidation in the 1950s and 1960s, the administration of Avam tundra's working population was moved to Volochanka, 90 kilometers east of Ust Avam, the center of the Avam district and Joseph Stalin State Farm *(sovkhoz)*.

In June 1971 ten million hectares were carved out of the territory of the Volochanka administration to create the *gospromkhoz* "Taimyrskii." At that time, the current settlement of Ust Avam, 13 kilometers upriver from Old Avam, was created. Novorybnoe and Old Avam were closed, and services at Kresty were restricted. Most Dolgan and Nganasan families were moved to the new settlement. The *gospromkhoz* had its main office in Norilsk and was administered under the Main Department of Hunting Industries and its Krasnoyarsk affiliate, *Kraiokhotupravlenie*, rather than the Taimyr Region's Agricultural Bureau. The main goal of the enterprise was to produce wild reindeer meat, fish, fur pelts, and crafts for Norilsk. Workers were no longer paid by the workday; they had seasonal or monthly plans and were paid minimum salaries whether they fulfilled the plan or not.

Figure 3.2 Brick apartment buildings in Ust Avam were built by the *gospromkhoz* in the late 1980s and early 1990s. Bricks, insulating concrete panels, and other materials were shipped to Ust Avam on barges. Construction workers were also of non-local origin, but many have settled in the community.

Cultural Encounters

The native population of the Taimyr Peninsula, relatively independent at the turn of the seventeenth century, quickly became exploited and dependent subjects of the fur-hungry Russian Empire. During this colonial period, there were many "loud years" across the north. Despite this resistance, political and economic institutions solidified under the czar's hierarchy, some of which included native representatives. In the twentieth century, communism promised a miraculous transformation. The Soviet state canceled debts due to merchants, and autonomous national regions were created for native Siberians. Soon after, however, the repressive policies of the Stalin regime were met with resistance among the native people of the Taimyr Region. The dissidents were easily handled, and native collaborators with the Communist party were rewarded with administrative posts. Newly developing Soviet institutions eventually transformed the Dolgan, Nganasan, Nenets, Enets, and Evenk into workers for Soviet agro-industry, supplying food and transportation to the growing industrial center. Dependencies on non-local energy, capital, and political forces increased, and many native people took advantage of the opportunities provided by Soviet society.

In rural Taimyr, since the breakup of the Soviet Union, the formal economic institutions that developed at a high human cost during collectivization are now disintegrating, and informal institutions of social mediation and control are developing in remote communities like Ust Avam. With high unemployment and inactivity in the labor force, it is no wonder that over 85 percent of the 79 adults in Ust Avam whom I interviewed in 1997 think their situation is worse than it was before 1991. The last two decades of Soviet power are now viewed, to some extent, as a golden age. In some respects, the breakdown of the formal economy is having a harmful outcome, and this is discussed in the next chapter.

Chapter Four

Alcohol and Violent Death

The Soviet government's goal of transforming the native Siberians from the "Stone Age" to socialism in one step was severe at its inception. The Dolgan and Nganasan were settled into permanent villages, eventually lost their domestic reindeer, and by the collapse of the USSR in 1991, most adults were employed in state-managed rural enterprises, hunting, fishing, trapping, and making crafts for the planned economy. The native peoples of the Taimyr Autonomous Region have been on the extreme end of a process of social and geographic differentiation, paralleling to some extent what has been occurring across the Russian Federation since the collapse of the Soviet Union. As a rule in the 1990s, people living in remote regions and territories have become worse off economically than those living in cities, while the greatest concentration of capital and jobs has been in Moscow (Ruble et al. 2000). With geographic differences in wealth and access to services and government, and regional variation in regulations, opportunities have been created for entrepreneurs to exploit those in less well-off locations (Humphrey 1998: 444–445, 1999: 34–42; Burawoy and Verdery 1999: 7). A product that has given one of the highest returns for speculators in the Russian north, where transportation costs have been increasing, has been alcohol. Speculative sale of alcohol has affected health in remote communities, such as Ust Avam.

The Alcohol Problem

For many years prior to the fall of the USSR, violent death rates in native Siberian communities had been higher than those in Russia as a whole or those among other native Arctic populations (Pika 1993: 62, Krupnik 1987: 101). Ironically, the change in mortality patterns began with settlement and employment of native populations and the stress of transition to settled life during Soviet rule. During this period, beginning in the 1930s and continuing through the 1980s, death due to infectious diseases among children diminished rapidly with regular access to medical care and more varied diet; fatalities due to violent causes, however, increased among the middle-aged across native Siberian communities (Bogoyavlinskii 1997, Krupnik 1987). The concept of violent mortality used here includes accidents, poisonings, trauma, homicide, and suicide (Vishnevskii 1999: 83). Natural deaths are defined as fatalities due to infectious or internal maladies. Even in the late Soviet era, violent deaths showed pronounced seasonality, correlated with periods of inactivity and holidays, when alcohol was most available (Pika 1993: 64–68, 74). Since 1991, the mortality trend that began with settlement has intensified in Ust Avam and other native northern communities. This chapter explores the problem using basic demographic data.

At the Third Congress of Native Small-Numbering Peoples of the Far North, Siberia, and the Far East, held in Moscow in March 1997, many challenges to the goal of self-determination were identified. A number of delegates discussed the interrelated problems of unemployment, violent death, and alcoholism. For example, Irina Eliseevna Afanas'eva, President of the Association of Kola Saami, Murmansk Region, said:

> Today, 50 percent of our Saami population is without work. Who is being thrown away first of all? A native people. There is one reason: alcoholism. We did not invent this blight. The Russian government that held the monopoly, controlling the sales of spirits, has now let it go from its hands. Commercial structures are feasting, while we die in this 20th-century plague. Today, this is an unannounced execution of the population, whether Saami, Russian, or Ukrainian. . . . The government should take cardinal measures for the alcoholic population. Why, this is not only drunkenness, it is a worsening of health. . . . Today in Labozero, where the majority of the population is Saami, there is not a week that goes by when we do not bury one or two people. They leave voluntarily from life, because they are at a dead end. There is no work, no normal life, no social protection. It is not rare that they go to the other world with a noose around their neck.

Along with indigenous political statements, the previous anthropological and demographic literature suggests that inactivity in the native Siberian labor force is related to increased alcohol abuse and violent death among working-aged adults. In the 1990s, as food production for the regional market economy all but ceased, efforts have focused on subsistence, which requires less time than that needed to fulfill government hunting plans. As a result, hunters and families spend more time in the settlement, where they are more susceptible to joining the "alcoholic population." A large number of adults are effectively unemployed in Ust Avam—registered as workers, but rarely or never receiving pay. This hidden unemployment contributes to low morale.

Overall, Russia's Arctic territories are among its most economically depressed since the fall of the USSR. The severity of the depression in the Siberian Arctic has to do in part with the structure of Russia's budget system: Only a few of Russia's regions are net contributors to the federal budget, which is partially redistributed to the remaining regions (Bikalova 1999, Stoner-Weiss 1997). For example, the Taimyr Autonomous Region contains sites of rich nonrenewable resources that are exploited industrially—now by companies whose stock is traded in the Russian and international stock markets. However, taxes on profits from these companies are collected in Krasnoyarsk, sent to Moscow, and redistributed from there. The Dolgan and Nganasan had little input on privatization of the Taimyr Region's mining and metallurgical industry in Norilsk.

Census information for this chapter originates from my review of the Ust Avam village council's 1997 registration book. The registration book lists community members by household and gives each individual's date of birth, date of death, adoption, education, place of work, and pension status, if applicable. The structured interviews served as a check of the demographic and genealogical information taken from Ust Avam's registration book. The registration book's information turned out to be impeccable, although interviews did augment it.

The village council maintained a separate registry for causes and dates of death in Ust Avam. I was allowed to copy the information going back 11 years. I also asked participants about dates and causes of death for family members during my interviews in Ust Avam. I recorded this information in my field notes and added it to my community census at a later date. I noted some divergence between the administration information on causes of death and my interview information. For example, in one case the official cause of death was listed as "heart attack," but the cause of death for that person communicated in an interview was "did not wake up after a night of drinking." Attributing such a death to heart attack has been standard procedure in Russia (Bogoyavlinskii, personal communication), and the procedure may have served to underestimate the record of violent death in Ust Avam.

The demographic information provided here is presented according to the comparative standards suggested by Hern (1995) for small-scale societies. After preparing this information and making some comparisons with other Siberian peoples and Russia overall, I found a distressing change in Ust Avam's fertility and mortality profile immediately following the collapse of the planned economy. In other anthropological case studies, analysis of the population-age structure has revealed problems in the demographic health and fertility of native communities (e.g., Chagnon 1998: 243–251). Similarly, Ust Avam's demographic profile adds to anecdotal sources and results from structured surveys on the direction of socioeconomic change.

Ethnodemographics of Ust Avam

The Ust Avam village council records the ethnicity, or *natsional'nost'*, of indigenous people registered to live in the area and reports this information to the regional statistical bureau annually. *Natsional'nost'* has been recorded on all internal passports (Soviet and Russian Federation) when individuals apply at the age of 16; if a person is of mixed ancestry, he or she can specify which ethnicity he or she prefers. Under the age of 16, people are considered to be the nationality of their mother for official reporting purposes. In 1996 in Ust Avam, there were 307 people counted as Nganasan in the official report, and there were 381 individuals registered as Dolgan. In 1997, my census of Ust Avam had, in addition to several Evenks and Nenets from other areas of Taimyr, 24 registered Russians and four people from Kirgizia, Kalmykia, and Azerbaijan. The Russians, Kirghiz, Kalmyks, and Azeris mostly came to work in the construction brigades of the 1970s and 1980s. They all are married, or were married, to local native women and many have offspring in the community. According to my review of the Ust Avam registration book in 1997, there were 127 individuals of mixed ancestry (table 4.1.); official statistics count most of these children among the native categories following the nationality of the mother.

In table 4.1, the ethnicity listed first is that of the father and the ethnicity listed second is that of the mother. For example, there are three individuals whose father is Azeri and whose mother is Dolgan. Interestingly, there are 56 people who have Russian fathers and native mothers, while there is only one person with a Russian mother and a native father. The 56 people of Russian/native ancestry are the product of 23 adult pairs. The fact that native women have had children with non-native men significantly more often than the reverse appears to be evidence of hypergamy—women marrying men of higher social status. Social and economic ties to Russia's dominant culture and location in the village may have increased the attractiveness of non-native men as mates before the collapse of the Soviet Union (cf. Humphrey 1998: 34–35, Dickemann 1979: 363). Table 4.1 shows 33 children with Dolgan fathers and Nganasan mothers and 22 children with Nganasan fathers and Dolgan mothers. These children are the result of 13 and 9 adult pairs, respectively. The absence of a clearly hypergamous marriage trend between the Dolgan and Nganasan suggests that there has been little status difference between them in Ust Avam.

Ninety percent of Ust Avam residents with mixed ancestry are under the age of 18. While this may partially be due to the fact that nationality was historically chosen at the age of 16, individuals with mixed ancestry make up a large portion of the community in any case. Friendships and kinship relationships overlap

Ethnicity	Number
Azeri-Dolgan	3
Dolgan-Nganasan	33
Dolgan-Russian	1
Evenki-Dolgan	2
Kalmyk-Dolgan	5
Kirghiz-Nganasan	2
Nganasan-Dolgan	22
Nganasan-Evenk	1
Russian-Dolgan	21
Russian-Nganasan	35
Tartar-Dolgan	2
Total	127

Table 4.1 Mixed ancestry in Ust Avam, June 1997 census.

ethnic identity. There are many individuals that bridge the ethnic groups, which may be why organized ethnic violence has not developed.

The Ust Avam administration provided summaries of census information for the years 1993 through 1996. It included lists reported to the regional statistical bureau of the number of men and women in three age categories (0–15, 16–55, and 56+ years old for men, and 0–15, 16–50, and 51+ years old for women) for indigenous residents of each ethnicity, and the total number of non-natives. I generated similar data for 1997 from my records of the Ust Avam registration book and structured household interviews. The 1997 information shows a significant decline in Ust Avam's total population compared with 1993–1996 (table 4.2).

According to the official information for 1993 through 1996, by January 1997, when the new registration book was started, 45 non-native individuals (62 percent of the 1996 set) had left the Avam tundra. Also in that year, 57 native individuals (8 percent of the 1996 set) were no longer registered in Ust Avam. There were 14 births and 15 deaths in 1996, and thus

Year	Total Population	Non-Natives	Community Composition (%)	Natives	Community Composition (%)
1993	750	50	6.7	700	93.3
1994	768	58	7.6	710	92.4
1995	763	58	7.6	705	92.4
1996	766	73	9.5	693	90.5
1997	662	28	3.9	636	96.1

Table 4.2 Summary census statistics for Ust Avam, 1993 through 1997.

the crude birth rate was 20/1,000 people, and the crude death rate was 22/1,000 people. In the first half of 1997, there were nine births and five deaths (crude birth rate 14/1,000 and crude death rate 8/1,000). For these 18 months averaged, the crude rate of natural increase was 1/1,000 (0.1 percent). At this rate, it would take 7,000 years for the population to double—a slow but positive growth rate. Birth-rate and death-rate differences cannot account for the reduction in the population in 1997.

The loss of population between 1996 and 1997 appears to be due largely to out-migration, especially by non-native residents with no local marital ties and by young native adults. I am aware of at least one young native family of three that moved to another village in 1996. Also, three native women moved to the regional capital of Dudinka, one ran away to an unspecified location, and another moved to a neighboring settlement. Three men from Ust Avam were in prison: one Russian and two native men. In addition to real migration out of the community, it is likely that a number of individuals already living in Dudinka changed their place of legal residence. The Soviet system of registration, still in practice today, requires each citizen over the age of 16 to be registered with the local authorities of his or her place of residence. For example, during my research in 1996, temporary non-native residents, such as teachers, were registered as living in Ust Avam. By 1997, a number had moved away and their replacements in Ust Avam were maintaining their legal residence in the city.

Figure 4.1 shows the population distribution for Ust Avam in 1997. There are fewer children in the youngest age category than would be expected historically for this population. In 1997, there were a total of 59 infants and young children (0–4 years old), composing 8.9 percent of the population. At the same time, there were 116 children in the 5–9-year age category, composing 17.5 percent of the population, and 95 children in the 10–14-year age category, composing 14.3 percent of the population. It appears that there are approximately half as many infants and young children (0–4 years old) as there should be. Male and female sex differences within each of these age categories are likely an artifact of the sample size.

There also appears to be a slightly lower total number of young adults (20–24-year age category) than would be expected from the number of people in the age categories immediately preceding and following it. Within the 20–24-year age category, there appears to be an especially low number of women (20, compared with 41 in the 15–19-year category and 30 in the 25–29-year category). Combined with low fertility rates in the 20–24-year age category (table 4.3), the 1993–1997 period signaled a significant decrease in community reproductive potential. With more than half (51.2 percent) of the community 19 years old or younger, Ust Avam's recent history is one of a relatively young, healthy, and fertile population. Something appears to have changed during the 1993–1997 period.

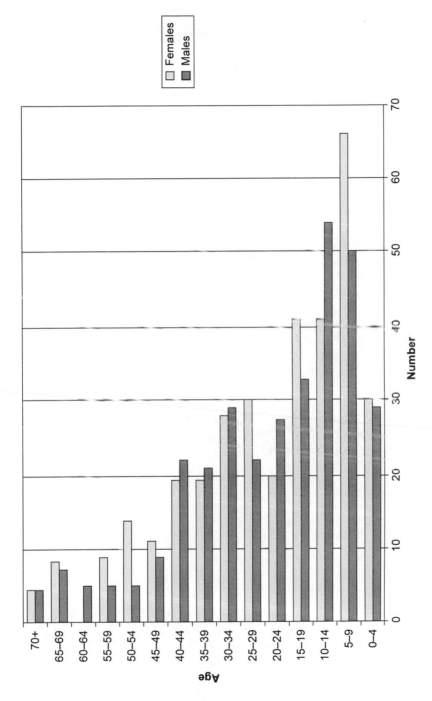

Figure 4.1 Age-sex distribution, Ust Avan, June 1997 census.

Fertility

Compared with the 1980s, the annual number of births in Russia decreased significantly during the 1990s. Russian demographers attribute this decrease, in part, to the lower number of women in the 18–28-year category, a result of low fertility rates in the 1960s—the generational echo of World War II (Vishnevskii 1999: 34, 1998: 112). While the number of women in Russia's 18–28-year category has gone from approximately 13.5 million in the early 1980s to 11 million in 1997, the total number of births has dropped from approximately 2.5 million per year in the mid-1980s to 1.26 million in 1997 (Vishnevskii 1999: 34). Thus, an 18.5 percent reduction in the 18–28-year female category was associated with a 50 percent reduction in the annual number of births. The number of women in Russia cannot be the only factor affecting fertility.

Ust Avam has also experienced a significant reduction in fertility, which began alongside fundamental economic changes in the settlement. Figure 4.2 shows Ust Avam's effective fertility rate (EFR) from 1987 to 1997. Effective fertility is calculated by dividing the number of children under 5 years old by the number of women 15 to 49 years old (Hern 1995). The numbers of women and children were calculated by reconstructing annual censuses for 1986 through 1996 using the records of death provided by the village administration and the June 1997 census as a starting point. There appears to have been a significant drop in the effective fertility rate from the 1987–1993 period to the 1994–1997 period. The average EFR for the 1987–1993 period was 0.73, whereas the EFR for 1994–1997 was 0.57.

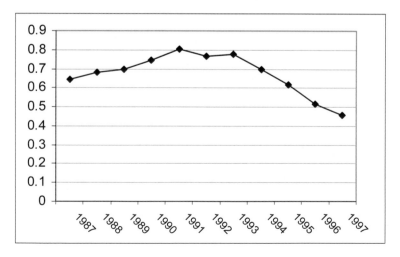

Figure 4.2   Effective Fertility Rate, Ust Avam, 1987–1997.

Another measure of fertility, the general fertility rate (GFR)—calculated on the number of live births every year divided by the number of women 15 through 49 years old—indicates a sharper difference between fertility in Ust Avam prior to and following the collapse of the USSR (see figure 4.3). This yearly statistic suggests fairly consistent rates before 1993 (average 0.16) and lower, less consistent rates after 1993 (average 0.08). In both cases, analysis by effective fertility rates and by general fertility rates, there appears to have been a major shift in 1993. This change in fertility coincides with a significant economic change in the state enterprise's relationship with hunters in Ust Avam. The *gospromkhoz* stopped paying hunters for fish that year and eliminated planned hunting. Fishing was an activity that generated income for hunters during the summer and winter fishing seasons, keeping them busy much of the year with fishing, packing and/or salting, and the maintenance of equipment. With much less disposable income and low morale in the community, Ust Avam's families appear to be limiting their reproduction.

Table 4.3 shows 1997's age-specific birth rates, in standard five-year increments, and female birth rates for women ages 15 though 49 in Ust Avam. One feature of the age-specific birth-rate information is the relatively low fertility of young women (ages 15 through 24). The highest fertility rate is for women in the 30–34-year age category. Most of the children born in 1996 (shown in this 1997 census) were born to women between 25 and 34 years old. This pattern of age-specific fertility indicates that the fertility of women in the 15–19- and 20–24-year age categories is much lower than one would expect for a high-fertility, rapidly growing tribal population (Hern 1995).

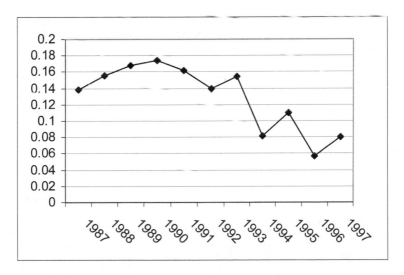

Figure 4.3   General Fertility Rate, Ust Avam, 1987–1997.

Ust Avam's overall fertility is very low, and women in the younger age categories are not having children as their counterparts did in the past. Table 4.4 summarizes several key fertility indices. Ust Avam's general fertility rate (0.071) is lower than the lowest rate provided by Hern (1995) based on World Health Organization statistics (0.088). Ust Avam's gross reproduction rate (GRR), generally considered one of the most accurate and reliable indicators of group fertility, is also lower than documented GRRs for other societies: 1.120 as compared with 1.255 (Hern 1995). Ust Avam's total fertility rate is slightly higher than the lowest comparative figure provided by Hern (1995): 2.695 as compared with 2.573. While the Ust Avam data represents only one community, the point is that fertility is especially low, and the scarcity of 0–4-year-olds appears to be a post-1992 phenomenon.

Ages	Women's YOB	Number of Women	Male Live Births	Female Live Births	Total Births	Birth Rate	Female Birth Rate
15–19	1978–1982	40	1	0	1	0.025	0.000
20–24	1973–1977	20	1	0	1	0.050	0.000
25–29	1968–1972	30	1	4	5	0.167	0.133
30–34	1963–1967	26	4	1	5	0.192	0.038
35–39	1958–1962	19	1	1	2	0.105	0.053
40–44	1953–1957	19	0	0	0	0.000	0.000
45–49	1948–1952	11	0	0	0	0.000	0.000

Table 4.3   Age-specific and female birth rates, Ust Avam, 1997 census.

Fertility Index	Calculation	Ust Avam 1997 Census	High Comparison[a]	Low Comparison
General Fertility Rate	Number of Live Births/ Number of Women 15–49	0.071	0.305	0.088
Effective Fertility Rate	Number of Children under 5/Number of Women 15–49	0.355	1.300	n/a
Total Fertility Rate	Sum of Age-Specific Birth Rates x 5	2.695	9.935	2.573
Gross Reproduction Rate	Sum of Age-Specific Birth Rates x 5	1.120	4.933	1.255

[a] Comparative figures are from Hern (1996).

Table 4.4   Fertility Indices, Ust Avam, 1997.

Low fertility rates, along with crude birth rates that barely exceed crude death rates and significant migration out of the community, are strong indicators of individual stress in Ust Avam. This period of transition is likely not the first such period in the Russian North, and the population should be expected to recover when conditions improve. For example, another turbulent period in Ust Avam's history—the period of collectivization and repression (1933–1937)—was followed by a recovery, and that is visible in Ust Avam's age structure (see figure 4.1). Currently in Ust Avam, there are no living women and only five living men who were born during the 1933–1937 period. In comparison, there are a total of 14 in the next youngest age group and 15 in the next oldest age group.

Mortality

Table 4.5 shows the age-specific mortality rates by sex for all 18 deaths in Ust Avam during 1996. Birth dates for six of the 18 people who died in 1996 are estimated. Four of these people were not in my census or genealogical database, indicating that they had few, if any, close relatives in the community. I excluded one individual who drowned in 1994, as the death was registered when the body was found in 1996.

The infant mortality rate in Ust Avam for 1996 and the first half of 1997 was 87 per 1,000; two deaths for 23 live births, a rate higher than the average annual rates in the late 1960s (78 to 83 per 1,000) and about double the annual rates for the late 1980s and early 1990s (35 to 40 per 1,000) for all Siberian native peoples considered together (Vishnevskii 1994: 156). However, the age-specific mortality rates for 1996 show that the rate of infant death was approximately the same as other child and young-adult mortality rates. Above the age of 40, there is an increase in the risk of death as people reach middle age. This pattern of age-specific mortality has been documented for a number of indigenous Siberian groups (Bogoyavlinskii 1993, Krupnik 1987) and in Russia as a whole for 1995–1997 (Vishnevskii 1999: 84–87). In Ust Avam, many of these violent fatalities in the middle-age categories (ages 40 through 54) were alcohol-related, and this phenomenon is discussed below.

The overall male mortality rate (0.037) in Ust Avam is higher than the overall female mortality rate (0.015). The community mortality rate is 0.026. The difference in mortality rates between men and women could be in part due to the riskier activities, such as hunting and fishing, in which males participate. Hunting accidents, however, accounted for less than 10 percent of violent deaths. A better explanation involves the economic depression, which began in the community in 1993. This depression affects men more than women, since they were the ones employed with the *gos-*

Age	Males			Females			Total		
	Number	Deaths	Mortality Rate	Number	Deaths	Mortality Rate	Number	Deaths	Mortality Rate
0–4	29	1	0.035	30	0	0.000	59	1	0.017
5–9	50	0	0.000	66	0	0.000	116	0	0.000
10–14	54	1	0.019	41	0	0.000	95	1	0.011
15–19	33	0	0.000	41	1	0.024	74	1	0.014
20–24	27	0	0.000	20	0	0.000	47	0	0.000
25–29	22	1	0.045	30	0	0.000	52	1	0.019
30–34	29	0	0.000	28	0	0.000	57	0	0.000
35–39	21	0	0.000	19	0	0.000	40	0	0.000
40–44	22	2	0.091	19	0	0.000	41	2	0.049
45–49	9	0	0.000	11	3	0.273	20	3	0.150
50–54	5	2	0.400	14	1	0.071	19	3	0.158
55–59	5	0	0.000	9	0	0.000	14	0	0.000
60–64	5	1	0.200	0	0	0.000	5	1	0.200
65–69	7	2	0.286	8	0	0.000	15	2	0.133
70+	4	2	0.500	4	0	0.000	8	2	0.250
Total	322	12	0.037	340	5	0.015	662	17	0.026

Table 4.5 Age-specific mortality rates by sex, Ust Avam, 1997 census.

promkhoz in the production of tundra foods and raw materials. With the post-Soviet transition, hunters' inactivity and time in the settlement converge with binge drinking when cash and alcohol become available. These factors may lead to the higher overall male mortality rate. Semyon Yakovlich Palchin, the head of the Taimyr Agricultural Bureau, put it this way: "The situation here has gone from worse to cataclysmic. There is no budgetary support for the State enterprises. Alcoholism is rampant as an effect of this lack of jobs." Women's employment is split more evenly across income sectors (state hunting enterprise, civil service positions, pensions), and they still receive cash income, if irregularly. This may partially account for the lower overall female mortality rate.

Violent deaths of various types are more common than natural causes of death in Ust Avam. Table 4.6 shows the relative importance of violent and natural deaths for the period 1986 through September 1997. This preponderance of violent deaths existed before the breakup of the Soviet Union but appears to have intensified since 1991. The impact of violence as a cause of death is likely even greater than shown here, since the six cases in which the cause of death was not listed or "not determined" were probably cases of violent death. Also, several of the deaths attributed to diseases, such as heart attack, were actually alcohol related violent deaths (table 4.8). Table 4.7 shows a breakdown of the types of violent deaths I recorded in Ust Avam for 1986 through September 1997. I compiled this information from a review of the death registry of the Ust Avam village council and informant interviews. A number of the deaths (eight of the 117) were not listed in the Ust Avam registry.

Year	Violent Deaths	Illness	Cause Not Determined	Total Deaths
1986	2	3	1	6
1987	5	2	0	7
1988	1	4	0	5
1989	3	2	0	5
1990	6	9	0	15
1991	2	1	1	4
1992	10	4	1	15
1993	6	6	2	14
1994	8	5	2	15
1995	5	4	0	9
1996	8	9	0	17
1997 (through September)	3	2	0	5
Total	59	51	7	117

Table 4.6   Causes of Death, Ust Avam, 1986 through September 1997.

Year	Drowning	Suicide	Alcohol Poisoning	Murder	Lost or Froze	Hunting Accident	Infanticide	Violent Deaths Total
1986	1	1	0	0	0	0	0	2
1987	0	2	2	1	0	0	0	5
1988	1	0	0	0	0	0	0	1
1989	0	0	1	0	1	0	1	3
1990	3	0	1	1	0	1	0	6
1991	1	0	0	0	1	0	0	2
1992	2	5	2	1	0	0	0	10
1993	1	1	1	0	2	0	1	6
1994	3	1	2	1	1	0	0	8
1995	2	1	0	1	0	1	0	5
1996	5	0	0	1	0	1	1	8
1997 (through September)	1	0	0	0	1	1	0	3
Total	20	11	9	6	6	4	3	59

Table 4.7   Violent deaths, Ust Avam, 1986 through September 1997.

There are fewer hunting accidents and accidental shootings than one might expect for this heavily armed, economically depressed population. The low incidence of hunting deaths in Ust Avam (6 percent of violent deaths from 1986–1997) speaks to the qualifications of the hunters. Two main factors play into the low incidence of hunting accidents: absence of alcohol on hunting excursions and gun safety. On the more than 100 hunting trips that I participated in or observed from 1993 though September 1997 in the Avam tundra, alcohol was never present. The fact that alcohol is never consumed while hunting, but often consumed in the village, points to the resolution of the problem of alcohol-related death in northern Russia; keeping people at their preferred job in the tundra may reduce alcoholism and its violent consequences. Also, hunters keep rifles, shotguns, and ammunition locked in steel cabinets far away from children and adolescents. I observed no handguns in Ust Avam except for those with the occasional police patrol.

Drowning is the most common type of violent death. One-third of violent deaths recorded from 1986 to 1997 were due to drowning. There are several factors that play into this pattern. First, drowning occurs mainly from mid-June through September, when the water is ice-free. July and August are the months during which supplies are brought to Ust Avam by boat. Along with supplies such as diesel fuel, coal, and food, the crews running the supplies now bring vodka and grain alcohol to sell to the natives, an activity that would have been strictly controlled during the Soviet period. "The whole village roams" is a local expression used to describe the large number of drunk people wandering from house to house after the barges arrive. Second, there are numerous small aluminum boats (14–20 feet), most with outboard motors (15–30 horsepower). Prior to 1991, the state supplied these boats to the village for the summer fishing season, which has been officially closed since 1993. When alcohol is present in the summer, it is common for people to go on joyrides, many of which turn out to be fatal. Third, there are no personal flotation devices available to the population of Ust Avam. Fourth, there is no instruction in water safety. No swimming lessons are available to the youth of Ust Avam. Small children play unattended by the river, and a few have fallen in and drowned. When the population was still herding reindeer and wearing traditional clothes made from reindeer and caribou hides, death by drowning was not as great a problem, since reindeer hair has a hollow shaft that provides excellent insulation and floats in water. Traditional clothes were natural life preservers, so there was little need for safety equipment. Now, traditional clothes are worn only during the winter, if at all.

Suicide is another form of violent death that is likely related to both binge drinking and the depressed economic situation, as mentioned by Afanas'eva at the 1997 Congress. The majority of the suicides in Ust Avam were hangings, and they occurred in the winter and spring. Pika (1993: 67) documented a springtime rise in suicide among other northern native groups in Russia, correlating with the major Soviet holidays in the winter and spring. The nine deaths recorded as alcohol poisonings in Ust Avam were the only official recognition of the drinking problem in the mortality records. Four murders were committed by knife stabbing, and two were shootings. The infanticides were recorded as "being pressed to the chest." Apparently, suffocation is the preferred means of infanticide. As far as I am aware, no one was prosecuted for committing infanticide. Many of the homicides in Ust Avam were associated with binge drinking, according to informants. Thus, the importance of alcohol in violent death is greater than the alcohol-poisoning figures would indicate.

Of natural causes of death in Ust Avam from 1986 to 1997 (table 4.8), cancer is the most common form (57 percent). Within this category, most of the deaths were attributed to lung cancer (14 cases) and stomach cancer (11 cases). The other four cases were described as throat cancer or esophagus cancer. The lung-cancer and esophagus-cancer deaths are most likely caused by cigarette smoking, which is still very popular in the north among both men and women. During household interviews, informants were asked what they purchased at the store; many answered, "Flour, sugar, tea, and cigarettes." There is no cancer screening in Ust Avam, and the health-care system in Dudinka is not geared toward dealing with cancer.

Within the heart-disease category, most of the deaths were due to heart attack or arteriosclerosis, with two cases not further specified. A number of alcohol-induced deaths were officially recorded as heart attacks, but informant interviews and my observations illustrated that these tragic cases were actually caused by months of heavy drinking.

Year	Cancer	Heart Disease	Old Age/ Non-Specified Disease	Alcohol-Induced Illness	Childhood Illness	Tuberculosis	Illness Total
1986	3	0	0	0	0	0	3
1987	0	1	1	0	0	0	2
1988	2	1	0	0	0	1	4
1989	1	0	1	0	0	0	2
1990	8	0	1	0	0	0	9
1991	1	0	0	0	0	0	1
1992	2	0	2	0	0	0	4
1993	4	0	0	0	2	0	6
1994	4	1	0	0	0	0	5
1995	1	1	1	1	0	0	4
1996	3	5	0	1	0	0	9
1997 (through September)	0	0	0	2	0	0	2
Total	29	9	6	4	2	1	51

Table 4.8   Natural deaths, Ust Avam, 1986 through September 1997.

While tuberculosis is a chronic problem in Ust Avam and has been a serious challenge to public health in Russia since 1991, there was only one registered death due to tuberculosis in the 1986–1997 period. The Taimyr Region has an adequate, if austere, tuberculosis-care center. If a person in a native village is identified with active tuberculosis, he or she is sent to Dudinka to stay 18 months in the "Tub-Dispansor," the inpatient tuberculosis clinic.

Despite the relative equality of mixed marriages between Dolgan and Nganasan and the rarity of ethnic violence, the demographic status of the two ethnic groups appears to be unequal within Ust Avam, with the Nganasan population being marginalized. While violent causes of death are common among both the Dolgan and Nganasan, Ust Avam's death records (1986 through September 1997) indicate that violent death is more of a problem for the Nganasan (table 4.9). There were a total of 117 documented deaths in the community during that period. Just over half of these (50.4 percent) were among the Nganasan. Less than half of these deaths (43.6 percent) were among the Dolgan, and six percent were among the non-native residents of the community. Comparing known causes of death, there is a significant difference between Dolgan and Nganasan.

One startling aspect of the information presented in table 4.9 is that violent death was almost twice as common among the Nganasan as natural death in the 1986–1997 period. This was due, in part, to the high violent-death rate among Nganasan females. Violent death among Nganasan females was almost as common as among Nganasan males (54 percent vs. 66

percent of total female and male deaths, respectively) and was more than double the rate for Dolgan females (24 percent of total female deaths). This fact is significant, since it is the females that provide the reproductive base for the population. The high rate of violent death among Nganasan women indicates a critical demographic situation for this ethnic group.

The violent-mortality problem was not quite so critical among the Dolgan, where natural deaths outnumbered violent deaths. With Dolgan females, violent death accounts for four of 17 documented deaths (24 percent). Violent death was slightly more common than natural death among Dolgan males (accounting for 18 of 34 deaths, 53 percent), while these causes were equal for the small non-native male population of Ust Avam.

Table 4.10 shows the distribution of violent, natural, and undetermined death in Ust Avam for the period 1970–1985 by ethnicity and sex. The data include only deaths that occurred in Ust Avam and do not include the deaths of Ust Avam residents that occurred in other locations or the deaths of non-indigenous people in Ust Avam. While there were more registered fatalities in Ust Avam for this period than for 1986–1997, and more fatalities per year (12 on average, vs. 10 on average), the proportion of violent death to natural death is approximately the same for both native groups. Also, the proportion of violent death to natural death for Nganasan females was lower than that of Dolgan females for the 1970–1985 period. Thus, for the 1970s and 1980s, the mortality data suggest more equivalent pressure on the Nganasan and Dolgan. A statistical comparison of known causes of death for the two groups in this time period shows no significant difference. The major challenge at that time was adapting to a sedentary lifestyle in Ust Avam, and it appears to have affected both groups equally. Comparing tables 4.9 and 4.10, it appears that the Nganasan are experiencing a significantly more difficult time now than during the 1970s and early 1980s.

In examining this differential mortality among the Nganasan, I believe that hunting territory (*ugod'ia*) assignments may have played a role. At the time of my research, the distribution of hunting parcels within the Ust Avam division favored Dolgan over Nganasan hunters. Approximately half of Ust Avam's 55 hunters were still officially assigned to 16 hunting *ugod'ia* in 1997. Within the Avam division, only two hunting *ugod'ia* comprised exclusively Nganasan hunters. Four territories were mixed with both Dolgan and Nganasan hunters, and Dolgan hunters and their households maintained land use over eight hunting territories. Two territories were assigned to both Dolgan and non-native hunters together. This distribution may represent a historical difference between the numerical strength of the two ethnic groups within the Ust Avam division or the Dolgans' greater willingness to adapt to the Soviet economic model of commercial hunting. As a result, in the early 1990s, when mechanized transportation from the socialist period was still serviceable, hunters maintained some access to their remote tundra bases. With cabins and

Cause of Death	Nganasan			Dolgan			Non-Native		
	Males	Females	Total	Males	Females	Total	Males	Females	Total
Violent	22	14	36	18	4	22	3	0	3
Natural	11	8	19	16	11	27	3	1	4
Not Known	0	4	4	0	2	2	0	0	0
Total	33	26	59	34	17	51	6	1	7

Table 4.9 Causes of death in Ust Avam (January 1986–September 1997) by ethnicity and sex.

Cause of Death	Nganasan			Dolgan			Other Native Taimyr Peoples		
	Males	Females	Total	Males	Females	Total	Males	Females	Total
Violent	26	17	42	36	19	55	2	1	3
Natural	17	14	32	33	22	55	2	0	2
Not Known	2	0	2	0	1	1	0	0	0
Total	45	31	76	69	42	111	4	1	5

Table 4.10 Causes of death in Ust Avam (1970–1985) by ethnicity and sex.

equipment to take care of in the tundra, the hunters with *ugod'ia* had more labor activity, which may have increased household morale as well as consumption security. With decreasing predictability of salary and pension payments in the 1990s, and given that Nganasan households and mixed non-native-Nganasan families were more dependent on this unpredictable cash income, internal household conflicts of interest could have been more intense. Such conflicts may be responsible for the relatively high female mortality rate among the Nganasan.

Pitfalls in the Post-Soviet Transition

We have seen that the dismantling of socialism in Russia has led to an extended economic depression in Arctic territories, especially among the numerically small indigenous populations. While Russia's economic depression appears to be influencing the demographic structure of the country, it has had more impact in communities like Ust Avam. Russia's total population decreased from 148,673,000 in 1993 to 146,861,000 in 1998 (Europa World Yearbook 1995, 1998). The annual growth rate in 1997 was –0.31 percent. Ust Avam's total population declined by 15 percent in 1996–1997.

Ust Avam's age-sex distribution is characterized by a large number of children and adolescents and a smaller number of adults and elderly people. The exception is the youngest age category, children up to four years old. These children were born from 1993 through 1997, the toughest economic years in the Avam tundra since collectivization in the 1930s. The number of children born at that time was approximately half of what would be expected from the previous birth trends.

The low number of births in this age cohort is one indicator of the seriousness of the economic depression there. Ust Avam's overall fertility rates were low, and reproduction was scarcely beyond replacement. Women between the ages of 25 and 34 had the highest fertility rates in the community, and women below the age of 25 had low fertility rates. It appears that fertility rates for women of all age categories are lower than they were five or ten years earlier. This change is representative of the fertility trends of the Russian Federation in the mid-1990s (Vishnevskii 1999: 34).

External, or violent, causes have historically characterized a large proportion of Ust Avam's mortality. Between 1987 and 1991 there were 17 violent deaths, 16 natural deaths, and one death of undetermined cause in Ust Avam—slightly more than 50 percent of deaths were due to violent causes. This pattern intensified after 1991, and violent death in Ust Avam is beyond that of the Russian Federation average, especially among the Nganasan (Vishnevskii 1999: 85). Between 1992 and 1997 in Ust Avam, there were

40 violent deaths, 30 natural deaths, and five undetermined deaths. The number of deaths in the community doubled after 1991, and the relative number of violent deaths increased to close to 60 percent of all mortalities. Fatal illness in Ust Avam was mainly due to cancer and heart disease, and these affected the Dolgan, Nganasan, and non-native populations equally.

Russian society in the 1990s has been going through fundamental changes with the abandonment of the planned economy in favor of the free market. This economic breakdown appears to have significantly affected the demographics of indigenous communities in northern Russia like Ust Avam. Underlying the violent-death and fertility statistics are the fundamental problems of alcohol distribution and labor inactivity. The decline in the demographic health of Ust Avam is affecting Nganasan males and females and Dolgan males to the greatest extent. The Nganasan are one of the numerically smallest native peoples of Siberia, and this health trend adds to the obstacles preventing the maintenance of their language and culture.

Many informants stated that people do not drink like they used to. In the past, it was acceptable for men and elderly women to drink. Drinking occurred on holidays, such as May Day, and on occasional trips to the store for provisions. At that time, families lived the year out in the tundra, herding domestic reindeer, trapping, or fishing. Now, the lack of alcohol in the Ust Avam community store, which one might think would reduce alcoholism, makes it a high-priced commodity when traders sell it (Saggers and Gray 1998). Alcohol is brought to the settlement along with salaries and pensions, which are often delayed for weeks or months. This practice means that on paydays, when people have the money, alcohol is made available at high prices. Some deaths occur during these payday drinking binges. Additionally, depression is a problem for those who spend their money, and the money of their relatives, on alcohol. They have little left to spend on basic necessities.

Individuals with connections to transportation from urban centers have the opportunity to bring alcohol to Ust Avam and other indigenous communities in the Russian North. These individuals are capitalizing on their positions to sell alcohol to native people who cannot afford it. Alcohol speculation keeps the people in Ust Avam in poverty and adds to violence and death in their community. These factors have been reported for many rural areas of Russia, and therefore it is likely that the demographic effects are analogous. The worsening health of Ust Avam is symptomatic of growing socioeconomic differentiation along geographic continua in post-Soviet Russia. People in more isolated settings are suffering to a greater degree than those in urban areas or places along major transportation conduits. Most everyone I spoke to in Ust Avam told me that they need jobs in the community in order to improve their situation. If they had jobs and received regular pay, then there would be less inactivity and presumably better self-confidence and morale.

Chapter Five

Shamans, Ancestors, Sin, and Sacrifice

Cosmology, in the sense used here, is a doctrine that explains the natural order of the universe. The Dolgan and Nganasan have rich cosmological traditions, and this chapter focuses on how these traditions manifest themselves today, after the breakdown of the Soviet Union. One could write an entire book about the history of these traditions, and there are a number of publications that deal with the topic in great detail (e.g., Dolgikh 1968; Gracheva 1979, 1981; Gurvich 1968; Popov 1981), but the purpose of this chapter is different. Dolgan and Nganasan cosmological traditions are essentially religions, or as social anthropologist L. B. Steadman (n.d.) defines it, the communicated acceptance of another person's supernatural claim. The traditional doctrines of the Dolgan and Nganasan combine different forms of belief and practice. For example, the Dolgan are ostensibly Russian Orthodox, while they also retain ancient beliefs and practices inherited from the time before the missionaries. Defining these systems of belief as a religion would be simplistic. Until recently, the Dolgan and Nganasan could be considered separate ethnic groups, each with its own distinct religious traditions. Now, as the Dolgan and Nganasan are merging into one population, there is much variation in the beliefs and practices within and between families in Ust Avam. Some traditions, such as the Dolgan epic narrative *olonkho*, are no longer practiced. Still, native cosmology remains important for social relationships, economy, and land tenure in the Avam tundra.

The cosmologies of the Dolgan and Nganasan both include legends about and practice of shamans. The word *shaman* comes from the Evenk word *saman*, meaning "to know in an ecstatic manner" (Shirokogoroff 1935). In anthropology, the word has been widely adopted to describe religious specialists in traditional kinship-based societies. Animism is a belief in spirits, and shamans often contact, manipulate, and cooperate with spirits of nature and deceased ancestors (Tylor 1924 [1871]: 23). Following evolutionist theories about the history of humankind such as those of Marx and Lenin, shamanism was actively repressed as primitive and backward during the years of Communism in the Siberian Arctic. However, some shamanistic traditions remain, especially those dealing with ancestors and social sacrifice. During my year and a half in the Taimyr Region, I got to know and became friends with the only remaining Nganasan shamans, members of one family. Nganasan shamanism was one of the reasons I decided to work in this region of Siberia, and I, as many others, was distressed when the head of the family died in 1996. Their practice today differs significantly from that of a generation ago and beyond, but it is an important part of what defines the Ust Avam community.

Despite the officially agnostic policy of the Soviet government and its efforts to eliminate traditional religious beliefs such as shamanism, there is evidence that traditional cosmological knowledge is still being transmitted across generations among the Dolgan and Nganasan. This knowledge is codified in myths, stories, and parental advice, as well as the occasional shamanic performance and traditional burial. Traditional cosmological knowledge is important because it contains information about strategies for survival, such as cooperation between co-descendants and the traditional use of the land and its resources.

Dulsimyaku Kosterkin and the Ngumtuso Clan

When I began my research in Ust Avam, Dulsimyaku Kosterkin was the oldest man in the Ngumtuso clan; he was the nephew of a famous Nganasan shaman, Tibiakou Kosterkin (Milovskii 1992). Tibiakou and his brother Dimnimei managed to keep their shamanic practices active through the periods of collectivization and settlement in Ust Avam, and thus Nganasan shamanism managed to be transmitted to the present generations. Dolgan shamanism was effectively eliminated during the collectivization period. Tibiakou passed away in 1988, a number of years after his brother, and Dulsimyaku inherited Tibiakou's shamanic costume and accoutrements, at one time kept in the Taimyr Regional Studies Museum. Traditionally, it was expected that a shaman would make a new costume or have one made according to the instructions of his or her spirit guide. Dulsimyaku used his uncle's implements—partially due to the fact that there was virtually no production of new traditional clothing among the Nganasan at that time. I was introduced to Dulsimyaku in 1994, but I really did not get to know him until returning to Ust Avam in the fall of 1995. It was through Dulsimyaku and his sisters that I became exposed to Nganasan shamanism firsthand.

At one of our first meetings, Dulsimyaku taught me about Nganasan musical instruments, including a bullroarer, an instrument that makes low vibrations when swung in a wide circle, and a whistle made from a goose feather. The Nganasan cradleboard also is used as an instrument. It has a piece of arched wood that crosses over the infant and is decorated and notched at regular intervals. A stick is used to rub against the notches and the rhythm is used in lullabies.

Later, I was invited to Dulsimyaku's for tea, and he talked about his hunting spot and the *balok* he had left there so that he and his sons could camp, not far from the village. Dulsimyaku was a reindeer herder in the 1950s and 1960s, and he worked in reindeer-herding brigades alongside Dolgan herders, many of whom were my close friends. He was an active hunter and was respected for that, and he did not want to talk about shamanism too much at first. We talked about setting up a *chum* outside the village to recreate a Nganasan ceremony. There always seemed to be a taboo on that, however, because of people that had just passed away, or some other problem. So I did not press the issue.

In the spring of 1996, Dulsimyaku and the Ngumtuso ensemble—named after their patrilineal clan—gave a public performance at a community holiday, sponsored by the City Department of Culture in Dudinka, whose representatives flew in for the occasion. I videotaped the performance, which occurred in the school gymnasium. The representatives organized and moderated the holiday, in honor of the ancient Nganasan rite of intensification, Aniu Diali, a celebration of the sun rising above the horizon. In addition to a performance by the Ngumtuso shamanic ensemble, the holiday included an art and craft show and a competition of native games. Prizes were given to participants and winners of the show, which included Dolgan, Nganasan, and non-indigenous residents of Ust Avam. Boiled caribou meat was distributed to all of the several hundred in attendance after the performance. The distribution of the meat was to signify respect to the caribou, the main source of food for the people of Ust Avam, and to encourage cooperation among those that live there.

Dulsimyaku made a short presentation expressing the meaning of what had been said in Nganasan:

> I will translate into Russian. They all do not understand Nganasan. Earlier, the whole world was all-all water. The entire empty planet was water. And then, there was a *gagara*, a baby loon, very small. This *gagara* swims and swims. She gets tired of swimming. Completely. "Well alright. Where, where is this dry land? It is nowhere to be found." She dives downward to the bottom. She dove, then she got,

Figure 5.1 Dulsimyaku Kosterkin (center) and the Ngumtuso ensemble, performing in the Ust Avam school gymnasium, May 1996.

what do you call it, she got silt, silt. Somehow she got this sacred (*shaitan*) dirt; that is what it is called. It has bush in it. Everything is in it. She put the silt on top of her head, and then thought, "Aha! Why did I forget that something will take the silt? A storm will get it—the wind blows. And then the other, I forgot the other one! Aha, I remembered it!" Then again, the *gagara* dove down to the bottom. She came back with more silt and a stone. This stone started drying the earth. Water started being dried by this stone, and then the land appeared, and rainbow, and the wind. The land feeds us. The land is our mother. And the sky that showers the land is her husband. Bread grows from the land. Seeds. Grain, they also feed from the land. From the land they grow, and you also grow from the land. Man grows from the land. It does not matter what nation you are—we are all together, we live by the land, live in unity. It does not count here, this nation, or another. We are all one, with one land we live. As one, we live. What kind of person there might be, American, Dolgan, this is not important. We are all brothers and sisters. Like flowers grow, it is all ours. Like flowers, we grow. Here, this is my legend, an old legend.

Traditionally, Nganasan ancestral spirits were represented by three-dimensional carved wooden idols, called *koika*. These were usually kept hidden, and I never saw one while I was in Ust Avam, although there were a number on exhibit in the Dudinka museum. Traditionally, the Dolgan also had carved idols, called *shaitany*. These were sacred symbols, usually a two-dimensional representation of an animal, that were often treated as family relics. In his speech, Dulsimyaku used the Dolgan word, *shaitan*, when he talked about the sacred dirt that the *gagara* brought to the surface. Dulsimyaku manipulated the traditional Nganasan creation myth to include everyone, including me, in one cooperative group of co-descendants, brothers and sisters, as he put it, children of one earth mother and one sky father. Ancestors, through their living representatives, encourage cooperation in this and similar messages constantly given to the younger generation in Ust Avam.

Dulsimyaku's sisters performed two shamanic séances while I was in Ust Avam. Their expressed desire was to have these performances videotaped so they could document their craft. Unlike the traditional séances that were most often oriented for healing, these were meant to guess certain things about my past and my future and to insure my safe road home. In both of these séances, they adorned special costumes, used a large flat drum (*buben*), and sang a long song that requested the spirits' presence. After the introductory song, when the shamans were translating to me what the spirits told them, I was asked to affirm their revelations by using a specially decorated stick and striking it against the rim of the *buben*—the correct behavioral acceptance of their revelations. Both of the séances ended with the Bear Dance in which everyone links arms and shuffles around in a circle making a rhythmic grunting noise. The holiday in the school gymnasium ended in the same way.

Figure 5.2   In the summer of 2001 I found a number of Nganasan *shaitany* and other personal items, such as the inverted bowl and the fish net, on an abandoned riding sleigh close to Ust Avam. Despite the proximity to the village, children had not upset or carried off these items, the belongings of a deceased person. My friends advised me not to touch anything, as that would certainly bring misfortune—an example of the power of ancestors transmitted through elders.

Figure 5.3 Nina Logvina (Kosterkina), her son Igor Kosterkin, and her grandson before a shamanic séance in the Logvins' apartment, Ust Avam 1997.

The bear, a powerful and dangerous animal, is important in the cosmology of both the Dolgan and Nganasan. Both refer to bears as relatives, and hunting of them is very limited. This totemic reference to the bear may be a holdover from an ancient bear cult that was widespread across Eurasia. Evidence of the spiritual importance of bears has been found in Eurasian archaeological contexts dating back thousands of years, as well as among modern indigenous people. Those that subscribe to the bear taboo are sacrificing a potentially valuable source of nutrition (bear meat). Taboos on certain parts of animals, or the whole animal, appear to be related to a number of ecological and traditional factors, such as relative abundance, herding behavior, size, potential hazard, "humanity," accessibility, taste, and percentage of edibility (Dentan 1981). Following Steadman's hypothesis (n.d.), such a sacrifice could have benefits in terms of cooperation among those that subscribe to the proscription.

Dolgan Shamanism

Currently in Ust Avam there are no Dolgan people that claim to be shamans. However, there are a number of people with putative powers, or personality peculiarities, who are sometimes referred to as shamans by others. One of my best informants in Ust Avam told me a story about her uncle and his *shaitany*. When the Dolgan were still reindeer herders they kept personal items packed in bundles tied onto a sleigh. In a *myagchaga* (decorated, caribou-leg-fur bag), which he always kept on top, he had *shaitany* that were tied together in a bundle. She did not take too good a look at her uncle's *shaitany* because she did not know how to deal correctly with them, but she described them as metal birds and fish tied in a bundle. Before her uncle died, she asked him about what to do with them. He said that they should remain with her. She brought the *myagchaga* into her storeroom after he died and hung it on the wall. Her husband cursed her for bringing these inside the house, as they would bring bad luck. After this, she and an elderly lady-friend took all of the uncle's bags, with the *shaitan* bag tied on top, out into the tundra. The lady-friend said that they should take the stuff out to the tundra and leave it there. My friend was not sure she did the right thing, as two of her children have died since then. Traditionally, the *shaitany* were tied together when the shaman did a séance (*kamlanie*). Tying the *shaitany* together meant that all the members of the family would stay together. When a member of the family died, the shaman unbound the *shaitany*. If the *shaitany* were not properly cared for, this could bring about bad events for the family.

While many of the accoutrements have been disposed of, and ceremonies are no longer performed in public, shamanism is still alive in Dolgan storytelling. While in Ust Avam, I had the privilege of getting to know and interview Aksenya Maximovna Bezrukikh. Aksenya (Oksye) was 93 years old when I interviewed her, and she told much about life before and after the advent of Soviet power. One of her stories, The Underground Kingdom (*Annyky Doidu*) exemplifies Dolgan cosmology: a three-tiered universe with an underworld, living world, and sky world. Only powerful shamans could negotiate between the worlds and the spirits that inhabit them.

Annyky Doidu as told by Oksye Bezrukikh

One man had two sons. The man did not like to communicate with other people. He and his family lived alone. He did not allow his sons to visit with neighbors. And so, they lived alone with no neighbors—just their family.

Once, the man went to gather his reindeer. Having rounded them up, he turned the herd in the direction of his *chum*. He started to look at the surroundings and back from where he had walked. He saw that the earth was ripped. A deep cavity appeared where he had just walked on solid ground. He began to walk by the edge of the canyon and he asked himself, "How is it that I did not notice this? I almost killed all my reindeer."

At that point the man himself fell into the void. He fell. He fell a long time in the nothingness. He fell until he perceived the ground, solid under his legs. It turned out to be solid earth.

The man saw three *chums* in the semi-darkness. Farther off in the dusk he saw a big herd of reindeer. The *chums* were big, gigantic, in fact. Near the central *chum* he saw two people blacksmithing. The man walked up to the camp, approached the two men, and said, "How do you do?"

One of the men asked the other, "What happened?" The other blacksmith said, "Why is our fire trying to tell us something?" (*Ot kepseter*)

The man said to them in surprise, "Ah, hey! What happened to you?" And again he said, "Hello."

The two blacksmiths did not see the newcomer. One said, "Something is going to happen. We need to stop working." They paid no attention to the man from the center world. "Let's go home," they said. And the blacksmiths went into their *chum*. The man followed right behind.

The man looked around and saw a beautiful girl sitting on her bed in the back of the *chum*. Her parents were sitting on the right side. The visitor stood next to the perpendicular pole near the center of the *chum* and next to the fire pit. Again, he introduced himself. "How do you do?" he said to the parents.

The old woman demanded, "What happened? What is our fire saying? You've done some kind of sin old man!"

The stranger thought, stood there in the center of the *chum*, and exasperated, "Eh-beh!" He then thought in surprise, "To where have I come?" He asked of his hosts, "You really do not see me?"

Again, the grandmother said, "The fire cracks. Even the coals are flying apart." The woman went over to her buffet, opened the door, and began to look for fat to put into the fire.

She put fat into the fire, made a cross out of firewood, and put the cross into the fire. The fire immediately caught, glowing brightly and evenly.

The newcomer said to himself, "Well, they are not paying attention to me, I'll go over to the girl." He went over to her and accidentally brushed her leg. Her legs were out in front of her. The grandmother said, "Eh-beh!" in surprise. The girl began to cry and scream, "My leg hurts. My leg hurts." She began to shake her leg.

The stranger was surprised, "What happened to her? Interesting."

The girl's mother, the old woman, said, "Eh-beh! About this, the fire spoke. Our daughter got sick." The mother started asking her daughter about her leg. Was it getting better? Was it all right? The pain went away and the girl felt normal.

The newcomer sat a bit away from the girl, and then decided to touch her in order to find out what would happen to her if he touched her. He decided to reach to her. When he approached the girl she began to scream, as if she was standing in a deathly fire.

The girl's mother said to her daughter, "You've gotten sick. Come here and sit with us." And the newcomer said, "She's not sick. It's me approaching her."

Again the people heard the fire talking. The coals began to fly out of the fire pit. Again, the old lady threw fat into the fire, and mixed it into the coals. While doing so she made several requests of the fire,

"Oh, grandfather fire, please help us grandfather, so that our daughter would not be ill."

The girl's parents sat her nearby. The newcomer sat alone on the girl's bench. He looked around the *chum*. Benches were as benches. Bedding was as bedding. People were like people. Everything was just as it was with his people.

The newcomer needed to urinate. He walked out of the *chum*, and saw that these people live next to a wide river on a large flat plain.

A big white reindeer approached the man. It snorted, "Brrr!" It was a very beautiful reindeer with large antlers. He caught the reindeer by the antlers and was going to pet it. The animal died immediately. The man thought to himself, "What happened to the reindeer?" The man walked up to another reindeer and petted it. The second reindeer also died and cooled immediately. It did not breathe or anything.

At that time, all the people came out of the *chums*. The owner came up to the white reindeer and said, "My lead reindeer! What happened? Why did he fall and die? He was walking just a few minutes ago. Earlier, reindeer suddenly died from some disease. Maybe he died from this disease." The people stood there talking amongst themselves. The owner told the young men, "Take the reindeer away. Take them farther. Don't touch the dead reindeer." The young men took the herd off to graze. The rest of the people stood there discussing the situation. "That is why our fire was talking."

The newcomer wanted to eat. He thought that he should go into the *chum*. He walked inside. The girl was sitting on her parent's bench. He decided not to approach her since she might die like the reindeer.

He approached the girl's parents and the fire began talking again. The old lady again stirred the coals. Then she pulled out of her buffet a big copper pot. Then she pulled out some old, old bones. She broke them up with an ax, and then boiled them. The family started to eat. What they ate, the newcomer did not understand. There were just bones in the soup. What would he eat? He only looked. After they ate the bone soup, the old lady gathered up the bones and gave half to their dogs. The other half she put back into the cupboard, and said that she would make soup again tomorrow. The newcomer remained hungry. No one even looked at him.

The old man said, "Well, my daughter is sick. What is ailing her? We have an old shaman. We need to call him. Maybe he will tell us what is wrong. I'll go after him." And the old man walked out of the *chum*, and walked to the shaman's *chum* to find out what was ailing his daughter.

He brought the shaman over to their *chum*. The shaman had a big drum. He began to beat the drum, and make requests among the spirits. He could not portend anything. He said, "I do not see anything. But there is a reason why your daughter fell ill. I can not tell you what the exact cause is."

The girl's father said to the shaman, "If you can't do anything, see anything, then on the other side of the river there lives a young shaman. We'll go ask him. We'll go after him. In the morning we'll get up and go. The young shaman will see why our daughter fell ill. You've gotten old. That is why you cannot see. In the morning we'll go after the shaman."

They went to sleep. The newcomer did not know what to do. He decided to lie on the girl's bench. But he stayed close to the wall so as not to touch her. As he breathed on her she could not stand it, and she began to scream. She got sick.

In the morning they rose and ate breakfast, leftover bone broth. The family still did not see the newcomer. They got ready to go for the shaman. The newcomer noticed again that the girl was beautiful. Her parents went out. He followed. He saw three or four *vetki* (canoes) leave the riverbank. Not too much time passed when he saw the boats returning, heavily loaded. On the first canoe, the shaman's clothes and attributes were loaded. They banked the *vetki*.

The newcomer saw the shaman come up to the camp. The shaman walked up to him, put out his hand, and greeted him. The newcomer said, "How do you do? These are what kind of people? To where have I fallen? I am dying from boredom." The man recounted to the shaman how he came to their land.

They walked into the *chum* where the newcomer spent the night. The people brought in the attributes, the clothes, drum, bells, and everything that is needed for the shaman.

The shaman began the séance. He told the girl's parents, "Bring *ehmek* (soft, dry wood from a dead tree). And carve from it a reindeer. Then make a model of a person from that material. Bring these into the *chum*."

The shaman continued the séance. The parents left to find *ehmek*, and carve the models. They returned after some time. The shaman told them to put the model of the person on to the model of the reindeer, and to orient them to the east. The shaman told the people, "I, having been a shaman, do not see anything horrible. Simply, a person came from the sunny world. There are no evil spirits here."

The stranger heard the words of the shaman. The shaman told the man, "Now I will return you to your home, the land from where you came." The shaman told him, "I made a model of a person and a reindeer. Look at them." And the man saw before him a big white living reindeer and a person in white clothes. The shaman said, "Sit with this person on his lap." The shaman had called the good spirit *Aiyi*.

The man sat on *Aiyi*'s knee and did not remember what happened next. After some time, he woke up, and the sun was shining in his face. He stood up, and was standing on the same place where he fell to the underground world. He silently thought, "It seems that I fell into the underground world. What a shaman! He returned me to the earth, my home."

The man thanked God. He returned home. His boys and wife came out to meet him. "Where have you been?" they cried out.

The man told his family about his experience in the underground kingdom. He told his family that the next day they would *argish* (caravan) to other people. He said that it is impossible to live alone, without people. He said that it was a big sin to live alone.

> In the morning, they argished, and came into the biggest camp. The man told his family, "People always need to live with people. Earlier, I did not like people. I lived to the side from them. Now, I will always live with my nation."

Oksye's story has a number of important points. First, it gives the reader a wonderful glimpse into the way cause-and-effect is interpreted traditionally among the Dolgan. This story is similar to hero myths as described by Joseph Campbell (1968[1949]). In Campbell's hero cycle, the hero goes out into the world, where he or she is tested by supernatural powers. If successful, the hero receives a revelation during his or her quest, and then returns to the world to communicate the prophecy. In the case of the *Annyky Doidu*, the message was cooperation; a family cannot survive on its own. The hero in this story was sent to the underground kingdom for his sin of living apart from other people. There, his presence was deadly, and when he could not get the people of the underground to see him or feed him, he realized he really needed other people. He was lucky there was a powerful shaman that could see him and facilitate his return.

Second, the story contains messages about how to deal with nature. Fire is extremely important for maintaining human life in the Siberian Arctic. Without it people simply would not be able to live throughout the winter. The importance of fire is symbolized by sacrifice to it. On my first trip to the Taimyr Region, I realized this when I visited Khantaiskoe Ozero. In that village, I went visiting relatives with my friend Boris Molchanov. Before we sat down for dinner with his sister and her family, we sacrificed a tablespoon of vodka to the kitchen fire. The more traditional sacrifice is animal or fish fat, and this occurred quite often in Ust Avam. Fat is an important nutrient for the Dolgan and Nganasan. They burn a lot of calories keeping warm in the harsh climate. Cuts of caribou meat with fat and whitefish that have a fatty layer are highly valued. To place some of this fat into a fire is to treat the fire as kin. Among the Dolgan, it is often said that fire talks (*ot kepseter*) when the wood or coal cracks and pops. What is the fire saying? It could be good or bad news, obviously. But if the fire talks too much, then something is surely wrong. The situation requires interpretation and possibly a sacrifice.

Third, the story reinforces the importance of shamanic power. The story includes two shamans. The old local shaman knew there was a reason for the unexplained sickness of the young girl, but could not see the problem. The young powerful shaman from across the river could see and talk to the man from the "sunny" world. He was able, with the correct sacrifice, to call upon the good spirit Aiyi to take the man back home. The importance of this part of the story is that shamans have different powers. Some can cure, others perform rites of intensification, such as the annual "new *chum*" ceremony, and still others can send evil spirits to do harm. Accepting such supernatural claims means that one agrees that it is important to keep shamans as mediators with the ancestors and spirits.

▲▼▲▼▲▼▲▼▲▼▲▼▲▼▲▼▲▼▲▼▲▼▲▼▲▼▲▼▲▼▲▼▲▼

Individuals and Shamanic Power

The Soviet government did its best to eliminate shamanism in the 1930s. Even though I did not observe shamanism as a regular religious specialization among the Dolgan and Nganasan, the people still attribute supernatural power to individuals in varying degrees and functions. In this way, shamanism is still alive in Ust Avam.

One of my very close confidants told me that her father foretold his own death. He foretold a lot of things, even though he was not a real shaman. This may be because he spent a lot of time in the tundra. He could forecast the weather a week in advance and was accurate. Once he brought an *argish* (reindeer caravan) into the camp during a fierce snowstorm. The storm was so bad they could not see their hands in front of their faces. It was a big *argish* with many sleighs. One of the women did not have a *sukhui* (a reindeer hide or canvas poncho with hood), and snow got into her clothes—she got wet, and could not steer her sleigh. The old man tied her to the sleigh, and wrapped her in a reindeer hide. He tied all the sleighs together and brought them right into camp. The reindeer would not go by themselves; he had to lead the reindeer on foot. The woman asked her father how he knew where the camp was, and he said that he knew where to go, since he knew his orientation.

This man also foretold his daughter's future life. He told her that she would raise a lot of children, but that he did not know how many of the boys would grow up to be men. This turned out to be true; two of her sons died as adolescents. Their deaths were very difficult for her. Also, he said that she would always have a lot of guests, and this turned out to be true as well.

He also foretold his own death. One spring, when they still were herding reindeer in Ust Avam, the man had a dream, about which he told his daughter. He said that an old man, a relative, came to him in his dream and was making something with his hands, but could not complete it. Also, he saw that his *balok* was broken into small pieces. According to Dolgan belief, both parts of the dream were bad signs. The man said to his daughter, "Soon I will die. Maybe I will live through the summer, but I don't know. Don't cry too much when I die, or I will take you with me." That the old man came to him meant that he might live a little longer. That the sleigh was broken into pieces meant that his death was imminent.

That very day he and a nephew, who he was helping to raise, were bringing a house *balok* and a freight *balok* from Taganari to their camp. Taganari is a series of lakes by which one can gain access to the Volochanka and Khatanga Rivers. This portage was important until mechanized transportation became available, and there are archaeological sites

Figure 5.4 Igor Falkov, demonstrating a model *argish* that he crafted. This *argish* includes (from left to right) a storage sleigh, men's riding sleighs, women's riding sleighs, children's riding sleighs and a living balok.

in this area that date back 6000 years. On the way back to camp, an ermine jumped on the nephew's lead reindeer, walked down its back, and jumped off its nose. This was an *aku* reindeer, or the reindeer that stays close to the tent and eats bread from their hands. That an ermine even came close to a person is a bad sign, as they usually keep their distance from humans. My friend told me that it is said that the ermine was possibly the helper of a shaman that was sent to eat a soul.

The man and his nephew stopped to talk it over. When a *balok* stops, it is always picked up and moved so the runners are at a slight angle with the trail; otherwise the runners will freeze in the trail. The man thought that the ill deed was meant for his nephew, since the ermine was on his reindeer. He sent the nephew on ahead, so that he could keep watch over him. The nephew had already started down the trail, but he thought that his uncle could use some help getting his large *balok* moving again. He turned back, and saw that the *balok* was standing at the bottom of a hill. He went over to it, and saw his uncle lying in the snow, paralyzed. The nephew got his uncle, and they rode into camp on a light sleigh. The daughter saw them coming into camp on a riding sleigh, and told her husband that something must be wrong. Her husband ran out of their *balok*. The old man could not move at all. After getting him inside, his daughter tried feeding him bouillon, and he swallowed a bit. The woman said that she could feel a slight movement in his hand when she held it. They brought him to the hospital in Ust Avam, and he died after three days. The woman said that her father did not die his own death, meaning that he died prematurely, and from the ill deed of someone, possibly a shaman.

This woman's mother died while she was still young, also because of a shaman. Her husband, the man that later in life foretold his death, was a brigadier of a reindeer-herding unit that specialized in producing fawns. It was a warm spring that year, and the water on the river was already pushing the ice up. The brigadier needed to hurry to get the reindeer on the north side of the Dudypta River before it was impassable. They were somewhere near a spot called Tundravaia, a hundred or so miles west of Ust Avam, where earlier that winter a shaman had been buried. Before the shaman died, she had told the community not to go around her grave or pass by too closely for a three-year period. However, the brigadier took the herd, his family, and some other families in that brigade across the Dudypta River near the shaman's grave. It would have meant a delay of several days to go to another spot suitable to cross, so he crossed there, not heeding the shaman's warning. Soon after they crossed the river, the mother gave birth to twins, a boy and a girl. It was a difficult birth, and she bled to death. Afterward, they called a shaman to find out why the woman died. She said that the mother died because they did not obey the wishes of the dead shaman. At the father's funeral, the director of the *gospromkhoz* came and made a eulogy. Someone had told him this story, and he mentioned it in the eulogy. The director said that the man did everything for the *kolkhoz*; he even sacrificed his wife. He was that kind of man, a local legend.

It is said among the Nganasan and Dolgan that shamanic powers run in families. I met a great-nephew of an individual that had foreseen the collapse of the Soviet Union in a dream several years in advance. The great-nephew was on his way to Dudinka but he ended up spending a week in Ust Avam. He was definitely peculiar, saying many things that did not make much sense to me, and his sentences were jumbled. He sat outside on the porch, and walked the village, talking to himself and singing Dolgan songs. I was told by Ust Avam residents, "Maybe he is a real shaman."

Traditional Cosmological Knowledge

Commonly in Ust Avam, behavior is framed and evaluated in terms of sin. "It's a sin" to do this or that. These sins do not have much to do with the Ten Commandments of the Judeo-Christian tradition. For example, it is a sin to feed *meshok* (reindeer tripe) to children: It may cause them to get lost in the tundra. The sin concept is used to channel behavior and is another example of traditional cosmological knowledge among the Dolgan and Nganasan. In Oksye's story of the Underground Kingdom, the hero's isolation was a sin and the mother of the underground household told her husband that he must have done some sin when the fire began to talk. Adults and elders are the ones that usually make statements about sins, and they make these statements to, or in the presence of, youngsters. In this way, they set up proscriptions and prescriptions about behavior. Many of these are likely meant to facilitate cooperation among co-descendants and long-term sustainability of resource use. If someone commits a sin, they are not following the proscription, that is to say they are not making the sacrifice.

For example, on a walk across Ust Avam, a Dolgan elder told her granddaughter and me that women were not supposed to walk on ash. She was commenting on the state of the village—people had spread out their winter ash piles when they cleaned up their yards in the spring. In the old days, people were careful to pile their ash in one place or put it in a pit. The fact that the ash piles were spread out made it difficult for her to walk to her friends' and relatives' houses. She told me that it is a sin for women, especially fertile women, to walk on ash. Since they are the ones that take care of the fire, and fire is very important here, they need to respect it. If they walk on ash, they show disrespect to the fire, and this can affect their ability to give birth.

Another informant, an Ust Avam hunter, told me that there are "essences" in nature. These essences understand and protect people if they treat nature correctly, and can punish people if they treat nature incorrectly. For example, if people do not treat nature with respect, they may die prematurely or have some other unfortunate thing happen to them. There was a Russian hunter on the Saniteh territory to the north of my friend. That hunter was well known for catching about 1000 Arctic fox every winter. He had 2000 traps, and he drove around his territory on a tractor. The native hunters in Ust Avam do not have access to this kind of equipment, and tractors rip up the fragile, slow-growing tundra mosses and lichens, which then take many years to recover. The Saniteh hunter bought a Volga, a full-size Russian car, with the profits from his hunting. The year before my interview in 1996, this hunter died at the age of 53. My friend's grandmother always told him not to hunt too many animals. The Russian hunter did not follow this rule, and his death was interpreted as a result of his breaking the laws of nature.

This story has a number of important points. First, my friend did not say that it was a particular spirit or personality that was responsible for this hunter's death. The essence of nature about which he refers (and that of the previous ash example) is a supernatural force, like karma. This kind of belief could be classified as animatism, or a belief in a supernatural power. In these cases, if a person's actions do not follow the laws of nature, they create a supernatural imbalance that can come back to penalize the person. In the fox hunter example, it was my friend's grandmother that gave him this information. Supposing that she gave this information to her other descendants, and that other grandmothers and grandfathers gave the information to their descendants, this essence of nature would provide a supernatural leveling mechanism among Ust Avam hunters. If one person hunts too many animals, then there would be fewer animals for the other hunters and their families, most of whom are related genealogically. A greedy hunter would be taking away opportunities from the ancestors' other descendants. There are plenty of examples of economic, social, and religious leveling mechanisms in hunting-and-gathering societies (Woodburn 1982). With these traditions, individuals make some kind of sacrifice for the common good. When the community is made up of kin, this sacrifice makes sense on a number of levels.

Many Ust Avam hunters explicitly stated that it is their practice to help one another. This help occurs within the community and is often extended to relatives and friends in other communities and Dudinka. The mutual aid can include sharing food, supplies, services, and information.

> I give meat and fish to my parents and they redistribute it. I think I give them the same amount as I did before 1991. We help each other out with money too. I help other people. If their motor breaks down I help them out and might even bring them into the village. I ask for no payment. We help each other out this way (*vsaimno-obratno*) more often now than before 1991. Gas and spare parts are hard to come by now. The law of the tundra is: Don't do evil to one another. It rarely

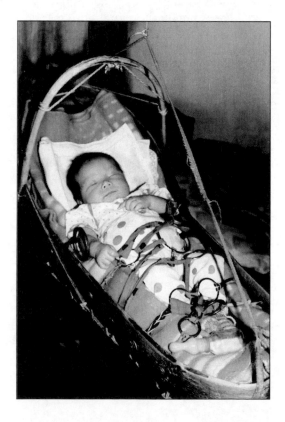

Figure 5.5 Dolgan and Nganasan families use the traditional cradleboard for their young children. These are often suspended from the ceiling so that the infant can be rocked while the parents do something else.

happens now and rarely happened before 1991. In the tundra we live and help each other.

Anufrey, Ust Avam, 1996

In Ust Avam, ancestors encourage sacrifice among co-descendants using stories and the sin concept. If a sin is committed (i.e., the sacrifice is not made), there is the potential for supernatural retribution. The likelihood of supernatural retribution is real, since when something bad does happen, the cause is easily related to the breaking of the laws of nature (and cooperation). Similarly, in the ash-pile example, it was an elderly woman talking to me in the presence of her young granddaughter. Obviously, it is an effort to dig a pit to bury the rather large ash pile that builds up outside everyone's apartment in Ust Avam. The Dolgan and Nganasan did not have this problem when they were semi-nomadic reindeer herders, and it was easier to observe the taboo. Still, the grandmother was emphasizing the traditional moral strategy, through the power of the "laws of nature," that facilitates the future cooperation of her grandchildren.

Sacred Places

Members of both the Dolgan and Nganasan groups made sacrifices at sacred places, sometimes at the same place and at the same time. These sacred places required regular visits, usually with a shaman, and sacrifices of reindeer meat or personal items, such as a button, a bullet, matches, or cigarettes. Strips of fur were also tied to trees or to a pole and crosspiece (*törö* in Dolgan). These ritual visits are not made anymore because of the distance—the sacred places were in the mountains or the foothills, at a location passed on the annual reindeer-herding migration. They are still talked about, however, especially on hunting trips when elders point out their locations and instructions for traveling to them. In practice, when the Dolgan and Nganasan travel to a new place in the tundra, it is said that it is important to make a sacrifice to that place. I have observed such sacrifices. If the sacrifice is not made, it is said that the hunting or fishing will not be productive, and that something bad may happen to the people. This practice could be interpreted as symbolic reciprocity with nature. Nature provides for people, so people should give something back to nature in order to maintain a balance between people and nature. Reciprocity with prey and nature is an important part of the cosmological traditions of many hunting-and-gathering peoples (Bird-David 1992).

In addition to symbolic reciprocity with nature, the Dolgan and Nganasan used sacred places for rites of passage. Certain rock formations that resembled humans or man-made items, such as an anvil or a table, were the venues for rites, around which children, for example, would pass three times in order to prevent illness. In the case of both sacrifices and rites of passage, participation in the ritual symbolizes the people's acceptance of the ancestrally defined contract with nature: respect and mutual sacrifice.

In 1997, heads of households in Ust Avam were asked a series of questions about their use of the tundra and sacred locations as part of my survey of the community. Of the 35 men and 30 women who answered the question "Did or does your family have special or sacred spots in the tundra or mountains?" 19 men and 16 women stated that they did have such locations; 16 men and 14 women said that they did not. When asked, "Do you work in the tundra?" the respondents' positive responses were just about equally divided between those who answered yes and those who answered no to the first question. Some answered that their parents had such places but that they did not know where they were (this counted as a yes to the first question). Knowledge of family history, rather than presence in the bush, is likely the main factor in whether respondents knew about sacred places, which points to the importance of transmission of traditional knowledge from ancestors.

As an example an informant told me a story from when they still had reindeer and argished to a spot in the Putorana Mountains. There was a block of granite there shaped like a house, longer than the Ust Avam House of Culture, which turned into a hill when they approached. There was also a stream and a lake there. When they came to the spot one of the older youths found *shaitany*. They were metal birds and fish. The leader of the reindeer brigade told them to collect them and check the area—there were to be no *shaitany* under the *chum* or where anyone would step on them. Later, after the *chum* was set up, my informant, another woman, and her mother went to check out the territory. In a small lake nearby, they found a scarf that was like new and a shaman's *buben*. At night her father was watching the herd. He fell asleep, and in a dream a voice said to him, "Chuno! Your reindeer are far away, and there is a wild bull down the stream." He woke up, and went outside. He walked down the stream, and there was a caribou bull with a new coat feeding at the end of the stream. He killed the bull and rounded up the reindeer. He brought back the meat, and they feasted. They found a place with good *shaitany*, and they tried to remember whose they were. Maybe they were those of a woman, a relative of the brigade leader's mother. This woman was a shaman.

The most sacred Nganasan places are their graves. Traditional Nganasan graves are open air. The deceased is dressed in a special parka and placed on a sleigh with many personal belongings. The person and the sleigh are enclosed inside a conical pole structure. Unlike a *chum* used to live in, these grave *chums* are completely made out of poles. The Nganasan are to avoid returning to the graves of their deceased, or it is said that the deceased could bring harmful consequences to the living. The Dolgan also avoid Nganasan graves. It is said that one must not make a complete circle around a Nganasan grave *chum,* or the spirit of the deceased will be offended and cause harm to come to the person.

Sacrifice and Cooperation

The communicated acceptance of supernatural claims is a part of daily life among the Dolgan and Nganasan in Ust Avam. While historic changes have caused many traditional practices to go into disuse, and the recent amalgamation of the Dolgan and Nganasan into a large settled community has intensified this process, the cosmology that is developing is both syncretic and functional. The cosmology is syncretic to the extent that Dolgan, Nganasan, and non-native beliefs, such as the infrequent display of Russian Orthodox crosses and icons, are joining together. The cosmology is functional in that people are encouraged to cooperate with one another and to limit their individual exploitation of the tundra's resources.

Dolgan and Nganasan cosmology facilitates relationships between people, between people and nature, and between people and the spiritual world. In all three areas of cooperation, one can observe, at least in stories, the importance of sacrifice, encouraged by ancestors; the avoidance of sin, defined by ancestors; and shamans, representatives of spirits and dead ancestors. Sacrifice is symbolic of future cooperation. Sacrifice is made in the form of gifts of meat and fish within the community, as well as little presents to special rock formations and fat fed to the fire. Many of these sacrifices are performed in public—a way to show acceptance of a supernatural declaration. In order to avoid committing sin, one must often make some kind of sacrifice, albeit some of these are symbolic. The sin concept is a way to encourage agreement among co-descendants. It is said that shamanic powers run in families and that the specific power can vary from individual to individual. Shamans are important in that they mediate between and transmit traditional knowledge from the spirit world of dead ancestors and the living world of descendants, thus providing a conduit for cooperation.

Chapter Six

The Law of the Tundra

Property is an important concept in human economic systems, as it defines people's access to land and resources. For some societies, property rights are defined by a formal written title, which confers to individuals or corporations the right to sell land. In other societies, or sectors within a society, property is traditionally assigned to kin groups or clans, and an individual within that unit has no right to sell. Property rights may be more or less informally negotiated in these cases. Cross-culturally, property varies as to whether it is defined as a relationship between people and a "thing" or as a relationship primarily between people (Hann 1998). As a result, attitudes, values, and practices that recognize the need for access to land are part of understanding a society's economy and social organization. To what extent humans were territorial in ancient environments is the subject of some speculation. However, in most modern hunter-gatherer societies, the resident group controls at least some surrounding lands and resources. For the Dobe Ju/'hoansi (Lee 1993), in the unpredictable Kalahari Desert, rights to waterholes are important and requests to the "owners" must be made to in order to camp and use resources near the waterhole. The exchange of *hxaro* valuables among the Ju/'hoansi helps maintain kinship and friendship ties in a number of areas and facilitates reciprocal access to waterholes (Wiessner 1977). As we will see in this chapter, Dolgan and Nganasan property relations include analogous means for reciprocal access to resources.

Among the Dolgan and Nganasan, the formal system of property relations implemented during the Soviet Union has been breaking down since the 1990s. In remote villages like Ust Avam, it is being replaced by an informal system, in some respects very similar to other hunter-gatherer societies in a variety of climates. The development of informal institutions to regulate resources among hunters in Taimyr, a process running counter to the global trend toward economic formalization, is a topic of applied and fundamental importance, especially considering current plans for developing environmental reserves in the Siberian North. The case of the Dolgan and Nganasan in Ust Avam may be one in which social relationships and ecological conditions favor informally managed property. As is the case in many hunting-and-gathering societies, economic independence is discouraged, and survival is dependent on the productivity of the tundra and cooperation in social networks.

Assigned Territories, Family/Clan Holdings, and Common-Pool Resources

A range of property relations can be identified among the Dolgan and Nganasan in the first post-Soviet decade: 1) Hunters and their families maintained use rights to state-enterprise hunting lands assigned to them during the Soviet period; 2) Sets of families and individuals established family/clan holdings; 3) Hunters used the sports-hunting territory immediately surrounding the settlement—an informally managed common-pool resource.

Ironically, the first property relation listed above—maintaining use-rights to assigned state-enterprise territories—involved decreasing contact with the regional economy. The management of what remained of the state enterprise allowed native hunters to continue to use the hunting territories allocated to them during the Soviet period, and kept them on the employment rolls even though the hunters did not receive regular salaries. This strategy allowed the hunters to practice household subsistence foraging, occasionally turn in products for cash, receive ever-decreasing allotments of fuel and equipment, and maintain eligibility for state pensions upon retirement. Rather than make a formal land claim, these hunters are practicing what might be thought of as a risk-minimizing strategy, the economic foundations for which were discussed in chapter 2.

As introduced in chapter 1, family/clan holdings were a new form of property, initiated by a 1992 decree of President Boris Yeltsin and created to protect traditional lands and economic activities for Russia's indigenous Siberian peoples. As a result of lobbying efforts of the Association of Peoples of the North and international and Russian academic pressure, Yeltsin issued decree No. 492 in April 1992, ordering northern regions to design procedures for returning land and property to native Siberian families and communities (Yeltsin 1992). In the Taimyr Autonomous Region, land claims under this new property category were called family/clan holdings or clan/community holdings (*semieno/rodovoe* or *obshchino/rodovoe khoziastvo*). Because of Yeltsin's decree, there was no property tax or rent on family/clan holdings, but the regional tax authority was able to collect taxes on profits from commercial sales, and obtaining legal documents, bank accounts, and licenses for the holding required regular contact with the regional center. From the regional perspective, family/clan holdings were to be incorporated into the newly developing capitalist economic system as producers of traditional products and rational users of the tundra.

The third property type, which could be characterized as a common-pool resource, was present during the Soviet era in the form of "sport-hunting" territories, small parcels of land surrounding remote villages that were to be used by those not employed as hunters in the state enterprise. Historically, hunting licenses were required to use the sport-hunting territory. In remote communities, these territories have expanded in recent years at the expense of assigned territories. Common property poses an anthropologically significant management dilemma: Where access is open it is impractical to keep people from misusing the common resources. When people compete for use of common-pool resources, the resultant increasing utilization leads to the degradation of the commons and its resources (Hardin 1968). Common property also is viewed as an impediment to capitalist development in Russia (Greenspan 1997). However, an assumption that there is no control in the commons is misleading in the case of the Dolgan and Nganasan. While currently there is little or no formal management of the Ust Avam commons—

Figure 6.1 Ilja Bezrukikh (left) hunts on the common hunting grounds surrounding Ust Avam. Ilja gave the meat from two and a half caribou to the other men, who came along but do not own firearms and have families to feed.

hunting licenses are not easy to obtain since the cost of transportation to the regional capital is so high—informal negotiation among the community's hunters generally results in beneficial allocation of hunting spots in the common zone. With distribution of the catch through kinship and friendship networks and traditionally reinforced economic leveling of other wealth, production for profit is not common, and thus, competitive utilization is minimized. With common-pool resources expanding in the Taimyr Autonomous Region, we have an opportunity to describe the conditions under which groups of resource users create and maintain viable systems of commons management, an important anthropological and environmental issue (Feit 1973, Ostrom, 1990, McCay and Jentoft 1998, Eerkins 1998).

Formal Land Claims

Despite the opportunities offered by family/clan holdings, the majority of native households living in 17 remote settlements in the Taimyr region have not taken claim to the land. From 1992 through 1997, less than 50 family/clan holdings were formed in the region's native communities, and many of these had been rarely used for reasons discussed below. The way the transfer worked was that a set of indigenous nuclear-family members and their relatives and friends assembled and voted to form a voluntary association that would pursue a land claim on which traditional economic activities could occur. The association typically had a head, or *glava,* and members, and the territory was generally, but not always, in areas where the members' ancestors had lived before collectivization. The Dudinka City Committee on Land Use was to continue managing land funds, however, and it required the holding to follow criteria of rational resource use and ecological safety. While this approach sounded promising for native self-determination, a disjunction appears to have formed between the intent of the family/clan holding and practical applications of it.

Family/clan holdings were understood to be a form of business that was, in part, replacing the state-enterprise system. Land was taken from state-enterprise holdings and transferred to family/clan holdings. This transfer of land, and the resources on it, was often viewed as a zero-sum game, meaning one side's win was another's loss, especially by those still involved in and managing the state enterprise. Reflecting this interpretation, the members of early family/clan holdings were referred to derogatorily as *arendatory,* or renters. Family/clan holdings' articles of incorporation specified that traditional activities could include commercial sales. In this respect, the private holdings were in competition with the state enterprise, an organization with a history of commercial relationships and big budgets. Without commercial sales, however, the question remained: How were the members of the holdings to purchase the equipment and fuel that would be needed to access the territory and harvest wild food resources? This question was reflected in both informal interviews and structured surveys in the Avam tundra.

> To start a family/clan holding I would need a big loan. What bank would give it to me? I have nothing to secure it. The *gospromkhoz* will strangle me. The *gospromkhoz* has power and finances, I would be starting from nothing. If I would have a financial position, I might be able to do it. It's one person versus the mafia. Why do hunters live poorly? The *gospromkhoz* is the mafia now.

> Gospromkhoz *hunter, July 1997*

In the Taimyr Autonomous Region, only people of aboriginal descent are allowed to create family/clan holdings. Individuals of non-aboriginal descent can claim land for "peasant-hunting holdings," however, and a number of these have been granted. Family/clan holdings have a number of advantages over peasant-hunting holdings. Native individuals with five years of professional hunting experience can create family/clan holdings. Non-native individuals are required to have 10 years of professional hunting experience. The regional government does not want novices running around and risking death in the tundra. Peasant-hunting holdings are granted only by lease, and lessees must pay land taxes. Family/clan holdings are granted in a number of forms, and payment of land taxes or lease payments is never required. Both types of holdings are required to pay

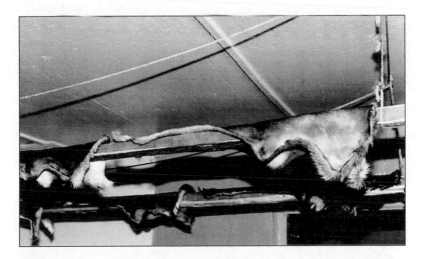

Figure 6.2 *Kamusa*—the hide from the lower limbs of the caribou—drying on racks in an apartment in Ust Avam. *Kamusa* are used for making traditional leather-soled footwear, as well as the uppers for *untaiki*, or rubber-soled fur boots previously sold in the Taimyr Region's cities.

taxes on profits from any sales, to open a commercial bank account, and to have the cooperation of the Committee on Land Resources, the Agricultural Bureau, the Association of Peoples of Taimyr, and the state enterprise in their area. Up to 11 documents have to be prepared in order to complete the land claim.

While native-run business could be interpreted as a sign of revitalization, supporting the neotraditionalism model of social change (Pika and Prokhorov 1994), the actual distribution of the holdings revealed a more complicated situation. A simple way to evaluate the distribution of family/clan holdings was to analyze their location. I reviewed 110 district decisions in which land was taken from or assigned to newly formed holdings at the Government Archive of the Taimyr Autonomous Region and the Dudinka City Committee of Land Resources. Only a few of these decisions were made for non-native (peasant) hunting, trapping, and fishing holdings, which were not included in this analysis. The majority of the family/clan holdings have been located near, or with good water access to, the Taimyr Region's urban centers, Dudinka and Norilsk. Few family/clan holdings are located in and around the 17 rural settlements, where the majority of the native population lives. Of 46 holdings in Dudinka District, 29 were on land contiguous with the city of Dudinka. Twelve holdings were on lands more distant from the city, but three of these had access to Norilsk by water. Five holdings were on unspecified lands. Proximity to Taimyr's urban centers likely facilitated access to services, markets, and government, which was necessary for active use of the holding.

Proximity to the regional capital appears to have been a major factor in the location of family/clan holdings (table 6.1). Most of the family/clan holdings registered in Dudinka district are within 100 kilometers of

The Source of Land	Number of Family/Clan Holdings
Contiguous with City of Dudinka	
Yenisei State Farm	11
Tukhard State Farm	9
Piasino State Farm	5
Land Resources of the City	2
Potapova Experimental-Production Farm	1
Shelmovskii Government Reserve Fund	1
Discontiguous with the City of Dudinka	
Government Hunting Farm Taimyrskii	4
Volochanka State Farm	4
Khantaiskii State Farm	4
Other	5
TOTAL	46

Table 6.1 Source of land for family/clan holdings in Dudinka District (1992–1997).

Dudinka or Norilsk. Of the holdings in areas discontinuous with the urban centers, three holdings, located on the Piasina River, have good access to Norilsk. The river historically has significant summer traffic with tugboats and barges, 30-ton freighters, and small aluminum boats that provide some ability to get goods to the Norilsk market.

Four holdings are located near the community of Volochanka. Transportation to Volochanka is expensive because of its location in the Central Taimyr Lowlands—transport by river is only possible during a short period of the summer from Khatanga. However, there are a number of villages that provide meat and fish more easily in that eastern district of the Taimyr Region. As a result, access to markets is difficult for these holdings, and they are used generally for subsistence foraging. One family/clan holding near Ust Avam is in a similar transport situation to that of the Volochanka holdings. There is virtually no large-scale transportation available to these holdings except by air.

The rate of formation of family/clan holdings has decreased significantly since 1994. Figure 6.3 shows the number of family/clan holdings registered per annum in Dudinka district. Because of this dynamic I felt it was important to investigate hunters' motivations for claiming or not claiming family/clan holdings.

In a structured survey of Ust Avam hunters in 1997, I asked, "Why did you or did you not claim a family/clan holding?" I asked this question to 25 individuals who are hunters in the Avam tundra and along the Piasina River and who have either a family/clan holding or work on an assigned territory. I interviewed at least one hunter from each of the 16 active hunting territories in the *gospromkhoz*, as well as the heads of three family/clan holdings and two individuals who work at surrounding state enterprises. In all but three cases, these individuals are the leaders of the hunting brigades or holdings. These hunters represent approximately half of those in Ust Avam and, according to my observations, they are generally

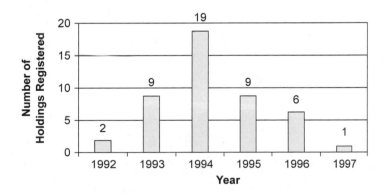

Figure 6.3 The Dynamics of Family/Clan Holding Establishment, Dudinka District (1992–August 1997).

the most active native hunters in the area. Twenty-two of the 25 respondents were not associated with family/clan holdings. The responses to these questions are grouped in table 6.2.

Of the three individuals with family/clan holdings, one stated that he hoped to live better. This individual alone admitted entrepreneurial motivations in claiming a family/clan holding. The reality is that taxes consume all his profits, however, and his holding is barely active. Another individual stated that the main reason for starting a family/clan holding was to feel more liberty. Being one's own boss is a reason why many individuals in the United States start businesses, too. This family/clan holding was the only active one in the Avam tundra, and the two members were constantly shuttling back and forth between their hunting territory on the Piasina River; Norilsk, where they sold their fish and meat; and Dudinka, where they had to deal with the tax police and regional hunting authorities. The third individual with a family/clan holding stated that he did not know why he started it. Currently, the head of this holding has returned to "work" for the government hunting enterprise by contract during certain seasons, and his family/clan holding is inactive.

Five of the 22 responses to the question "Why did you not claim a family/clan holding?" dealt with the notion of the family/clan holding. Three of these individuals said that they did not understand what a family/clan holding was, or how it could actually work. These responses point to the lack of information and the disintegrating infrastructure in the region. The other two said they doubted that it was possible for them to take a family/clan holding. This response underscored the difficulties associated with getting the necessary approvals, completing the paperwork, and dealing with government officials.

Reason	Number of Responses
No Family/Clan Holding	
Money	10
Problem with Concept	5
Intention to Make Claim	2
Listed as Member of Family/Clan Holding	1
Land is Poor	1
Non-Local	1
Too Much Paperwork	1
Does Not Know	1
Family/Clan Holding	
To Live Better	1
Liberty	1
Does Not Know	1
TOTAL	25

Table 6.2   Reasons for claiming or not claiming family/clan holdings, 1997 interviews.

Money was the main factor in not starting a family/clan holding for 10 respondents. There were three kinds of problems these informants associated with money. The first had to do with the absence of adequate money to establish the organization and make the land claim. Four informants mentioned the lack of starting capital as the main reason for not claiming land. The second aspect of money was generally phrased, "It's not profitable." Five informants stated that clan holdings are monetarily disadvantageous. Their concerns were probably justified, since two of four holdings in the area were inactive, a situation that has been repeated in other parts of the region. The third problem informants associated with money had to do with obtaining supplies, such as gas, coal, and consumables, along with conducting the distribution and marketing. Five informants mentioned these infrastructural problems as the first or second reason for not starting a clan holding.

One informant stated that he had no reason to make a family/clan land claim. He clarified that the land is poor (i.e., resources are migratory). In addition, he mentioned the problems with obtaining supplies and marketing his products.

Another hunter stated that he had no right to lands there since he was not local. He clarified that he "never thought about it." He is married to a local woman, however, and there are prior instances of family/clan holdings being granted to non-local native and non-native men married to women from the local native community. He could apply for one if he believed there would be some kind of benefit.

One hunter mentioned overwhelming paperwork as the main reason for his not making a land claim. It is true that it took several weeks, if not months, to complete the paperwork and get the approvals necessary for starting a family/clan farm in the Taimyr region. This process must be conducted in Dudinka, difficult for hunters that spend months on end in the tundra.

One individual stated that he did not know why he did not decide to start a family/clan holding. This hunter spends most of his time in the bush and has rarely visited the regional capital or Norilsk. It was not surprising that claiming a family/clan holding was not in his interests.

Most hunters were busy hunting, and they did not have the time nor the political capital necessary to push their land claims through the system or to market their products. In addition, there was little competition for hunting grounds, still officially held by the *gospromkhoz*, and those individuals with family/clan holdings made little, if any, material gains. The economic situation in a remote village such as Ust Avam was characterized by decreasing access to urban centers and markets. In sum, there was insufficient time and money, and little apparent benefit, for residents in the Ust Avam community to pursue official land grants under the current regulations and economic conditions in the Taimyr region.

I informally interviewed a number of heads of family/clan holdings whose lands were closer to Dudinka and Norilsk. For several years, the more prominent holdings had produced up to several tons of fish and caribou meat annually for sale in the cities. Their use of the land differed little from the Soviet-period hunting brigades, except that they lived most of the year in the city, where they had to manage transportation, sales, and payments.

Forms of Ownership and Politics

The creation of family/clan holdings is best interpreted in terms of Russia's overall process of privatization and state-enterprise devolution. In 1992, two family/clan holdings were registered by the city of Dudinka. As part of this and other early decisions regarding family/clan holdings, the city cited existing law. One piece of legislation, cited in the Dudinka decisions, was a law of the Soviet of People's Deputies of the Taimyr Autonomous Region "about a program of development for villages and hunting/ trapping holdings in the region under conditions of economic transition to market relations." This regional decree was issued December 25, 1991 with the goal of increasing individual responsibility for the condition, protection, and rational use of hunting and trapping resources. From the regional perspective, family/clan holdings were created to use the land effectively. This orientation differed significantly from the intent of the April 1992 presidential decree, which was to protect traditional lands and economic activities, supporting self-determination. Despite the 1992 presidential decree, the regional government retained the rational-use criterion.

During my review of the decisions of the City of Dudinka that created these family/clan holdings, I identified three forms of land grants assigned to the native people: lifetime inheritable property; leased property; and unlimited (continuous) use property. All three types are classed as family/clan holdings, but the specifics of the city decisions have different implications in terms of property. The type of property was not specified in all the archival documents. Nonetheless, I identified a shift in the type of property available to the native people of Dudinka district as time proceeded (table 6.3).

Form of Ownership	Number	Dates Issued
Lifetime inheritable property	8	May 1992 – June 1993
Leased property	9	April 1994 – April 1997
Unlimited (continuous) use property	7	January 1995 – December 1996

Table 6.3 Types of property for family/clan holdings in Dudinka District, Taimyr Autonomous Region.

These three forms of ownership were not granted simultaneously. Lifetime, inheritable ownership was granted to eight holdings from May 1992 through June 1993. Lifetime, inheritable ownership was secured with a document called a government act (*gosakt*), which was symbolized with a certificate of ownership. Ironically, the certificate that in effect granted private ownership of land displayed the insignia of the R.S.F.S.R., a political unit that did not officially condone private property. The R.S.F.S.R., or *Rossiiskoi Sotsialisticheskoi Federativnoi Sovietskoi Respublic* (Russian Socialist Federal Soviet Republic), was the first and largest of the former Soviet republics. At least two family/clan heads that received these certificates had received low-interest loans from the Taimyr Region and were involved in sales of country food to regional markets, as their land was not far from the city. Particularly proud of the *gosakt* and confident in the economic potential of their holding, the lifetime, inheritable ownership allowed these families to pass these holdings on to their descendants. The holdings were to maintain "effective use" of the land and to follow ecological demands and measures, as regulated by the City Committee on Land Use and Management and local village administrations.

Unlimited (continuous) use ownership (*vladenie*) was granted to seven holdings from January 1995 through December 1996. Less impressive than the *gosakt*, this type of ownership was more limited in the rights it conferred. It was not to be passed on to descendants automatically. The City Committee on Land Use and Management was to help set up a business plan and required the organization to follow rational use of natural resources and ecological requirements.

After President Boris Yeltsin's showdown with the Supreme Soviet of the R.F.S.F.R. in 1993, certificates of ownership with the Soviet insignia were no longer used in the Taimyr Region. From April 1994 through April 1997, nine family/clan holdings were granted land leases (*arenda*). The most significant difference between holdings granted on leases and those that received the other forms of ownership is that the lease specifies a termination point for the land tenure, usually 10 years. While no land payments were required because of the 1992 decree, "effective" use of the land was again required and regulated by the City Committee on Land Resources and Management. The Dudinka government favored land grants with lease agreements as time proceeded. City representatives pointed out to me that the lease arrangement was more logical, since some of the holdings were becoming inactive after a year or two and it was easier to reassign the land granted through a lease than land granted through the other forms. Occasional subsistence hunting was not necessarily sufficient for effective use. Interpreted as a lapse of effective or rational use of the land, the administration reasoned that others should have the chance to use the land if they had the ability.

This system of formal property relations in the Taimyr Region is quite different than collective bargaining and corporate land claims arranged in

Alaska and Canada. The shift in property towards leases appears as an erosion of rights that were to be granted the native peoples with the 1992 decree. Obviously, regular contact with the regional center is important, at least at the initial stages of making the land claims. From the perspective of native people in remote settlements, increasing costs of living and transportation made regular travel to the capital close to impossible, and filing a land claim even less feasible.

Assigned Territories

Figure 6.4 shows Ust Avam, the surrounding low-lying tundra, and the Putorana Mountains in the south. I recorded the location of the points represented on the map using an off-the-shelf Garmin GPS instrument. The unnumbered points on the Piasina River are hunting cabins and slaughtering facilities in the Kresty subdivision of the *gospromkhoz*. In the 1970s, the Piasina River became the main focus for the *gospromkhoz* fall "on-water" caribou hunt. By the mid-1980s, more than 30,000 caribou per year were being harvested, mostly on the Piasina River by non-indigenous hunters from Norilsk. The hunters were paid for the number of caribou turned in, of course, and they could make in a few weeks as much as or more than their annual salary. Assignment at one of the *gospromkhoz* seasonal brigades on the Piasina River was often achieved through personal favors to the *gospromkhoz* administration in Norilsk, according to indigenous hunters in the area.

The unnumbered points surrounding the white ring encircling Ust Avam represent cabins on hunting parcels in the Avam subdivision of the *gospromkhoz*. The indigenous population of the Avam tundra area was concentrated in Ust Avam through collectivization and amalgamation of collectives, a process completed in 1971. Sixteen brigades of hunters, usually members of extended families living in Ust Avam, were assigned to these territories. In three cases, however, pairs of unrelated hunters constituted the brigade. In most cases, the brigades originally assigned to the territory (or their sons) are still using the territory, where they are still responsible for the equipment and buildings, and occasionally turn some products in to the *gospromkhoz*. Most of these assigned territories (*ugod'ia*) are located some distance from the main waterways.

Points 1 and 2 are family/clan holdings, whose owners have apartments in Dudinka and live part of the year in the city. Points 1 and 2, and their considerable surrounding hunting grounds, were originally part of the Kresty subdivision of the *gospromkhoz*. The hunters at those spots, in effect, privatized an assigned territory.

Points inside the white ring are informally allocated hunting spots within the common-pool territory surrounding Ust Avam. Only a few of

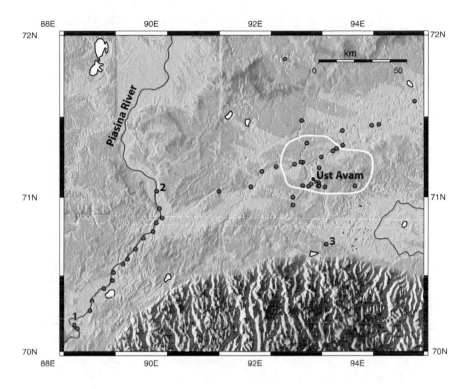

Figure 6.4 The Avam tundra with hunting cabins along the Piasina River (Kresty subdivision), cabins on hunting territories in the Avam subdivision of the *gos promkhoz*, and the Ust Avam commons (points inside the white ring are informally allocated hunting spots within the commons). Points 1, 2, and 3 are family clan holdings. Point 3 is the only family/clan holding within the Ust Avam subdivision.

the major points I visited are represented here. Since 1993, this common-pool zone has expanded since two contiguous assigned territories were not reassigned to other staff hunters or family/clan holdings when the brigade disbanded. In one case, the hunter assigned to the territory passed away. In another, the non-native brigadier that worked seasonally at the territory did not return after 1996. The *gospromkhoz* could reassign these open territories, and the capital equipment and buildings on them, to other hunters in Ust Avam. Conversely, a family could organize and claim the territories under the regional regulations for forming family/clan holdings. At present, the effectively unemployed hunters of Ust Avam use the buildings and territories on these abandoned parcels for subsistence hunting, thus expanding the community's common-pool resource. This growing communal-use area is regulated among the hunters. They decide amongst themselves when, where, and with whom they will hunt, usually making these arrangements before traveling into the tundra, similar to the land-tenure practice used before formation of state enterprises in the region.

> Earlier you could go anywhere to hunt. Trap lines belonged to individual hunters however. Everyone knew whose trap lines were whose. To hunt or to pasture caribou, they could go anywhere, but tended to avoid one another.
>
> *K. K., Ust Avam, 1996*

Point 3 is the only family/clan holding in Avam territory, and the owners live in Ust Avam. A large hunting parcel lies to the south and west of point 3—close to 8,000 square kilometers in the lowlands, foothills, and Putorana Mountains. The distance to these areas from Ust Avam, however, along with the degradation of mechanized transport, means that the owners and members of the holding rarely, if ever, visit the territory.

Management of Hunting Grounds and Resources

Since most of the hunters in Ust Avam did not pursue formal land claims, in the 1990s they continued to use hunting territories assigned to them during the Soviet period and/or they began to forage more often in the common-use land around the village. The practice of turning in products had become rather haphazard by 1997. There were no longer any production plans, and the *gospromkhoz* had not accepted fish since 1994. In 1997, Norilsk Nickel, and the *gospromkhoz* as one of its subdivisions, came under new management. Salaries for the whole company were frozen, and no one in Ust Avam was paid for furs delivered in February and March. Several hunters lost a whole season's work and gasoline. Later, in 1997, rifles previously given out every fall for caribou hunting were removed from the *gospromkhoz* office and the village; thus, the prospects for making cash from hunting diminished further for the majority of hunters.

The social context of property relations in Ust Avam is important for understanding the management of property in the post-Soviet period. Following recent discussions of property in economic anthropology (Hann 1998), I believe that a number of traditional cosmological proscriptions and prescriptions, discussed in the previous chapter, serve to subordinate individual maximization of land and resource use in Ust Avam. These traditions are not always agreed upon within the community, as there is significant variation from family to family, not to mention between the Dolgan and Nganasan. While there may, for example, be some disagreement between traditions on whether a moose should be hunted or not, if one is killed, then the meat is distributed to a wide circle, thus fulfilling a different land-management tradition. The fact that families may disagree about which traditions are important reveals the significance of ancestors and elders in the process of transmission, since many of the specifics are limited to one extended family.

The first important tradition in Dolgan and Nganasan property relations is what is known in Ust Avam as the law of the tundra (*zakon tundry*). The law of the tundra sets two basic requirements for hunters. First, hunters should help one another with food, labor, and other goods and services. Mutual aid, known in anthropology as delayed or balanced reciprocity, something that the Communist Party attempted desperately to stop among native Siberians as a vestige of primitive communism, is viewed as an integral part of the hunter's contract with the tundra. A number of hunters stated to me that if they did not give food to other people, then the tundra would prevent them from successful hunting. In addition, living nearby and helping other people is the lesson of traditional Dolgan and Nganasan stories, such as Oksye's "Underground Kingdom." Second, hunters must not overuse the tundra's resources. Ancestors have told members of the present generation that the "essences" of the tundra will punish those that hunt too much. The early death of a hunter or the misfortune of a relative are taken as evidence of supernatural retribution for the hunter's overhunting. The law of the tundra is a powerful ancestral force for most Dolgan and Nganasan, encouraging sharing and discouraging behavior to accumulate individual wealth.

A belief in sacred places is widespread among the native people of Siberia (cf. Gurvich 1986, Humphrey 1998, King n.d.), and this also is relevant to property relations. Two types of activities—a ritual sacrifice and a rite of passage—occurred traditionally at sacred spots of the Dolgan and Nganasan. Ritual sacrifices and rites of passage at sacred places are examples of ancestral encouragement of proper relations with the land. This tradition continues today with the giving of a small present to the tundra or to a lake before hunting or fishing.

Following the law of the tundra, another of the rules of Dolgan and Nganasan property relations is related to food distribution and consumption, which is viewed as property-sharing rather than economic exchange (cf. Woodburn 1998). Food and other resources from the tundra are distributed within the community, and many types of people are included in the distribution networks: relatives, friends, pensioners, single mothers, and other people that request help. Because of the distribution of raw food products, accumulation is limited and the maximization of return from hunting, which provided large cash benefits in the Soviet period, provides only increasing drudgery at present (Chayanov 1966). The lack of a market sector for country food limits the competitive use of natural resources. Many people in Ust Avam told me that half the village was related to them in some way or another and, if need be, they could go around to a different relative for every meal. In that way they would visit a given relative's household to eat less than once in a month or so (assuming half the 160 households in Ust Avam were related and they visited two to three house-holds a day). In reality, few people visit relatives' houses only to eat. How-ever, visiting relatives and friends is an important part of daily life in Ust Avam, and hosts are always hospitable, covering the table, as they say, with some food to go along with tea. Visiting is one of the main social ac-tivities in the village, and relatives and close friends are apt to knock on the door and walk in at almost any time of the day. More rarely, unrelated people and more distant friends will stop in to visit. Since tea and food are almost always served to guests, foods that the hosting household has, but the guests might not have, will be equalized to some extent. Food distribu-tion after a hunt, as well as visiting, provide venues for economic leveling in Ust Avam, and thus management of resources for the long term rather than for short-term profit.

Physical and Social Territoriality

In semi-structured interviews of 31 hunters in Taimyr I included a number of questions about the level of exclusivity hunters perceived for their territory. Exclusivity is important because it allows the owner to limit competitive use of the property and its resources. Certain resources were considered more "private" than other resources, and requests to use them were expected. Hunting lands themselves were not viewed as exclusive property, however.

The first question I asked was, "Have you ever demanded that some-one leave your hunting territory?" Four hunters answered yes, and 27 an-swered no. I asked a follow-up question for those that answered yes: "If so, what happened?" While I cannot relate the details of their answers be-cause of confidentiality, they boiled down to personal differences and con-flicts between brigade members. The use of the hunting territories in the Avam tundra is generally friendly.

In reply to the question "Do you feel that you can stop someone going through your hunting territory, even if they do not appear to be planning to hunt?" seven hunters answered yes, 22 answered no, and two hunters said they did not know, likely implying that it depends on the situation. From their answers, it appears that trespass is not a widespread problem among Avam hunters. Hunters added that travelers usually stop and visit in any case, and a few stated that it is more interesting when they do. When a traveler stops, the hunter typically finds out what the traveler in-tends to do, where he is going, and whether he has seen any animal tracks. A visitor may also stay a few days to hunt or do some other work. They may also bring news and gifts. This visiting in the tundra is important for setting up and maintaining friendship and reciprocal obligations.

The next question was in the form of a table that listed different types of resources, and for each resource there was a column of use for oneself (subsistence) or for sale. The hunter was asked to determine whether a visitor to his territory should ask permission to use the resource for each of the economic goals. I asked, "Should someone coming to your hunting territory ask your permission to obtain the following resources (wood, hare, ptarmigan, caribou, moose, bear, wolverine, wolf, other fur-bearing animals, fish, and goose) for oneself or for sale?" Twenty-two hunters answered yes for at least some resources. Of particular concern for most hunters answering yes were Arctic-fox trap lines. Trap lines are usually named (e.g., Ivan's first trap line, Ivan's second trap line) and considered the personal property of an individual, as there is considerable investment in their set-up. Some trap lines have been handed down from ancestors, and thus form an important part of the kinship estate. If a hunter was in pursuit of prey and crossed into another territory, on the other hand, he need not ask permission to cross (tables 6.4 and 6.5). The borders are often fairly remote and virtually impossible to patrol. However, if the hunters were going to "sit on" someone's territory to hunt or fish, especially for hunting caribou and fishing on lakes, a request of permission would most certainly be expected. Eight hunters answered no, they did not expect requests for permission to use any of the listed resources. One hunter commented that he did not "own" the land. One hunter did not know. One resource about which I did not ask was the hunting cabin itself. Some hunters did seem concerned about people using their cabin without their permission, as they kept it locked when they were not there. In an emergency, however—if someone's life depended on it—these hunters stated that they would certainly not object if someone broke into their cabin, shed, or *balok*. One hunter mentioned that during the Soviet period, hunters were expected to check the hunting licenses of unfamiliar people that showed up at their territory, especially during goose season, and to report them if they were unlicensed. Hunting Arctic fox was most strongly associated with personal property, the trap line. There was some indication that the hunting cabin and valuable resources such as fuel were becoming increasingly private. In the past, houses and cabins were closed and a board was placed at an angle to the door or a bucket was placed in front of the door. Now locks are increasingly used.

Finally, I asked, "Do you know of anyone that took resources from your hunting territory without your permission?" Four hunters answered yes. These were hunters with cabins on the Dudypta River, the main transportation route from Kresty to Ust Avam. Gasoline and oil were the resources most often cited as having been taken. Twenty-seven hunters answered no. Thus, if resources are taken from a hunter's territory without permission, in most cases the hunter is not aware of it.

The answers to these preliminary survey questions about property indicate that exclusion of potential beneficiaries from hunting territories is difficult or impossible, while there are clear potential benefits from including visitors. Borders are not easily patrolled, and if a hunter is chasing prey he may not have the opportunity to ask permission. Locations with significant capital improvements, such as trap lines and cabins, are the most sensitive, along with fishable lakes and caribou migration routes. While these questions were posed specifically to hunters with assigned territories, there is evidence that there are similar relations to the commons.

Informally allocated hunting and fishing spots are distributed fairly evenly along the major rivers throughout the commons. Positions of goose blinds, for example, are agreed upon among hunters before goose season, and hunters do not travel as far as their assigned land for goose season, at present. Many hunters have built small sheds throughout the commons that they use as lookouts and base camps. These are especially useful during the caribou migration. Everyone knows to whom these sheds belong, and if a hunting party is headed in that direction, the hunters will ask the owner about using it. In this way, there is little competition for hunting spots most of the year, even in the commons.

The next series of questions dealt with whom hunters preferred to have visit and who would disturb them the most if they visited and hunted on their land. Since the ability to maintain physical exclusion is limited, social preferences for partners may be the place to look for regulation in the Dolgan and Nganasan property-management scheme. Hunters were asked who they prefer to have hunt on their territories. A number of categories of people were presented to the hunter: certain individuals; local people (*mestnyi*)/non-local people (*priezhii*, or newcomers); Dolgan/Nganasan; a neighboring-brigade member/distant-brigade member; close relative/relative/non-relative; and no one. This was an open-ended question, and hunters tended to have multiple answers. A compilation of the answers is presented in table 6.4. Two hunters preferred that no one come to their territory. Twenty-four of 29 responding to this question preferred a more familiar person, including locals (*mestnie*), a neighboring-brigade member, or a relative. Close relatives were mentioned in about half of the responses. Three hunters stated that they would accept any "normal" person.

As there are two indigenous ethnic groups in Ust Avam that have been living in the same community for 30 years, I expected to find a much greater emphasis on ethnicity in statements about hunting-partner preferences. The results surprised me, although they seem to confirm the importance of inter-ethnic marriages and friendships in the low incidence of inter-ethnic group violence. Instead, the hunters emphasized indigenous status in general (local person), personal characteristics (normal person), and kinship in partner preferences.

Hunters were then asked what types of people would disturb them the most if they hunted on their territories. The same categories of people as above were suggested. Again, the question was open-ended, and there were a number of respondents with multiple answers. A compilation of the answers is presented in table 6.5. Fifteen hunters said that it would not disturb them if people visited to hunt on their territory. Nine hunters mentioned non-local people (either *priezhie* or truck drivers) as potentially disturbing them. A couple of specific individuals were trouble, as well as a couple of people from the neighboring brigade. These cases again were on

Category	Rank Order of Answers			
	1st	2nd	3rd	4th
Local person[a]	8	0	0	0
Normal person/friend	7	0	0	0
Relative	4	5	0	2
Close relative	4	0	3	1
Dolgan[b]	0	4	0	0
Neighboring-brigade member	2	1	2	0
No one	2	0	0	0
Non-local person	1	0	0	0
Distant-brigade member	0	1	0	0
Non-relative	0	0	0	1

[a] This response also includes those respondents (3) who answered both Dolgan and Nganasan, meaning both types of *mestnyi*.
[b] There was no clear trend for preference of visitors of the same ethnicity: two respondents were Dolgan, one Evenk, and one Kalmyk (a Mongol nationality from southern Russia).

Table 6.4   Rank order of answers to the question "Who do you prefer to have visit to hunt on your territory?" Ust Avam, 1997.

Category	Rank Order of Answers			
	1st	2nd	3rd	4th
No one	15	0	0	0
Non-local person	5	1	0	0
Truck drivers	3	0	0	0
Specific individuals	2	0	0	0
Neighboring-brigade member	2	0	0	0
Nganasan[a]	1	1	0	0
Dolgan[b]	0	1	0	0
Local person	0	1	0	0
Non-relative	0	0	1	0
Drunks	0	0	0	1
Does not know	1	0	0	0

[a] One of these respondents was Dolgan and the other one was Kalmyk.
[b] Again, there is no clear trend as concerns preference by ethnicity; this respondent was Dolgan and suspected a Dolgan hunter from the neighboring brigade in borrowing, and not returning, a radio from his cabin.

Table 6.5   Rank order of answers to the question "Who would disturb you the most to have visit to hunt on your territory?" Ust Avam, 1997.

the Dudypta River, where there is considerable traffic. The specific mention of members of the other ethnic group was relatively low. This result is surprising, but consistent with the results from the previous question.

Based on the results of these two survey questions, Ust Avam hunters prefer locals, friends, and relatives as hunting partners, and are potentially most disturbed by non-locals. Thus, the social boundary defining the in-group of hunting partners is fairly wide in Ust Avam. Why are non-locals most feared? Non-locals are most likely not to subscribe to similar traditional proscriptions and prescriptions regarding land tenure. They are in the easiest position to maximize short-term gains and then defect on the social network, since their ties to the community are ephemeral at best. The most surprising result is that the majority of hunters stated that there was no one whose presence hunting on their territory would be a worry.

Preferences aside, kinship appears to be a significant factor in the social organization of the hunting territories surrounding Ust Avam. Bilateral kinship or affinal ties were prevalent among the brigade membership of 13 of 16 occupied hunting territories (table 6.6). Bilateral kinship means that genealogical reckoning occurs through both the father's and mother's sides of the family. These bilateral relationships structure Ust Avam's land tenure and production. The one family/clan holding in the Ust Avam subdivision of the *gospromkhoz* contains members of three families, which were distantly related. In 1994, the mayor of the village, a Dolgan, wanted to rebuild the caribou-herding station "Dolgany" and move anyone who wanted to go. With this ultimate goal, the mayor worked to form the family/clan holding Dolgany. The majority of this territory had been a biological reserve within the *gospromkhoz* during the Soviet period, although a natural-gas-explor-

Figure 6.5 Ust Avam hunter searching for caribou on a *maiak* (sighting platform) built by the Soviet geological survey. The same hunter shooting at a caribou on a fall on-land subsistence hunt.

Figure 6.6 Ust Avam hunter pursuing a wounded caribou. The same hunter, cutting the spinal cord of the wounded caribou—the most efficient, but dangerous, way to euthanize it.

atory expedition maintained a semi-permanent facility that was removed in 1996. The mayor was not a hunter, however, and the head of the holding, his father, was too old to travel to the holding. As a result, the holding was used very infrequently. The large number of people listed as members of the holding includes a large number of children and non-hunters. Similarly, if all the family members of the other brigades were listed too they would have even longer lists (compare the numbers of consanguineal relatives).

Elizabeth Cashdan's (1983) social boundary defense model for hunter-gatherer territoriality helps to explain this phenomenon. Where territories are large, resources dispersed, and perimeter defense is costly and has little benefit, control of land conducted through social means is the most effective (figures 6.5 and 6.6). It makes sense to restrict access on the basis of social ties to maintain access rights to resources and gain reciprocal privileges to other resources in the future. In the Avam tundra, access to hunting grounds is managed primarily through social and kinship relationships, and reciprocal arrangements with people associated with other assigned territories and spots in the commons.

In the Ust Avam commons, exploitation of resources by any one individual is socially limited. For example, if an individual is especially productive, some of the food gets shared within the community. If an individual arrives in the village with a big catch from fishing on the river, news about this achievement travels, and other fishermen might go out and try their luck. As many of the food resources are migratory, limiting one's hunting to a specific territory could be a liability. Social relationships based on friendship and kinship extend territories and ecological zones within

Name of Holding	Head		Members			
	ID	Number of Living Relatives	ID	Number of Living Relatives	Kinship to Head/ Brigadier	Kinship among Brigade Members
Bataika	496	22	306	29	n/f	MMBS of 498
			498	72	S	FZDS of 306
Dolgany/Oz. Sakhatinoye	724	9	727	9	B	
Ebennak	101	72	88	72	B	
Elgen	188	49	190	92	S	
			193	92	S	
Gusinii Yar (empty)						
Kol'sto	329	4	554	15	n/f	
			331	5	S	
Koral	183	59	118	60		ZH of 183
Krasnoye Oz.	542	31	380	15	n/f	
Letovya	84	6	83	2	H	
			342	13	n/f	
			429	5		B of 430, 431
			430	5		B of 429, 431
			431	5		B of 429, 430
Luga	94	60	89	68	B	
Muksunakh	38	6	539	22	n/f	
Mukulai (Russian couple, now empty)						
Novorybnoye	72	19	518	19	B	
			519	19	B	
Oz. Glubokoye (empty)						
Sakhyr Kuel	506	22	513	76	S	
Starii Avam (empty)						
Taganara	446	7	217	3	n/f	
Tundravaya	627	4	714	2	n/f	
Ugarnaya	289	46	262	46	B	
			265	46	B	
			335	14	ZH	
			357	46	B	
Yergalakh	1	5	302	29	n/f	
			521	22	n/f	
			591	46	n/f	brother of 610
			610	46	n/f	brother of 591
			451	6		WFZS of 1

(continued)

Table 6.6 Ust Avam hunting territories, head and brigade members, number of living consanguineal relatives in the Ust Avam community, and kinship relationships.

| Name of Holding | Head | | Members | | | |
	ID	Number of Living Relatives	ID	Number of Living Relatives	Kinship to Head/ Brigadier	Kinship among Brigade Members
F/C Holding	725	8	726	8		W of 725
Dolgany			656	67	SD	SD of 726; also FMFBSDD of 177, 178
			722	1		SW of 725 and 726
			747	0	"distant" cousin	
			723	10	SS	SS of 726
			724	9	S	S of 724
			728	2		SW of 725 and 726
			729	10	SD	SD of 726
			730	10	SD	SD of 726
			176	2	n/f	M of 177, 178
			177	50	n/f	MFFBDSD of 656
			178	50	n/f	MFFBDSS of 656
			50	45	n/f	BS of 49
			49	45	n/f	FB of 50; cousin of 726

Table 6.6 *continued*

which hunters forage. A few landmarks, such as high river embankments, are often associated with individuals or ancestral camps. Association with these locations is not exclusive, however, since many residents of Ust Avam do not live in the tundra year-round anymore. Hunters are regularly establishing shelters and blinds throughout the communal-use area (figure 6.7). These are considered that person's property, and permission is usually sought before using them, except in emergencies. While most economists might think of it as market failure, common-pool management is a viable property strategy in post-Soviet Taimyr. By controlling access to common-pool resources and kinship estates through social relationships, Ust Avam hunters appear to have implemented a sustainable, risk-minimizing, and ecologically sensitive land-tenure institution.

City and Tundra Law

The establishment of family/clan holdings appears to have had multiple purposes. First, family/clan holdings ostensibly were intended to be lifetime, inheritable lands protected from industrial development, reserved for

Figure 6.7
Repairing an old
living *balok* to
use as a base
camp in the Ust
Avam commons.

native people and their traditional economic activities. Second, family/clan holdings were a unique Russian government solution for aboriginal land claims. The native people were allowed to take land, not as nations on reservations, but as individual families and their kin. Third, as an undercurrent in the administration's practice, establishment of family/clan holdings was the logical continuation of the process of privatization of state farms occurring across rural Russia. If privatization did not lead to rational use, the land could be reclaimed by the state and reassigned. Fourth, in some cases, family/clan holdings were granted for political reasons—i.e., to native members of regional or local administrations, or high-profile native families in the city. With these functions in mind, the distribution of family/clan holdings in Dudinka district is biased. Access to transportation services and markets necessary for maintaining efficient use of the land (from the perspective of regional officials), and proximity to government and administrative institutions is necessary to establish and maintain the holding.

The changes in the type of family/clan holding available from the administration demonstrate the diminishing position of the remote indigenous communities in regional politics. As the Russian economy has experienced crisis after crisis, and the wars in Chechnya have brought ethnic divisiveness to the forefront, indigenous Siberian self-determination has come under greater scrutiny by the public and government. Regional land grants to native families have become more provisional.

In the heart of the Taimyr tundra, capital-intense production strategies are now unsuccessful, where during the Soviet era thousands of tons of food were produced there for the urban centers. Family/clan holdings could not widely operate under the economic conditions of the 1990s as producers, distributors, and marketers. Rather, hunters and their families have reoriented to a foraging economy with opportunistic and supplemental exchange in the larger economy. As part of the subsistence economy, non-market reciprocal exchange and altruistic gifting of meat and fish occurs under the tundra code, "Give it, if you have it." As part of reciprocal exchange arrangements, some land has been developed for communal use with informal negotiations determining hunt locations and party composition. Formal land claims are too costly for hunters and their families, considering their potential economic benefit from sales in urban markets. Without an organization that provides distribution and marketing, the least risky strategy for native hunters in remote communities is to practice subsistence hunting and minimize involvement with the formal economy.

Chapter Seven

The Future Is in Their Hands

Divergence and Convergence

The Dolgan and Nganasan, indigenous peoples of the Siberian tundra, have become increasingly reliant on hunting and gathering in recent years. This experience shows that an economy and social institutions based on subsistence foraging is viable and appropriate. If they are given the choice, it is likely that Dolgan and Nganasan will continue to live and make do in the tundra that they love so much. The contemporary implementation of a hunting-and-gathering economy has implications for our understanding of human origins and human nature, as well. Sharing in Ust Avam occurs mainly with relatives, but also includes unrelated people who are in need, as well as friends and neighbors. Informal sharing economies reflect human decision-making preferences, and may be a key to long-term sustainable development and human survival (Dugatkin 2000).

In areas where family/clan holdings were granted, generally within 100 kilometers of an urban center, these organizations may represent a process of socioeconomic differentiation of the native population, thereby supporting Pelto's (1987) snowmobile-revolution model, but on a regional scale. By formalizing ownership of territory and assigning the property to sets of individuals, the family/clan holding must produce and sell goods in order for the owners to afford travel to their holding, and thus the unit is to some extent oriented to the market. The regional government uses its own framework of land tenure, and if the holding goes unused for several years, the government can return the land to its account and reassign it. For the majority of indigenous households in the Taimyr Region, family/clan holdings have not been an issue because of high costs, low benefits, and distance from the market and regional government. This apparent differentiation in land-tenure strategies resulting from Yeltsin's 1992 decree is yet another example of the unpredicted effects of the economic reform process in the former Soviet Bloc (Burawoy and Verdery 1999). Similarly, other rural people and low-income sectors of Russian society have become increasingly involved in non-market and barter economies, while the major cities have experienced an influx of Western goods, technology, and cash.

Given their remote location in the central Siberian Arctic and the dismantling of the factory-state in the early 1990s, the Dolgan and Nganasan are more isolated now than at any time in the last 30 years. Subsistence hunting, fishing, and gathering now provide the main source of protein for local households, whereas prior to the breakup of the Soviet Union, caribou meat and fish were available for purchase in the local store or state enterprise, as well as stores in urban centers. With a growing domestic subsistence economy and non-market distribution of food products, land tenure has to some extent reoriented to informal and communal use, rather than following formal ownership procedures through family/clan holdings. Land tenure, a subject of importance for the native political association, has changed in unexpected ways since 1991 in Dolgan and Nganasan settlements.

In practice, the Dolgan and Nganasan in remote villages such as Ust Avam rely more on informal cooperation and non-market distribution of food than they did when groceries were available in the store and they made money in a cash-based formal economy. Provisioning between relatives accounts for the bulk of food sharing, although some meat and fish enter reciprocal food exchange between households that are generally not closely related by kinship. Reciprocal food sharing also occurs among non-producers. For example, retired women mentioned that they share with their friends, and vice versa, when they have bush food. In some hunting tasks, food is divided immediately after the hunt. Presumably these hunters increase their output by cooperating with the other hunters and dividing the catch. These small economies of scale appear to be related to certain foraging activities, such as seine fishing, which requires four people. Finally, when hunters have large surpluses, they share food with almost any person that expresses a need. Typically, this food goes to single mothers, invalids, pensioners, neighbors, and other people who ask. Moral prescriptions for sharing mean that accumulation and isolation are socially costly. For example, there is a likelihood that derogatory public statements would be made if one did not simply share (Peterson 1993). And there could be non-food-related benefits for sharing, such as heightened status or desirability for intimate relationships (Hawkes 1993).

The situation in this Siberian community contrasts significantly with those in many native and rural communities around the world, where contact and integration with the global economy is increasing. The fragmentation of post-Soviet Russia has left the native peoples of remote Taimyr settlements at the edge of a depressed economy, where local social processes encourage subsistence foraging, food gifts, and communal land tenure. The development of institutions that regulate common-pool resources among hunters in Taimyr, a process running counter to the global trend, is a topic of applied and fundamental importance, especially considering current plans for developing environmental reserves in the Siberian north. The case of the Dolgan and Nganasan in Ust Avam may be one in which social relationships, and ecological conditions, favor expanding the locally managed common-property resource. As is the case in many hunting-and-gathering societies, economic independence is discouraged, and survival depends on the productivity of the tundra and cooperation in social networks. A cynic might say they have finally made it to the stage of communism, only it is not the planned state communism of Marxist-Leninist philosophy, but the underlying human adaptations for cooperation.

Within the Ust Avam community, a process of ethnic convergence is occurring. There have been many interethnic marriages and relationships over the last 30 years, and as a result there are many young people that have multi-ethnic ancestry. Ninety percent of Ust Avam residents with mixed ancestry are under the age of 18. Since these individuals make up a large portion of the youth of the community—the most volatile sector—friendships and kinship overlap ethnic identity. As one informant put it, "We are not Dolgan and Nganasan anymore. We are peoples of the former Soviet Union." Krivonogov (1999), reporting on his 1993 and 1994 surveys of the Nganasan in three communities in Taimyr, came to similar conclusions: The population was becoming a mixed Nganasan-Dolgan-Russian population, with Russian as the native language. Finally, the importance of interfamilial and inter-ethnic cooperation was emphasized in Oksye's story "Annyky Doidu" and Dulsimyaku's speech. There are many individuals that bridge the ethnic groups, which may be why organized ethnic violence has not developed.

Kinship and Social Organization

I have saved a discussion of kinship for this final chapter because, in some respects, it is one of the most difficult issues to deal with for the Dolgan and Nganasan. Kinship is relevant to the previous discussions of land tenure, economy, and cosmology. The nature of kinship among the Dolgan and Nganasan, especially its formal structure, has changed significantly during the last century, partly as a result of changing social organization and intermarriage. Many of these changes were imposed from outside. I have been able to document some of the changes of the last century through informant interviews, comparing the kinship terms presently used with those documented earlier in the twentieth century (Popov 1946). In the 1920s, the Dolgan had at least 32 kinship terms in their classification system, many of which were used to address a number of different kinds of relatives. Today, many of these terms are no longer in use. For example, a specific term, either *taai* or *hürdü* (depending on the group), was used in the past to address the mother's brother. Today, the term for "elder male relative" (*ehe*), including father's elder brother, father's father, and mother's father, has been extended to include the mother's brother. Changes in kinship structure that resulted from Russian colonial expansion are even harder to document, but the Russian ethnographers B. O. Dolgikh (1960, 1962, 1963) and G. M. Afanasieva (1990) have dealt with the issue, based on archival materials from the *yasak* collection books (cf. Anderson 1998b, 2000).

A confounding problem is that Russian colonial representatives often used the terms *clan* and *tribe* interchangeably. In anthropology, a clan is conventionally viewed as a unilineal descent group, or a set of co-descendants identified by a name that has been inherited from a common ancestor. Clans have important organizing functions in many traditional societies, and specific rights and obligations often go along with clan affiliation. A tribe is a classification of society having more complex sociopolitical integration than a band, often including clans among other features, such as chiefs and age grades (Service 1962). After the 1822 Speranski reforms, clans became official administrative units in Russian Siberia, and the czar chose the clan leaders (*kniazok*, or little king), who passed their affiliation to their descendants. Thus, within each geographic area of Russian administration, one family became politically dominant, and political organization became ranked; that is to say, that status was ascribed by birth. The whole administrative area began to be referred to by the name of that "clan," and this continued into the early Soviet period, when clan councils (*rodovie soviety*) were created. I believe that for some of the minority Siberian peoples, such as the Dolgan and Nganasan, clans were created by the Russian administration. Before Russian colonization, they may or may not have had true unilineal descent groups. Some Siberian peoples, such as the Buryat and Sakha, did have unilineal descent prior to Russian contact, and they fit into the Russian political system more easily than did their less integrated neighbors (Forsyth 1992). The confusion between the terms *clan* and *tribe* continues to the present, especially among non-anthropologists and in Russian legal policy—for example, with the name of the family/clan holding. In the Avam tundra, I found that bilateral kinship ties were an important factor in the use and access of assigned hunting territories and family/clan holdings. Bilateral kinship connections are reckoned through both male and female ancestors, and thus, the term *clan* is incorrectly applied, but is probably used to emphasize native status.

During interviews with older informants in Ust Avam, I asked them about their clan affiliation. I found that "clan"—*rod* in Russian—was a problematic term here too, because informants used it to refer to both local groups and affiliation through unilineal descent. I began to use the Dolgan word, *tördü*, with Dolgan informants, which is translated as *rod*, or "clan," in the Dolgan-Russian, Russian-Dolgan dictionary. Many informants did not know this word, and 93-year-old Oksye Bezrukikh back-translated it into Russian as "generations" (*pokolenia*), and knew her clan affiliation; she was an Edyan. According to Dolgan lore, there were four clans from which they originated: Dolgan, Dongot, Edyan, and Koronto. The story among the Nganasan was different. Nganasan last names are more or less synonymous with their clan. Thus, a person whose father has the family name Kosterkin is a member of the Ngumtuso clan. The Nganasan had at least seven patrilineal clans, and they practiced exogamous sister-exchange marriages until the middle of the twentieth century.

While clan names appear to have lost much of their meaning for the Dolgan and Nganasan with the collectivization of local herding groups in the 1930s, informants still use and know identities, based on topographic features, villages, or east-west distinctions. A few of these terms for the Ust Avam Dolgan are: Uhagilar (Western Dolgan, including Ust Avam); Maragilar (Eastern Dolgan); Mastagilar (Woods Dolgan); Muoralagalar (Tundra People); Tasdegilar (Kamenskiye, or Mountain Dolgan); Baikalar (Chasovny Dolgan). These traditional local group names comprised a word referring to place or direction (e.g., *muora*—north) and the third-person-plural suffix *-alar/-ilar,* meaning "people of." It is likely that these toponymic categories were a way to express attachment to their locality and to distinguish local residential groups from surrounding groups (van den Berghe 1987). Similarly, modern settlement names are used in the Russian plural adjectival form to refer to the people of a certain community. For example, the word *Avamskie* is used to describe someone from Ust Avam, especially from the point of view of other communities. Nuttall (1992) identified a similar process of changing identity among the Greenlandic Inuit.

Students in introductory anthropology classes are sometimes mystified by anthropological studies of kinship, but it is Lewis Henry Morgan's discovery of kinship terminology systems (1870) that really set anthropology apart from other social sciences. One problem is that debates about kinship in anthropology have been operating on a number of non-exclusive levels. Kin terms, and the systematic ways that terminology systems are organized in human societies, are conflated with other topics, such as kinship cooperation (social sacrifice), actual genealogical relationships, and the emotions of kinship. Schneider (1984) argued that kinship is an artifact of anthropologists' approach to other cultures: Anthropologists have used their mode of classification to describe the meaning of social relationships in non-Western societies. This argument has impressed many anthropologists, and only recently has there been a renewed interest in this important topic within the field (e.g., Stone 1997). While kin terms may reflect particular material conditions in a society that may or may not have much to do with genealogical distance, it is actual social practice of relatives that makes kinship an interesting phenomenon.

Prior to asking questions about genealogical relatedness in Ust Avam, I asked about the role relatives (*rodstvenniki*) play in their lives. This was my first question during interviews of 79 household heads in the Avam tundra, and the answers to this question give us an idea of relatives' roles from the emic (or insider) perspective. These characterizations are presented in rank order in appendix A. The answers can be divided roughly into two sets: concepts about kinship (such as close/distant relatives, old/young relatives, number of relatives) and various roles of relatives. Most of the explicit roles imply an enduring social relationship (such as communication, friendship, and help). Many of these concepts also imply some kind of sacrifice of time, energy, emotions, and protein. Two answers, "land" and "origin," were not as frequent as one might expect. The answers "big role," "normal role," "positive role," and "little role" are frequent and hard to break down further. While there was much variance in answers about the role of relatives, it is clear that kinship emotions (nepotism or favoritism, love, sacrifice, compassion) are present. Kinship cooperation implies a social sacrifice, one that is based on birth, where emotional motivations are strong. For example, parental love ordinarily facilitates the flow of resources from parent to offspring and other potentially costly behaviors, such as protection against adult antagonists. Some people in Ust Avam made distinctions between close and distant relatives, and, other things being equal, one would expect that emotional ties would be stronger with close kin; however, kinship emotions and sacrifice can be extended to distant kin and non-kin. According to appendix A, kinship is important for most people in the Avam tundra, despite the recent history of state-enterprise building, forced settlement, and repression of ancient customs.

In a recent introductory anthropology course at University of Alaska Fairbanks, I asked the students, "Who here has a relative who is also registered for this class?" Four people raised their hands—we had two sets of siblings out of 75 students, a fairly high ratio compared to other classes I have taught. I asked a similar question for the populations of Ust Avam and Tukhard, so we can compare social environments in this way. The Ust Avam and Tukhard data are based on complete community censuses provided by the village administrations in 1997, and my genealogical survey of households. Tukhard has little direct historical connection to the Ust Avam community, and it provides an interesting point of comparison, since the majority of village households are involved in reindeer herding, which requires year-round mobility and many hands to help out. It is relatively easy to add another tent or *balok* for a Tukhard Nenets family, but it is virtually impossible for the Dolgan and Nganasan in Ust Avam to add a bedroom to their brick and log/stucco apartment buildings. These materials were brought to the village in limited quantities during its construction in the 1970s and 1980s.

At the time of my census of Ust Avam in June 1997, there were 673 people living in Ust Avam and the surrounding tundra. Only eight of these individuals were not related to anyone else in the village! As population is settled and most households are small, average household size is four people. In Tukhard (May 1997 census) there were 617 people living in the community, and there were 12 individuals who were not related to anyone in the village. Average household size was slightly bigger than in Ust Avam, at five people. For reindeer-herding families, mean household size was six people. For both communities I conducted a genealogical survey, double-checked the genealogies with a number of informants, and entered the information into a computer program that analyzes genealogical information (Chagnon and Bryant 1985). I thought that the results for Ust Avam and Tukhard would be significantly different because Tukhard is more homogeneous in terms of ethnicity. The majority of individuals are Nenets, with only a few Dolgan and Enets that married into the village in the 1930s and a dozen unrelated individuals.

Despite the significant differences in their economies and histories, both villages have a relatively low density of genealogical connections when compared with a Yanomamö village (Chagnon et al. 1997). However, in comparison to most contemporary towns, cities, suburbs, and college classrooms with which we are familiar, there is a considerable density of genealogical ties. Table 7.1 provides several etic (or outsider's perspective) kinship indicators for Ust Avam and Tukhard. The average of each individual's relatedness to all other members of the community (FgAll) is 0.012 for Tukhard and 0.007 for Ust Avam. These figures represent the average chance that two individuals chosen at random share a given gene by Wright's inbreeding formula (1922)—full siblings are related by 0.5, as are a parent and their offspring. In other words, if you pick two individuals at random in Tukhard, on average, they would be related to each other as a bit less than a second cousin, once removed. In Ust Avam, the average relatedness is slightly lower than that between third cousins. In comparison,

Community	Ust Avam	Tukhard
Population	673	617
Individuals in Database	906	713
Unrelated Individuals	8	12
Average Household Size	4	5
FgAll	0.007	0.012
Average Number of Relatives	35 (5%)	38 (6%)
FgCon	0.213	0.248

Table 7.1 Comparative kinship indicators for Ust Avam and Tukhard.

traditional Yanomamö villages show average genealogical relatedness at the first-cousin level.

The average number of genealogical relatives is another indicator of the kind of kinship density in these villages. In Tukhard, each individual, on average, has 38 genealogical relatives, approximately six percent of the population. Three individuals have 104 kin, the maximum number, and the mode, or most common number, of kin is 58; 22 people have 58 genealogical kin. In Ust Avam, each individual on average has 35 genealogical relatives, approximately five percent of the population. Two individuals have 118 kin, but the modal number is five in Ust Avam; 41 people have five genealogical relatives. According to the means, the villages appear to be about the same. The modes tell a different story: Ust Avam has more recent immigrants who have married and have had children in the community. Another indicator, the average relatedness of each individual to his or her consanguineal, or blood, relatives (FgCon), tells us how closely an individual is related to his or her genealogical relatives. In Ust Avam, the average FgCon is 0.213, slightly less than the relatedness of a person with their aunt, uncle, or half sibling, but more than that person and a first cousin. In Tukhard, the average relatedness of each individual to his or her consanguineal relatives is 0.248, or about that of a person with his or her aunt, uncle, or half sibling. Because many people have relatives in the village beyond the nuclear family, the average FgCon figures for Ust Avam and Tukhard are in the aunt/uncle/cousin-range.

There is a slight difference in the density of genealogical relationships for Ust Avam and Tukhard, but people in both communities have significantly more relatives in their social environment than people do in most U.S. communities. One indicator, FgAll, or the average relatedness of each individual with all members of the community, is 70 percent higher for Tukhard than Ust Avam. Ust Avam's bifurcated ethnic history and higher number of in-married immigrants appear to be the best explanations for this difference, since Tukhard has a higher number of totally unrelated individuals. On the community level, both these communities are significantly different from any urban setting. The proportion of related-to-not-related individuals is very high. It is my contention that this is a significant force in individual development, cooperation within the community, and identity.

In Ust Avam, individuals stated to me repeatedly that half the people of the village were relatives (*rodnya*). These individuals used the term *rodnya*, meaning relative(s) or relation(s) in a collective sense, rather than the term *rodstvenniky*, meaning relatives in a more specific sense. Both words are from the same Russian root, *rod-*, and its variants *rozhd-*, *rozh-*, meaning birth, tribe, nature (Wolkonsky & Poltoratsky 1961:304). Obviously, in both of these villages the proportion of individuals' genealogical relatives in the village is much less than 50 percent, according to their own genealogies. The indicators described in table 7.1 are only for consanguinal kin, or blood relatives. Why do they talk about all these people as relatives? Informants making these kinds of statements included their own affinal relatives, or in-laws. They also likely include the blood relatives of their affines. If affinal relatives are included, the proportion of relatives to non-relatives in the village quickly increases.

Affinal relatives are important to this discussion, since they were mentioned specifically in many interviews as people with whom the interviewee shared food and other resources, as well as communication and friendship. Thus, it should be noted that the "relative" concept for many people in Ust Avam includes individuals related through marriage. Affinal relatives are or have the potential to be the co-ancestors of common descendants, however, where there may be a relationship by birth, but not in the ancestral direction. As Radcliffe–Brown (1951) pointed out, kinship is not only descent, but is also common descendant. The Dolgan and Nganasan care for their relatives and friends, and the fact that there are a lot of them around in a small community makes people's activities more transparent, encourages frequent visiting, provides more opportunity for child care in a family setting, and facilitates other forms of cooperation.

Globalization and Circumpolar Cooperation

In the West, the end of the Cold War was celebrated as a victory of capitalism and democracy over socialism, which was viewed as an inferior system. The story is very different in some parts of the former Soviet Union and Eastern Europe, where the end of socialism is still being mourned as the end of a golden age of sorts, and we have seen, practically, the reverse of capitalist growth. In these remote and rural locations, large-scale economic institutions have been in a process of collapse, conditions for profit making are limited, and government support has been consistently dwindling. One significant lesson from this study is that globalization is a heterogeneous process. What has occurred in remote Taimyr villages, for example, is like an historical eddy in the global tide, where informal and non-market forms of cooperation are being instituted in response to a vacuum left by the dismantling of the Soviet economy and the lack of capitalist development.

This process may actually work to the advantage of the indigenous people. The term *malochislennie narody* is an official designation of the Soviet and Russian governments used for some indigenous minorities of the Far North, Siberia, and Far East. Together, these peoples number fewer than 200,000 people in 694 remote and rural communities (Semenova 2000). The Russian Association of Indigenous Peoples of the North, or RAIPON, represents these indigenous nations on the national level. In the last few years of the Soviet Union, this organization was formed to pursue greater self-determination for its member minority peoples (Sangi 1991, 1992). An early and hopeful sign was the 1992 decree Boris Yeltsin issued to allow indigenous families to claim title to traditional hunting and herding territories (Yeltsin 1992, Aipin 1994, Bol'shakov and Klokov 1997). With low-interest loans from the local or regional government, indigenous families began a multitude of businesses based on traditional practices, such as hunting, fishing, trapping, and arts. However, as Russia's transition progressed, it turned out that the government had difficulties supporting its soldiers or any rural people in Russia, especially the native communities distributed across thousands of miles of tundra. Loans became increasingly difficult to get after 1994, and at the same time, the state enterprise system that had for decades employed native Siberians to hunt, fish, trap, and herd reindeer became insolvent.

While supporting the United Nations International Decade of the World's Indigenous People, Russia's current policy toward its own indigenous groups appears somewhat ambiguous. The Russian Parliament never accepted as a law the decree that President Yeltsin issued in 1992 protecting indigenous Siberian territory and tradition, although in 1999 there was a law passed regarding the rights of native minorities (N82–F3). Few family/clan holdings have been formed in the Taimyr Region, and most of those that have been established are headed by the urban dwellers in relatively close proximity to the regional capital, Dudinka, or the region's industrial center, Norilsk. There currently is a program of socioeconomic development for the indigenous minority peoples of Siberia, Far North, and Far East, administered through the Government Committee of the North, and this program will be extended for another five years. In the remote native settlements people have not yet seen any real benefit to these programs, and there is not much optimism, since the money must filter through layers of Russian bureaucracy. In addition, most families in the tundra have little access to government services or information. The breakup of the Soviet Union and the dismantling of its planned economy have caused severe hardship among Russia's lower classes, generally located outside the major urban centers. The story of these people has gone largely untold, simply because of the difficulties of travel, lack of hotels and other services, and the general focus on business, economic, and military matters by journalists and policy makers in Russia.

Scholars have recently taken on the question of why Russia's free-market and democratic reforms did not work as well as expected in the early 1990s. Burawoy and Verdery (1999), for example, provide a number of case studies on the unexpected reactions to the transition in Eastern Europe and the former Soviet Union, and Wedel (1998) outlines the assumptions of those advising the Russian transition. Recommendations of Western experts and institutions, drastic moves by the Russian government, such as the closing of the national bank in 1991, and policies, such as shock therapy (removing price controls on most goods) and privatization of industry, combined with the inefficiencies of the Russian administrative and judicial systems, have led to rapid socioeconomic differentiation, shrinking population, and depressed economies in rural regions. The post-Soviet transition is an important topic, and scholars are also teaming up to address these issues through Internet lists and area studies organizations. Soyuz, the post-Communist research network of the American Anthropology Association, and the Association for the Study of Nationalities at the Harriman Institute, Columbia University, are two of these. Since Russian economic reforms began in the 1990s, remote native communities such as Ust Avam have become more isolated from the national economy than comparable populations in North America (cf. Ziker 1999, Condon et al. 1995). Conversely, urban communities in Russia have greater access to the world economy. Other scholars investigating the socioeconomic differentiation occurring in Russia have also found a geographic dimension to the distribution of poverty (Ruble et al. 2000).

Addressing these problems in April 2001, RAIPON had its fourth Congress, which I attended as a guest. The congress occurs once every four years. Forty ethnic groups were represented at the 2001 congress. The Association has a web page with information in English (http://www.raipon.org/). A major theme within RAIPON's lobbying effort is environmental protection, allowing for its constituent indigenous people to continue their traditional way of life for their descendants. Large-scale industrial development, which in Siberia is mostly focused on raw materials, is an impediment to environmental protection and indigenous rights. The situation is exemplified in western Siberia, where most of Russia's oil and gas are produced. Russia exports natural gas to Europe, about 25 percent of Europe's annual consumption. In western Siberia, the native people have suffered large losses of territory to the oil-and-gas industry, with little compensation. Starkly contrasting with this situation is the arrangement between the oil industry and native groups in Alaska, for example (Chance and Andreeva 1995; Novikova 1994, 1995; Balzer 1999).

Equitable use of natural resources and environmental protection is a concern of the indigenous Siberian movement because they are interested in long-term, sustainable development. These people's ancestors have lived in these regions for hundreds, if not thousands, of years, and as far as they know, their children and more distant descendants will live there, too. Given the opportunity, most would not move away. A few do move to the cities of their regions, and even fewer move to Russia's major cities. However, many go for a few years and then return to their homeland, frustrated with mainstream society. An orientation to past and future generations (kinship) is explicitly mentioned in the preamble of RAIPON's charter (appendix B).

As industrial-based societies require increasing non-local inputs, especially in energy and labor, expanded exploration and production in the Arctic could become more concentrated, especially if shortages become more common. The debate in the U.S. over whether to allow companies to explore for oil in Alaska's Arctic National Wildlife Refuge is an example of this trend. One might think that there is a natural convergence of interests among the indigenous-rights groups and environmental-protection interests, but in fact there have been many conflicts of interest. Anti-fur-trapping politics had a significant impact on indigenous northern peoples in Canada in the late 1980s. And conflict continues over subsistence hunting between environmental groups and indigenous peoples, for example in the case of the Washington State Makah and the revival of their traditional whale hunt. On the other hand, the activities of European and Russian environmental groups and RAIPON are to some extent converging in Siberia.

World Wildlife Fund (WWF) Russia, for example, has helped to set up 20 protected areas in the Russian Arctic with an area of 25 million hectares. The funding for these programs generally comes from European chapters of WWF (see http://www.wwf.ru for more information). WWF Russia's main goals are protection of rare species, of course, and environmental education. They are developing a closer connection with native peoples in Siberia, and are consulting with indigenous communities before initiating environmental programs. WWF Russia is training native people as inspectors of nature in areas where they are setting up reserves, and providing them with snowmobiles, boats, and communication equipment in order to enforce environmental protection. WWF is giving high school students living in remote communities scholarships to study in Siberian cities, with the expectation that they will return to their villages and work in nature protection.

International participation in projects with RAIPON and directly with indigenous Siberians appears to be on the rise. RAIPON participation in international organizations is also increasing. RAIPON now has a permanent position in the Arctic Council, as well as a membership in the UN's Permanent Forum on Indigenous Issues from the NIS region (former Soviet Union). RAIPON has been cooperating with groups like the Saami Parliament since the early 1990s, but this activity has intensified, and RAIPON representatives traveled to Finland at least twice in 2001 for meetings. The emphasis on international cooperation has been with Canada, the Scandinavian countries, and the UN. While not completely absent, there is little U.S. federal, Alaskan, or U.S. indigenous NGO funding for RAIPON or its regional affiliates. This is surprising, considering Alaska's proximity to east Siberia and the multitudinous personal contacts between Alaska and Siberia. A number of Siberian delegates to the congress mentioned to me that they had been to Alaska.

Overall, direct support of RAIPON from international organizations also is on the increase. The Inuit Circumpolar Conference (Canada) has a project in capacity building for RAIPON, and they have funded the outfitting of RAIPON's Moscow office with modern communications and computer equipment. RAIPON has done a good job at consolidating representational power for close to 700 communities of indigenous Siberians, although direct support of regional and district-level associations from outside sources also occurs in small amounts. RAIPON representatives acknowledge the importance of the consolidation in light of the increasing importance of the Arctic as a source of non-renewable resources for the global economy.

At the April 2001 congress, RAIPON president Sergei Kharuchi read a 45-minute report titled "Our Life and Our Destiny Are in Our Hands." His report, which was a summary of the group's work over the last four years and a call to self-improvement and traditional and contemporary training of native youth, listed RAIPON's priorities: strengthening of the organizational capacity of the movement; establishment of an information exchange system with the regional associations and with foreign partners; strengthening cooperation with Russian parliamentary committees, with the Presidential Administration of the Russian Federation, and with governmental agencies; strengthening partnerships with divisions of the UN and other international organizations and governmental agencies; formulation and implementation of policy at the federal level and the regional levels; establishment of professional and creative unions and organizations; establishment of contacts with the large Russian and foreign companies that conduct industrial activity on the aboriginal lands; and participation in the formulation, implementation, and monitoring of the federal programs for socioeconomic development of the indigenous peoples of the North, Siberia, and the Far East. Like other large indigenous movements, RAIPON will work with international nongovernmental organizations in attaining these goals. This international approach is a growing phenomenon among indigenous movements and is a subject that some anthropologists are pointing out as a promising topic for study (cf. Birdsell, April 2001 *Anthropology Newsletter*).

The growing international connections of the Russian Association of Indigenous Peoples of the North are facilitated by globalization. The Internet, for example, has simplified and accelerated the ability of indigenous groups to communicate. On the local level, however, indigenous communities in many parts of the Russian north are not significantly reaping the benefit of RAIPON's activities and government programs, and President Kharuchi mentioned this fact. Thus, there is a dichotomy between RAIPON's activities and connections and the social and economic situation in remote settlements.

Even more significant than globalization itself is the developing trend of Arctic/northern regionalism and the place of the indigenous peoples of the north in intensifying northern connections. The circumpolar North is increasingly becoming a "region" with a set of common interests. Multinational companies exploiting resources, nongovernmental organizations such as the Northern Forum—a group involved in creating region-to-region ties in the circumpolar north—as well as government-sponsored institutions like the Arctic Council, are helping to facilitate this regionalism. Sakha-Yakutia President Nikolaev brought up this issue during his address to the April 2001 congress, while his primary message was to promote the improvement of the general level of humanity in the north. Arctic regionalism with an emphasis on environmental protection, sustainable development, and indigenous rights appears to be a growing phenomenon, which ties into the international indigenous-rights movement and the environmental movement. The tendency for political fragmentation of indigenous northern populations on the local level needs to be counterbalanced with international and national indigenous movements in order for their voices to continue to be heard in the face of pressure, generally from the south, for industrial development.

Appendix A

Rank-ordering of responses by 79 heads of households of the Avam tundra to the question, "What Role Do Relatives Play in Your Life?"

Roles Relatives Play	Order Mentioned			
	1st	2nd	3rd	4th
Big Role	15	5	0	0
Close/Distant Relatives	4	8	2	0
Communication	3	1	2	0
Dependence	2	2	0	0
Don't Know	3	0	0	0
Fight	0	0	1	0
Friendship	1	1	2	0
Future	1	0	0	0
Help	13	14	3	1
Interconnectedness	1	0	0	0
Kinship or Parenting	1	2	0	1
Land	1	1	0	1
Little Role	3	0	0	0
Not Specified	3	0	0	0
Normal Role	11	0	0	0
Notoriety	0	0	1	0
Number of Relatives	10	0	0	0
Old/Young Relatives	2	3	0	0
Origin	1	1	0	0
Positive Role	2	2	0	0
Respect and Love	0	0	1	0
Sharing	0	2	1	1
Sincerity	1	0	0	0
Work	1	1	1	0

Appendix B

Charter of the Minority Indigenous Peoples of the North, Siberia and Far East of the Russian Federation

We, the indigenous peoples of the North, Siberia and Far East of the Russian Federation,

believe that:
The Air, the Land and Water are blessed,
Nature is the source of life,
Man is but a drop in the whirlpool of life,
The river of time is but a reflection of the past, present, and future and that how our ancestors lived in the past is how we now live and how our offspring will live in the future;

know that:
Man is a part of nature and bears responsibility for protecting the diversity of the environment;
Our home is the tundra, the taiga, the steppe and the mountains bequeathed to us by our ancestors, these are great, powerful, harsh, kind and generous manifestations but defenseless in the face of technical progress;
Use of knowledge can bring not only perfection and happiness but can cause pain and inflict injury;
Thoughtless work of human hands is capable of polluting and poisoning the air, the land, and the water, of destroying the living and of killing both large and small;

Economic growth, expanding wealth and assets for the few do not always improve life and prosperity for the majority;

Social, economic, and environmental policies of those now in power:

- do not eliminate need and injustice,
- do not protect the health of man and so the tree of life, of our kinfolk and our fellow countrymen, is rapidly withering away,
- do not renew the disrupted natural processes that forms our historical development,
- do not return the land of our ancestors, the lands of our traditional use;

Our way of life, based on time-honoured experience of communal, social organization, has been created from the original cultures and beliefs of our ancestors and is the one, true way of maintaining life and sustainable development;

No one, neither society nor civilization, will ever solve our problems and only we, and the good will of the government, are capable of accomplishing this task;

desire that:

- our unique cultures, our ancestral homelands and way of life be protected by the government;
- our legal rights be observed and that we can participate, as equal partners, in the planning strategies for the sustainable development of the North of our country;
- our experience, knowledge, interests and traditional approaches to the use of the environment be accounted for when decisions are made on how the lands of our ancestors shall be used.

Everything that we believe, everything that we know and all that we desire must serve as the basis for advancing our traditional way of life.

We speak of development and not simply of "preservation" or "government protection," emphasizing our desire to take part ourselves in the process of sustainably developing the North, our government and the world in general, using and improving on the accumulated wisdom of our ancestors.

Only in harmony with nature will humanity find a way out of its current crisis. We, the indigenous peoples of the North, Siberia and Far East of the Russian Federation, know this path!

Adopted at the IV Congress of Indigenous Peoples of the North, Siberia and Far East
Moscow
April 13, 2001

Glossary

Affine (in-law)   A relationship identified through marriage, not birth. Restricted usually to either a person's spouse or the kin of a spouse, but also extended to the spouse of distant kin and the spouse of spouse's kin.

Argish   A reindeer-herding caravan; the movement of a reindeer herding family, or brigade, along with their sleighs, *baloks,* and reindeer.

Balanced reciprocity   An exchange where the returns are made in the customary equivalent of the thing received (Sahlins 1972). Balanced reciprocity is less personal and more economic than generalized reciprocity, as "the relations between people are disrupted by a failure to reciprocate within limited time and equivalence leeways" (Sahlins 1972:195).

Balok   A small house constructed atop sleigh runners, similar by idea to a camper or covered wagon. The *balok* has a plank floor, a wooden frame, and slightly rounded on the top. It is covered with caribou hides that are sewn together and heat is generated with a small wood-burning stove. The *balok* is moved with a team of four to six reindeer.

Chum   A conical pole tent, traditionally covered with tarps sewn from reindeer or caribou skins.

Clan   A set of kinspeople, sharing a common ancestor and identified by the same ancestral name, which is inherited either through the male or female line.

Gospromkhoz   Government Hunting/Fishing/Trapping Enterprise, generally larger than a *sovkhoz* or *kolkhoz* and administered by the Ministry of Hunting of the Russian Federation, or as in the case of Ust Avam after 1986, the Norilsk Nickel company. *Gospromkhoz* property belonged to the government until Norilsk Nickel was privatized in 1995.

Generalized reciprocity   "Putatively altruistic" transactions of assistance given and, if possible and necessary, returned, occurs generally among close kin (1972: 193–194). Sahlins distinguishes generalized reciprocity by a "sustained one-way flow" of resources; failure to reciprocate does not cause the giver to stop giving. However, in an earlier discussion of reciprocity, Sahlins (1968: 88) states that it entails that one: (1) help those that have helped you; and (2) not injury those that have helped you.

Kin (genealogical or consanguineal relative)   Individuals related by birth: ancestors, so-descendants or descendants.

Kolkhoz **(collective enterprise or farm)**   A collective organization of peasants for socialist agricultural production; it was the main economic unit of 1930s collectivization programs. *Kolkhoz* property belonged to the collective.

Negative reciprocity   "The attempt to get something for nothing with impunity, the several forms of appropriation, as well as transactions opened and conducted to gain net utilitarian advantage" (Sahlins 1972: 195); expected between strangers or recognized enemies. Negative reciprocity is the most impersonal form of exchange. Not surprisingly, negative reciprocity may entail one-way flows, with reciprocation contingent on mustering countervailing pressure or guile.

Sovkhoz **(Soviet enterprise or farm)**   A large government agricultural enterprise that played a major role in the transformation of agriculture in the USSR. The number of *sovkhozes* quadrupled from 1940 to 1977. Government planning was conducted for intensification of production, specialization, and agro-industrial integration. *Sovkhoz* property belonged to the government.

Yasak   Tribute; the annual payment to the czar, usually in the form of furs, indigenous Siberians made during the colonial period.

References

Aipin, Eremei (1994) "Obrashchenie Vtorogo Vserossiiskogo S'ezda Korennykh Malochislennykh Narodov Severa, Sibiri, i Dal'nogo Vostoka k Prezidentu, Pravitel'stvu i Federal'nomy Sobraniyu Rossiiskoi Federatsii." ["Appeal of the Second All-Russia Congress of Native Small-Numbering Nations of the North, Siberia, and the Far East to the President, Administration and Federal Assembly of the Russian Federation."] *Severnie Prostory* 2: 9.

Afenasieva, G. M. (1990) *Traditsionaia Sistema Vosproizvodstva Nganasan (Problemy Reproduktsii Obosoblennykh Populyatsii)*. [*Traditional System of Reproduction of the Nganasan (Problems of Reproduction of an Isolated Population).*] Moscow: AN SSSR.

Alekseev, M. P. (1932) *Sibir' v Izvestiiakh Zapadno-Evropeiskikh Puteshestvennikov i Pisatelei*. [*Siberia in the Publications of Western-European Travelers and Writers.*] Irkutsk.

Alkire, William H. (1965) *Lamotrek Atoll and Interisland Socio-Economic Ties*. Prospect Heights, IL: Waveland Press, Inc.

Anderson, David G. (1998a) "Property as a Way of Knowing on Evenki Lands." Pp. 64–84 in C. M. Hann (ed.) *Property Relations*. Cambridge: Cambridge University Press.

——— (1998b) *Tundroviki: Ekologiia i Samosoznanie Taimyrskikh Evenkov i Dolgan*. [*Tundroviki: Ecology and Identity of Taimyr Evenk and Dolgan.*] Novosibirsk: Russian Academy of Sciences.

——— (2000) *Identity and Ecology in Arctic Siberia: The Number One Reindeer Brigade*. Oxford: Oxford University Press.

Bakhrushin, S. V. (1959) *Nauchnye Trudy*. [*Scientific Works.*] Volume 4. Moscow: USSR Academy of Sciences Press.

Balzer, Marjorie Mandelshtam (1997) *Shamanic Worlds: Rituals and Lore of Siberia and Central Asia*. Armonk, NY: M. E. Sharpe.

———— (1999) *The Tenacity of Ethnicity: A Siberian Saga in the Global Perspective.* Princeton, NJ: Princeton University Press.

Bashilov, V. N. (1989) *Nomads of Eurasia.* Seattle: University of Washington Press.

Berreman, Gerald D. (1981) "Social Inequality." In Gerald D. Berreman (ed.) *Social Inequality.* New York: Academic Press.

Béteille, André (1986) "Individualism and Equality." *Current Anthropology* 27(2): 121–134.

Bikalova, N. A. (1999) "K Voprosu o Sovershenstvovanii Mezhbyudzhetnykh Otnoshenii v Rosiiskoi Federatsii." ["To the Question of Perfecting Interbudgetary Relations in the Russian Federation."] In L. P. Kurakov (ed.) *Sovershenstvovanie Sotsial'no-ekonomicheskikh Otnoshenii v Sovremennykh Usloviakh.* [*Perfecting Socio-Economic Relationships in Contemporary Conditions.*] Moscow: Gelios Archive.

Bird-David, Nurit (1992) "Beyond 'The Original Affluent Society': A Culturalist Reformulation." *Current Anthropology* 33: 25–47.

Bliege Bird, Rebecca L., and Douglas W. Bird (1997) "Delayed Reciprocity and Tolerated Theft: The Behavioral Ecology of Food-Sharing Strategies." *Current Anthropology* 38(1): 49–78.

Blurton Jones, Nicholas G. (1987) "Tolerated Theft, Suggestions about the Ecology and Evolution of Sharing, Hoarding, and Scrounging." *Social Science Information* 26(1): 31–54.

Bogoras, Waldemar (1904–1909) *The Chukchee.* Jessup North Pacific Expedition, VII. Memoirs of the American Museum of Natural History, XII. New York: G. E. Stechert.

Bogoyavlinskii, D. D. (1997) "Native Peoples of Kamchatka: Epidemiological Transition and Violent Death." *Arctic Anthropology* 34 (1): 57–67.

Bodley, John H. (1990) *Victims of Progress.* 3rd ed. Mountain View, CA: Mayfield Publishing.

Bol'shakov, N. N., and K. B. Klokov (1997) *Rol' i Zadachi Tsentral'nosibirskogo Biosfernogo Gosudarstvennogo Zapovednika v Ustoichivom Razvitii Traditsionnogo Prirodopol'zovaniya Turukhanskogo Severa.* [*The Role and Goals for the Central-Siberian Government Biosphere Reserve in the Stable Development of Traditional Nature-Use of the Turukhansk North.*] Sankt-Peterburg: NII Geografii Sankt-Peterburg State University.

Brown, Donald E. (1991) *Human Universals.* New York: McGraw-Hill, Inc.

Burawoy, Michael, and Katherine Verdery (1999) "Introduction." Pp. 1–17 in Michael Burawoy and Katherine Verdery (eds.) *Uncertain Transition: Ethnographies of Change in the Postsocialist World.* Lanham, MD: Rowman & Littlefield.

Campbell, Joseph (1968 [1949]) *The Hero with a Thousand Faces.* Princeton, NJ: Princeton University Press.

Cashdan, Elizabeth (1983) "Territoriality Among Human Foragers: Ecological Models and an Application to Four Bushman Groups." *Current Anthropology* 24: 47–66.

———— (1989) "Hunters and Gatherers: Economic Behavior in Bands." Pp. 21–48 in Stuart Plattner (ed.) *Economic Anthropology.* Stanford, CA: Stanford University Press.

Chagnon, Napoleon A. (1998) *Yanomamö.* 5th ed. Fort Worth, TX: Harcourt Brace.

Chagnon, N. A., and J. Bryant (1984) "KINDEMCOM: The Fourth Style in the Study of Human Kinship Relations." Mimeographed, Department of Anthropology, University of California, Santa Barbara.

Chagnon, N. A., Ziker, J., Thompson, B., Price, M., and Eerkens, J. (1997) "The Density of Kinship in Tribal and Peasant Communities." Paper presented to the Ninth Annual Meeting of the Human Behavior and Evolution Society, June 5.

Chance, Norman A., and Elena N. Andreeva (1995) "Sustainability, Equity, and Natural Resource Development in Northwest Siberia and Arctic Alaska." *Human Ecology* 23: 217–240.

Chayanov, A. V. (1966) *A. V. Chayanov on the Theory of Peasant Economy*. D. Thorner, B. Kerblay, and R. E. F. Smith (eds.). Homewood, IL: Richard D. Irwin, Inc.

Condon, Richard D., Peter Collings, and George Wenzel (1995) "The Best Part of Life: Subsistence Hunting, Ethnicity, and Economic Adaptation among Young Adult Inuit Males." *Arctic* 48(1): 31–46.

Dentan, Robert (1981) "Ecology and Diet: Some Ecological Variables in the Choice of Food Animals Among Eighteen Circumpolar Cultures." Pp. 49–97 in James R. Leary et al. *Cross-Cultural Studies of Factors Related to Differential Food Consumption*. New Haven, CT: Human Relations Area Files, Inc.

Dickemann, Mildred (1979) "Female Infanticide, Reproductive Strategies, and Social Stratification: A Preliminary Model." In Napoleon A. Chagnon and William Irons (eds.) *Evolutionary Biology and Human Social Behavior: An Anthropological Perspective*. North Scituate, MA: Duxbury Press.

Dolgikh, B. O. (1960) *Rodovoi i Plemennoi Sostav Narodov Sibiri v XVII Veke*. [*Clan and Tribal Composition of the Peoples of Siberia in the 17th Century.*] Trudy Instituta Etnografii im. N. N. Miklukho-Maklaia, Novaia Seriia, Vol. 55. Moscow: USSR Academy of Sciences Publishers.

———— (1962) "The Origins of the Nganasans: Preliminary Remarks." Pp. 220–299 in Henry N. Michael (ed.) *Studies in Siberian Ethnogenesis*. Arctic Institute of North America/University of Toronto Press.

———— (1963) "Proiskhozhdenie Dolgan." ["Origin of the Dolgan."] Pp. 92–141 in *Sibirskii Etnograficheskii Sbornik V, Trudy Instituta Etnografii im. N.N. Miklukho-Maklaia, Novaya Seriia, Tom 84*. Moscow: USSR Academy of Sciences Publishers.

———— (1968) "Matriarkhal'nie Cherty v Verovanniakh Nganasan." ["Matriarchal Traits in the Beliefs of the Nganasan."] Pp. 214–229 in V. P. Alekseev and I. S. Gurvich (eds.) *Problemy Antropologii i Istoricheskoi Etnografii Azii*. [*Problems of Anthropology and Historical Ethnography of Asia.*] Moscow: Izdatel'stvo Nauk.

Dugatkin, Lee A. (2000) *Cheating Monkeys and Citizen Bees: The Nature of Cooperation in Animals and Humans*. New York: Free Press.

Durkheim, Emile (1933) *On the Division of Labor in Society*. New York: Free Press.

Eerkens, Jelmer W. (1999). "Common Pool Resources, Buffer Zones, and Jointly Owned Territories: Hunter-Gatherer Land and Resource Tenure in Fort Irwin, Southeastern California." *Human Ecology* 27(2): 297–318.

Eidlitz, Kerstin (1969) *Food and Emergency Food in the Circumpolar Area*. Studia Ethnographica Upsaliensia XXXII. Uppsala: Almquist & Wiksells Boktryckeri AB.

The Europa World Yearbook 1995. London: Europa Publications Limited.

The Europa World Yearbook 1998. London: Europa Publications Limited.

Feit, Harvey A. (1973) "The Ethno-Ecology of the Waswanipi Cree: Or How Hunters Can Handle Their Resources." Pp. 115–125 in Bruce Cox (ed.) *Cultural Ecology*. Toronto: McClelland and Stewart, Ltd.

Fienup-Riordan, Ann (1990) *Eskimo Essays: Yup'ik Lives and How We See Them*. New Brunswick: Rutgers University Press.

Fisher, Raymond H. (1943) *The Russian Fur Trade 1550–1700.* Berkeley: University of California Press.

Fondahl, Gail (1997) "Environmental Degradation and Indigenous Land Claims in Russia's North." Pp. 68–87 in E. A. Smith and Joan McCarter (eds.) *Contested Arctic.* Seattle: University of Washington Press.

——— (1998) *Gaining Ground? Evenkis, Land, and Reform in Southeastern Siberia.* Boston: Allyn and Bacon.

Forsyth, James (1989) "The Indigenous Peoples of Siberia in the Twentieth Century." Pp. 72–95 in Alan Wood and R. A. French (eds.) *The Development of Siberia.* New York: St. Martin's Press.

——— (1992) *A History of the Peoples of Siberia: Russia's North Asian Colony, 1581–1990.* Cambridge: Cambridge University Press.

Fortes, Meyer (1958) "Introduction." Pp. 1–14 in Jack Goody (ed.) *The Development Cycle in Domestic Groups.* Cambridge: Cambridge University Press.

Goody, Jack (1958) "The Fission of Domestic Groups among the Lodagaba." Pp. 57–91 in Jack Goody (ed.) *The Development Cycle in Domestic Groups.* Cambridge: Cambridge University Press.

Gracheva, G. N. (1979) "K Voprosu o Vliianii Khristianizatsii na Religioznye Predstavleniia Nganasan."["Addressing the Question of the Influence of Christianization on the Nganasan's Concept of Religion."] Pp. 29–49 in I. S. Vdovin (ed.) *Khristianstvo i Lamaizm u Korennogo Naseleniia Sibiri.* [*Christianity and Lamaism in the Native Population of Siberia.*] Leningrad: Nauka.

——— (1981) "Shamanstvo u Nganasan." ["Shamanism among the Nganasan."] Pp. 69–89 in I. S. Vdovin (ed.) *Problemy Istorii Obshchestvennogo Soznaniia Aborigenov Sibiri (po Materialam Vtoroi Popviny XIX – Nachala XX v).* [*Problems of the History of Social Consciousness of the Aborigines of Siberia (from Materials of the Second Half of the 19th through the Beginning of the 20th Century).*] Leningrad: Nauka.

Gramsci, Antonio (1985) *Selections from Cultural Writings.* Cambridge, MA: Harvard University Press.

Grant, Bruce (1995) *In the Soviet House of Culture: A Century of Perestroikas.* Princeton, NJ: Princeton University Press.

Gray, Patty A. (1998) *Pursuing a Native Movement in a Russian Space: The Predicament of Indigenous Peoples in Post-Soviet Chukota.* Ph.D. dissertation, University of Wisconsin-Madison. Ann Arbor, MI: University Microfilms International.

Greenspan, Alan (1997) "Greenspan is Skeptical on Russia's Transition." *The Wall Street Journal,* June 11.

Gurven, Michael, Kim Hill, Hillard Kaplan, Ana Hurtado, and Richard Lyles (2000) "Food Transfers Among Hiwi Foragers of Venezuela: Tests of Reciprocity." *Human Ecology* 28(2): 171–218.

Gurvich, I. S. (1968) "Kul't Sviashchennykh Kamnei v Tundrovoi Zone Evrazii." ["The Cult of Sacred Stones in Eurasia's Tundra Zone."] Pp. 230–238 in V. P. Alekseev and I. S. Gurvich (eds.) *Problemy Antropologii i Istoricheskoi Etnografii Azii.* [*Problems of Anthropology and Historical Ethnography of Asia.*] Moscow: Izdatel'stvo Nauk.

Hallowell, Irving A. (1960) "Ojibwa Ontology, Behavior, and Worldview." Pp. 19–52 in S. Diamond (ed.) *Culture in History: Essays in Honor of Paul Radin.* New York: Columbia University Press.

Halperin, Rhoda H. (1994) *Cultural Economies: Past and Present.* Austin: University of Texas Press.

Halstead, Paul, and John O'Shea (1989) "Introduction." Pp. 1–7 in Paul Halstead and John O'Shea (eds.) *Bad Year Economics: Cultural Responses to Risk and Uncertainty.* New York: Cambridge University Press.

Hann, C. M. (1998) "Introduction: The Embeddedness of Property." Pp. 1–47 in C. M. Hann (ed.) *Property Relations.* Cambridge: Cambridge University Press.

Hardin, Garrett (1968) "The Tragedy of the Commons." *Science* 162: 1243–1248.

Hawkes, Kristen (1993) "Why Hunter-Gatherers Work: An Ancient Version of the Problem of Public Goods." *Current Anthropology* 34: 341–361.

Hern, Warren M. (1995) "Micro-Ethnodemographic Techniques for Field Workers Studying Small Groups." Pp. 129–148 in Emilio F. Moran (ed.) *The Comparative Analysis of Human Societies: Toward Common Standards for Data Collection and Reporting.* Boulder, CO: Lynne Rienner Publishers.

Herodotus (1858–60) *The History of Herodotus.* Translated by George Rawlinson. London: J. Murray.

Hill, Kim, and Hillard Kaplin (1993) "On Why Male Foragers Hunt and Share Food." *Current Anthropology* 34: 701–710.

Høygaard, Arne (1941) *Studies on the Nutrition and Physio-pathology of Eskimos, undertaken at Angmagssalik, East Greenland 1936–1937.* Norske Videnskapsakademi i Oslo. Skrifter.

Humphrey, Caroline (1998) *Marx Went Away—But Karl Stayed Behind.* Ann Arbor: University of Michigan Press.

———— (1999) "Traders, 'Disorder,' and Citizenship Regimes in Provincial Russia." Pp. 19–52 in Michael Burawoy and Katherine Verdery (eds.) *Uncertain Transition: Ethnographies of Change in the Postsocialist Word.* Lanham, MD: Rowman & Littlefield Publishers, Inc.

Ingold, Tim (1995) "Notes on the Foraging Mode of Production." Pp. 269–285 in Tim Ingold, David Riches, and James Woodburn (eds.) *Hunters and Gathers Volume 1, History, Evolution, and Social Change.* Oxford: Berg.

Islavin, V. (1847) *Samoedy v Domashnem i Obshchestbennom Bytu.* [*Samoyeds in Domestic and Social Life.*]

Ivanov, S. V., M. G. Levin, and A. V. Smolyak (1964) "The Nivkhi." Pp. 767–787 in M. G. Levin and L. P. Potapov (eds.) *The Peoples of Siberia.* Chicago: The University of Chicago Press.

Jochim, Michael A. (1976) *Hunter-Gatherer Subsistence and Settlement: A Predictive Model.* New York: Academic Press.

Karachintsev, Mefodii (1892) *Ukazi I Predpicaniia 1825 Goda 1-oi Poloviny.* [*Orders and Descriptions of the First Half of 1825.*] Materials from the Archive of the Taimyr Regional Studies Museum (TOKM 01-21/17:3).

Karlov, V. V. (1991) "Narodnosti Severa Sibiri: Osobennosti Vosproizvodstva i Al'ternativy pazvitiia." ["Peoples of Northern Siberia: Peculiarities of Reproduction and Alternatives of Development."] *Sovietskaia Etnografia* 5: 3–16.

Kerttula, Anna M. (2000) *Antler on the Sea: The Yupik and Chukchi of the Russian Far East.* Ithaca, NY: Cornell University Press.

Khazanov, Anatoly M. (1984) *Nomads and the Outside World.* New York: Cambridge University Press.

Khlobystin, L. P. (1972) "Absoliutnyi i Otnositel'nyi Vozrast Pamiatniki Tagenar VI." ["Absolute and Relative Age of the Artifacts of Tagenar VI."] Pp. 130–133 in *Problemy Absoliutnogo Datirovaniia v Archiologii.* [*Problems of Absolute Dating in Archeaology.*] Moscow: Academy of Sciences of the USSR.

———— (1982) *Drevniaia Istoria Taimyrskogo Zapoliar'e i Voprosy Formirovaniia Kultur Severa Evrazii.* [*The Ancient History of the Polar Taimyr and Questions of the Formation of the Cultures of Northern Eurasia.*] Abstract of doctoral dissertation, Moscow State University.

———— (1984) "Exchange in the Neolithic and Bronze Age in the Territory of the Forest Belt of the USSR." *ISKOS* 4: 60–63.

Khlobystin, L. P., and G. N. Gracheva (1973) "Novie Dannie o Drevnosti Taimyra." ["New Data on Antiquity in the Taimyr."] *Archiologicheskie Otkrytiia.* [*Archealogical Discoveries.*] Moscow: Academy of Sciences of the USSR.

———— (1993) "Taimyrskie Kultury i Problema Zaseleniia Vostochnoi Sibiri." ["Taimyr Cultures and the Problem of the Settlement of Eastern Siberia."] Pp. 37–38 in *Ad Polus* (*Arkhiologicheskie Izyskaniia,* Vypusk 10). [(*Archaeological Investigations,* Issue 10).]

King, Alexander (2000) "Reindeer Herders' Landscapes and Culturescapes in the Koryak Autonomous Okrug." Paper presented to the Postsocialisms in the Russian North workshop, Max Planck Institute for Social Anthropology, Halle (Saale), Germany, November 8.

Krivonogov, V. P. (1999) "Sovremennye Etnokul'turnye Protsessy u Nganasan." ["Contemporary Ethnocultural Processes Among the Nganasan."] *Etnograficheskoe Obozrenie* 1: 67–79.

Krupnik, I. I. (1987) "Demograficheskoe Razvitie Aziatskikh Eskimosov v 1970-e Gody (osnovnye tendentsii i etnosotsial'nye yslovia)." ["Demographic Development of the Asian Eskimos in the 1970s (basic trends and ethnosocial conditions)."] Pp. 85–109 in V. V. Prokhorov (ed.) *Regional'nye Problemy Sotsial'no-demograficheskogo Razvitia.* [*Regional Problems of Socio-Demographic Development.*] Moscow.

Lee, Richard B. (1993) *The Dobe Ju/'hoansi.* 2nd ed. Fort Worth, TX: Harcourt Brace College Publishers.

Levi-Strauss, Claude (1969a) *The Raw and the Cooked: Mythologiques, Volume 1.* Chicago: The University of Chicago Press.

———— (1969b) *The Elementary Structures of Kinship.* Translated from the French by James Harle Bell and John Richard von Sturmer. Boston: Beacon Press.

McCay, Bonnie J., and Svein Jentoft (1998) "Market or Community Failure? Critical Perspectives on Common Property Research." *Human Organization* 57(1): 21–29.

Melnichenko, Vladimir (1996) "Ekologia i Ya." ["Ecology and Me."] *Zapoliarnaia Pravda,* (Norilsk), No. 317 (30 May).

Milovskii, A. S. (1992) "Tubiakou's Spirit Flight: A Siberian Shaman Adapts His Ancient Profession to Modern Times." *Natural History* 7: 35–41.

Moran, Emilio F. (1995) "Introduction: Norms for Ethnographic Reporting." Pp. 1–20 in Emilio F. Moran (ed.) *The Comparative Analysis of Human Societies: Toward Common Standards for Data Collection and Reporting.* Boulder, CO: Lynne Rienner Publishers.

Morgan, Lewis H. (1870) "Systems of Consanguinity and Affinity." *Smithsonian Institution Contributions to Knowledge* 17: 218. Washington, DC: Smithsonian Institution.

Murdoch, John (1887) "On Some Popular Errors Regarding the Eskimos." *The American Naturalist* 21.

Novikova, N. I. (1994) "Khanty i Mansy: Dva Puty Razvitiia?" ["Khanty and Mansy: Two Roads of Development?"] Pp. 113–128 in Z. P. Sokolova (ed.) *Narody Severa i Sibiri v Usloviiakh Ekonomicheskikh Reform i Demokraticheskikh Preobra-*

zovanii. [*Peoples of the North and Siberia Under Conditions of Economic Reform and Democratic Transformation.*] Moscow: Institute of Ethnology and Anthropology im. N. N. Miklyukho-Maklaya, Russian Academy of Sciences.

——— (1995) "Okhotniky i Neftianiki: Vozmozhnost' Dogovora." ["Hunters and Oil Workers: The Opportunity of an Agreement."] Pp. 43–63 in Z. P. Sokolova (ed.) *Sotsial'no-Ekonomicheskoe i Kul'turnoe Razvitie Narodov Severa i Sibiri: Traditsii i Sovremennost'.* [*Social-Economic and Cultural Development of the Peoples of the North and Siberia: Tradition and Contemporaneity.*] Moscow: Institute of Ethnology and Anthropology im. N. N. Miklyukho-Maklaya, Russian Academy of Sciences.

Nuttall, Mark (1992) *Arctic Homeland: Kinship, Community, and Development in Northwest Greenland.* Toronto: University of Toronto Press.

Okladnikov, A. P. (1968) *Istoriia Sibiri: Tom Btoroi, Sibir' v Sostave Feodal'noi Rossii.* [*The History of Siberia: Volume Two, Siberia in the Structure of Feudal Russia.*] Leningrad: Nauka.

Osherenko, Gail, and Andrei V. Golovnev (1999) *Siberian Survival: The Nenets and Their Story.* Ithaca, NY: Cornell University Press.

Ostrom, Elinor (1990) *Governing the Commons: The Evolution of Institutions for Collective Action.* Cambridge: Cambridge University Press.

Pelto, Pertti J. (1987) *The Snowmobile Revolution: Technology and Social Change in the Arctic.* Prospect Heights, IL: Waveland Press.

Pelto, Pertti J., and Gretel H. Pelto (1978) *Anthropological Research: The Structure of Inquiry.* 2nd ed. New York: Cambridge University Press.

Peterson, Nicolas (1993) "Demand Sharing: Reciprocity and the Pressure for Generosity Among Foragers." *American Anthropologist* 95(4): 860–874.

Petrova, S. A. (1982) *Istoricheskaia Spravka "Istoriia Osvoyeniia Eniseiskogo Severa XVII v."* [*Historical Information "History of the Assimilation of the Yenisei North in the 17th Century."*] Unpublished manuscript from the Taimyr Regional Territorial Studies Museum archive.

Pika, A. I., and V. V. Prokhorov (1988) "Bolshie Problemy Malykh Narodov." ["Big Problems for Small Peoples."] *Kommunist* 16: 76–83.

——— (1994) *Neotraditsionalism na Rossiiskom Severe.* [*Neotraditionalism in the Russian North.*] Moscow: Institute of National Prognosis, Center for Human Demography and Ecology, Russian Academy of Sciences.

Pika, Alexander I. (1993) "The Spatial-Temporal Dynamic of Violent Death Among the Native Peoples of Northern Russia." *Arctic Anthropology* 30 (2): 61–76.

Pitul'ko, V. V. (1996) "Oleny Brook Site: A New Contribution to Taimyr Archaeology." *Terra Nostra.* Schriften der Alfred-Wegener-Stiftung 96/9: 82–83.

——— (1999a) "Ancient Humans in Eurasian Arctic Ecosystems: Environmental Dynamics and Changing Subsistence." *World Archaeology* 30 (3): 421–436.

——— (1999b) "Archaeological Survey in Central Taimyr." Pp. 457–467 in H. Kassens, H. A. Bauch, I. A. Dmitrenko, H. Eicken, H. W. Hubberten, M. Melles, J. Thiede, and L. A. Timokhov (eds.) *Land-Ocean Systems in the Siberian Arctic: Dynamics and History.* Berlin: Springer-Verlag.

——— (2001) "Terminal Pleistocene—Early Holocene Occupation in Northeast Asia and the Zhokhov Assemblage." *Quaternary Science Reviews* 20: 267–275.

Polanyi, Karl (1957) "The Economy as Instituted Process." Pp. 243–270 in K. Polanyi, C. Arensberg, and H. W. Pearson (eds.) *Trade and Market in the Early Empires.* New York: The Free Press.

Popov, A. A. (1946) "Semeinaya Zhizn' u Dolgan." ["Family Life of the Dolgan."] *Sovietskaya Etnografiia* 4.

―――― (1966) *The Nganasan: The Material Culture of the Tavgi Samoyeds.* Bloomington: Indiana University Press.

―――― (1981) "Shamanstvo u Dolgan." ["Shamanism among the Dolgan."] Pp. 253–264 in I. S. Vdovin (ed.) *Problemy Istorii Obshchestvennogo Soznaniia Aborigenov Sibiri (po Materialam Vtoroi Popviny XIX – Nachala XX v).* [*Problems of the History of Social Consciousness of the Aborigines of Siberia (from Materials of the Second Half of the 19th through the Beginning of the 20th Century).*] Leningrad: Nauka.

Radcliffe-Brown, A. R. (1951) "Introduction." Pp. 1–85 in A. R. Radcliffe-Brown and D. Forde (eds.) *African Systems of Kinship and Marriage.* London: Oxford University Press.

Ruble, Blair, Nancy Popson, and Jodi Koehn (eds.) (2000) *Fragmented Space in the Russian Federation.* Washington, DC: Woodrow Wilson Center Press.

Saggers, Sherry, and Dennis Gray (1998) *Dealing with Alcohol: Indigenous Usage in Australia, New Zealand, and Canada.* Cambridge: Cambridge University Press.

Sahlins, Marshall D. (1972) *Stone Age Economics.* Chicago: Aldine Atherton, Inc.

Sangi, Vladimir M. (1991) "Konventsiia-26 Assotsiatsii Malochislennykh Narodov Severa Rossii." ["Convention-26 of the Association of Small-Numbering Peoples of the North of Russia."] *Poliarnaia Pochta* 3(5): 1–4.

―――― (1992) "Deklaratsiia Svobodnogo Razvitiia Narodov Severa." ["Declaration of Free Development of the Peoples of the North."] *Poliarnaia Pochta* 3(2): 1–4.

Schneider, David M. (1984) *A Critique of the Study of Kinship.* Ann Arbor: The University of Michigan Press.

Semenova, Tamara, Pavel Sulyandziga, and Tatyana Vlassova (2000) "Participation of Indigenous Peoples in Building a Russian Strategy for Sustainable Development." Paper presented to the workshop Postsocialisms in the Russian North, Max Planck Institute for Social Anthropology, Halle, Germany, November 8–9.

Sergeyev, M. A. (1964) "The Building of Socialism Among the Peoples of Northern Siberia and the Soviet Far East." Pp. 487–510 in M. G. Levin and L. P. Potapov (eds.) *The Peoples of Siberia.* Chicago: The University of Chicago Press.

Service, Elman R. (1962) *Primitive Social Organization: An Evolutionary Perspective.* New York: Random House.

Shirokogoroff, S. M. (1935) *Psychomental Complex of the Tungus.* London: Kegan Paul.

Sinor, Denis (1990) *The Cambridge History of Early Inner Asia.* New York: Cambridge University Press.

Sokolova, Z. P. (1990) "Perestroika i Sud'by Malochislennykh Narodov Severa." ["Perestroika and the Fate of the Small-Numbering Peoples of the North."] *Istoriia SSSR* [*History of the USSR*] 1: 155–166.

Steadman, Lyle B. (1994) "Social Behavior and Sacrifice." Paper read at the Human Behavior and Evolution Society Meetings, Ann Arbor, Michigan, June 16.

Stefansson, Vilhjálmur (1927 [1918]) "Observations on Three Cases of Scurvy." Pp 1–9 in *Meat Diet in Health and in Disease.* Chicago: American Medical Association.

Stahl, Henri H. (1980) *Traditional Romanian Village Communities: The Transition to the Capitalist Mode of Production in the Danube Region.* Cambridge: Cambridge University Press.

Stetsyuk, R. G., N. A. Tsytsyna, O. A. Yaruntsov, Yu. Ya. Myasnyankin, and N. A. Elagin (1990) *Taimyr—Tsifry i Facty.* [*Taimyr—Figures and Facts.*] Dudinka: Obshchestvenno-Politicheskii Tsentr OK KPSS [Social-Political Center of the Organizational Committee of the CPSU].

Stone, Linda (1997) *Kinship and Gender: An Introduction.* Boulder, CO: Westview Press.

Stoner-Weiss, Katheryn (1997) "Federalism and Regionalism." Pp. 229–250 in Stephen White, Alex Pravda, and Zvi Gitelman (eds.) *Developments in Russian Politics 4.* Durham, NC: Duke University Press.

Thomas, William A. (1927) "Health of a Carnivorous Race—A Study of the Eskimo." Pp. 14–18 in *Meat Diet in Health and in Disease.* Chicago: American Medical Association.

Tonkinson, Robert (1978) *The Mardudjara Aborigines: Living the Dream in Australia's Desert.* New York: Holt, Rinehart and Winston.

Troitskii, V. A. (1987) *Khatanga: Goroda i Poselki Krasnoyarskogo Kraia.* [*Khatanga: Cities and Settlements of Krasnoyarskii Krai.*] Krasnoyarsk: Knizhnoe Izdatel'stvo.

Tylor, Edward B. (1924 [1871]) *Primitive Culture: Researches into the Development of Mythology, Philosophy, Religion, Language, Art, and Custom.* New York: Brentano's.

Uvachan, V. N. (1971) *Put' Narodov Severa k Sotsializmy.* [*The Path of the Peoples of the North to Socialism.*] Moscow: Mysl'.

Vainshtein, S. I. (1991) *Mir Kochevnikov Tsentra Azii.* [*The World of Central Asian Nomads.*] Moscow: Nauka Publishers.

van den Berghe, Pierre L. (1979) *Human Family Systems: An Evolutionary View.* Prospect Heights, IL: Waveland Press, Inc.

——— (1987) *The Ethnic Phenomenon.* New York: Praeger.

Vishnevskii, A. G. (ed.) (1994) *Naselenie Rossii 1994: Vtoroi Ezhegodnyi Demograficheskii Doklad.* [*The Population of Russia 1994: The Second Annual Demographic Report.*] Moscow: Institute of Domestic Forecasting and the Center for Demography and Human Ecology, Russian Academy of Sciences.

——— (1998) *Serp i Rubl'.* [*Scythe and Ruble.*] Moscow: OMI.

——— (1999) *Naselenie Rossii 1998: Shestoi Ezhegodnyi Demograficheskii Doklad.* [*The Population of Russia 1998: The Sixth Annual Demographic Report.*] Moscow: Institute of Domestic Forecasting and the Center for Demography and Human Ecology, Russian Academy of Sciences.

Wallerstein, Immanuel M. (2000) *The Essential Wallerstein.* New York: New Press.

Weatherford, Jack (1988) *Indian Givers.* New York: Fawcett Columbine.

Wedel, Janine R. (1998) *Collision and Collusion: The Strange Case of Western Aid to Eastern Europe 1989–1998.* New York : St. Martin's Press.

Weller, Susan C., and A. Kimball Romney (1988) *Systematic Data Collection.* Newbury Park, CA.: Sage Publications.

Wiessner, Pauline (1977) *Hxaro: A Regional System of Reciprocity for the !Kung San.* Ph.D. dissertation. University of Michigan, Ann Arbor.

Wilk, Richard R. (1996) *Economies and Cultures: Foundations of Economic Anthropology.* Boulder, CO: Westview Press.

Winterhalder, Bruce (1997) "Gifts Given, Gifts Taken: The Behavioral Ecology of Nonmarket, Intragroup Exchange." *Journal of Archaeological Research* 5(2): 121–168.

Wixman, Ronald (1984) *The Peoples of the USSR: An Ethnographic Handbook.* Armonk, NY: M. E. Sharpe.

Wolf, Eric R. (1982) *Europe and the People without History.* Berkeley: University of California Press.

Wolkonsky, Catherine A., and Marianna A. Poltoratsky (1961) *Handbook of Russian Roots.* New York: Columbia University Press.

Woodburn, James (1982) "Egalitarian Societies." *Man* (n.s.) 17: 431–451.

——— (1998) "Sharing is Not a Form of Exchange: An Analysis of Property-Sharing in Immediate-Return Hunter-Gatherer Societies." Pp. 48–63 in C. M. Hann (ed.) *Property Relations.* Cambridge: Cambridge University Press.

Wright, Sewall (1922) "Coefficients of Inbreeding and Relationship." *American Naturalist* 56: 330–338.

Yeltsin, B. N. (1992) "Ykaz Prezidenta Rossiiskoi Federatsii o Neotlozhnykh Merakh po Zashchite Mest Prozhivaniia i Khoziaistvennoi Deiatel'nosti Malochislennykh Narodov Severa, No. 397." ["Decree of the President of the Russian Federation About Immediate Measures for Protection of Places of Residence and Economic Activities of the Small-Numbering Peoples of the North, No. 397."] *Rossiiskie Vesti* (Moscow), April, No. 4 (50): 4.

Ziker, John P. (1998a) "Kinship and Exchange Among the Dolgan and Nganasan of Northern Siberia." Pp. 191–238 in Barry Isaac (ed.) *Research in Economic Anthropology,* Volume 19. Greenwich, CT: JAI Press.

——— (1998b) "Land Tenure and Economic Collapse in Northern Siberia." *Arctic Research in the U.S.* Volume 12: 73–80. Arlington, VA: National Science Foundation, Interagency Arctic Research Policy Committee.

——— (1999) "Survival Economy and Core-Periphery Dynamics in the Taimyr Autonomous Region, Russia." *Anthropology of Eastern Europe Review* 17(2): 59–65.

——— (2001) "Land Use and Social Change among the Dolgan and Nganasan of Northern Siberia." Pp. 47–66 in David G. Anderson and Kazunobo Ikeya (eds.), *Parks, Property, Power: Managing Hunting Practice and Identity within State Policy Regimes. Senri Ethnological Studies No. 59.* Osaka: National Museum of Ethnology.

Ziker, John, and Ivan Shmetterling (1997) "Robinzony i Piatnisty, Odnako." ["Robinsons and Fridays, You Don't Say."] *Ekspert* 48: 82–85.

Archival Sources

GATAO = Government Archive of the Taimyr Autonomous Region

TOKM = Taimyr Regional Territory-Studies Museum Archival Fund

TOKM GIK = Taimyr Regional Territory-Studies Museum Main Inventory Book

TOKM NSKF = Taimyr Regional Territory-Studies Museum Scientific-Informational Card Index of Facts

Archival References

TOKM A: 1-2. "Dudinka Merchants and Their Morals." Copy of remembrances of Viktor Koreshkov from the Norilsk Museum.

TOKM 01-21/5a: 1. Copies of materials "About the 1932 Merchant Rebellion in the Khatanga and Avam Tundra" from the GATAO Archive: Letter addressed to "Everyone, Everyone, Everyone!"

TOKM 01-21/5a: 2. Copies of materials "About the 1932 Merchant Rebellion in the Khatanga and Avam Tundra" from the GATAO Archive: Telegram from Ustritskii.

TOKM 01-21/5a. 2a. Copies of materials "About the 1932 Merchant Rebellion in the Khatanga and Avam Tundra" from the GATAO Archive: Telegram 2 from Ustritskii.

TOKM 01-21/5a: 3. Copies of materials "About the 1932 Merchant Rebellion in the Khatanga and Avam Tundra" from the GATAO Archive: Telegram from Zolotukhin.

TOKM 01-21/5a: 4. Copies of materials "About the 1932 Merchant Rebellion in the Khatanga and Avam Tundra" from the GATAO Archive: Telegram of the Congress of April 4-6, 1932 on the Avam.

TOKM 01-21/5a: 7. Copies of materials "About the 1932 Merchant Rebellion in the Khatanga and Avam Tundra" from the GATAO Archive: Informational Letter No. 106/ss.

TOKM 01-21/5b. List of collective farms in the Taimyr National Region for June 20, 1937.

TOKM 01-21/5c. List of kulaks, shamans of Ust-Yeneseiskii raion, 1938. Copies of materials from the GATAO Archive.

TOKM 01-21/17: 1. Materials from the TOKM Archive: Alphabetical list of native tribes and nations living in Yeneseiskaia gubernia.

TOKM 01-21/17: 3. Karachintsev, Mefodii. File of inventories 1892, No. 134; "Towards information and a guide, volume 1 for 1825"—renamed case "Orders and descriptions for the first half of 1825."

TOKM 4696(1): 1–6. "Remembrances of the Events of 1932." V. Solovyov, former member of the management of the Volochanka Cooperative, 1979.

TOKM GIK 111. Edict from February 1, 1930 about the order of conducting the dispossession of the kulaks.

TOKM GIK 112. Edict from June 6, 1938 about the confiscation of reindeer from *kulaks* (Case No. 7 *Gosarkhiv*).

TOKM GIK 288. Protocols of the closed meetings of the presidium *Okrispolkoma* for 1938 about the transfer of reindeer of repressed kulaks, shamans, and kings to collective farms.

TOKM GIK 465. Acts for giving and receiving reindeer, 1938.

Study Guide

Prepared by

Ann McElroy

University at Buffalo, State University of New York

Change in contemporary indigenous cultures usually involves transformations from traditional patterns to modern forms. In *Peoples of the Tundra*, John Ziker introduces us to an alternative model of change dynamics in two Siberian populations, the Dolgan and Nganasan of the Taimyr Autonomous Region. These two groups, ethnically and linguistically distinct but inhabiting common territory, accommodated to programs and policies of the USSR government for more than 70 years. Both groups have undergone major economic reversals after the collapse of the Soviet Union in 1991. Without wage income or a dependable supply of consumer goods, many people have found it necessary to return to a subsistence economy as hunters, fishers, and trappers. Ziker's research in this region from 1992 to 1997 documents the survival value of traditional foraging practices and sharing patterns for people coping with economic uncertainty and political turmoil in a multi-ethnic Siberian community.

The Dolgan and Nganasan are two of 26 indigenous ethnic groups in the Siberian North. The total population of all 26 groups is about 160,000; Dolgans number about 6,000 and Nganasans around 1,000. Nganasans speak a Samoyedic language and about 70 percent also speak Russian; some also speak Dolgan. From Dudinka, there are radio broadcasts in Nganasan and in Dolgan. Dolgans speak a language that is closely related to Yakut, a Turkic language. About 73 percent of Dolgans also use Russian, and their children are educated in Russian. Unlike Nganasan, which is not written, there are published works in the Dolgan language. (This information is from Dirmid Collis' *Arctic Languages*, UNESCO, 1990.) Both the Dolgan and Nganasan languages are taught in the Ust Avam grade school as electives.

Page 1

Ziker suggests that understanding native responses to the economic instability of post-Soviet transition will help us learn about "the resiliency of tradition." What does the word "tradition" mean to you? Do you see tradition as a positive part of your life? Have the traditions of your family and community remained resilient during recent periods of crisis and uncertainty?

Pages 2-3

The Dolgan and Nganasan live in an *okrug* (a governmentally designated district), the Taimyr Autonomous Region, that is twice the area of California (332,850 square miles or 862,100 square kilometers). About 10,000 indigenous people and 45,000 Russians and Ukrainians live in this region. Using an atlas or the Internet to obtain the current population of your home state or province, calculate and compare its density to that of the Taimyr Autonomous Region. Chances are that you live in a region with a much higher population size and density than the area Ziker studied. Why does the Taimyr region have such a low population? What aspects of the climate reinforce its low density?

Pages 3-4

Looking at Figures 1.1 and 1.2, you can see that the Taimyr Autonomous Region is well north of the Arctic Circle (66° 33'). How cold do you think it gets in winter in this region? How warm in summer? How much snow falls each year? You may be surprised how little! Use your encyclopedia or other reference materials to learn about Arctic climates. An excellent source is *To the Arctic: An Introduction to the Far Northern World* by Steven B. Young (1994, John Wiley & Son, Inc.)

Page 4

Dolgan people call themselves *tiajono*, meaning "people of the tundra" in their language. The Nganasan people refer to themselves as *nya*, which simply means "people." Many indigenous people are called one term in the history books and a different term in their own language. The name by which an indigenous group identifies itself is called an ethnonym. In recent years, many groups have asserted the right to have their ethnonyms used in the media, in published materials, and especially in government documents.

Do you recognize these ethnonyms: Inuit, Yup'ik, Inupiat, Kalaallit, Dene, or Saami? If not, use library reference materials or do an on-line search to find these names (spellings may vary). What meaning do you think they have in common? Why do you think so many native peoples early in their contact history with outsiders such as explorers and missionaries were called a name that turned out not to be correct? What does this phenomenon suggest about the history of colonialism?

Pages 9–11

The bleak economic picture that Ziker describes for Ust Avam in 1997 is a microcosmic reflection of financial hardship in the entire Russian Federation. Do you think that the economy of Russia, and especially of the Siberian regions, has improved or deteriorated since 1997? Consult recent news accounts about the Russian political economy to obtain current information.

Pages 12–16

Anthropological fieldwork depends on the kindness of strangers. Ziker, a graduate student visiting Arctic Russia in search of a good site for doctoral research in 1992, found himself mentored by a network of indigenous people. One mentor was a Dolgan artist named Boris Molchanov; later Boris' widow and cousin helped Ziker find a field site. The cousin took Ziker, just arrived in the village of Ust Avam, on a one-week hunting and trapping trip in the bush in January, one of the coldest and darkest months of the year. It was critical that Ziker learn how to protect himself from freezing and to function at least half-competently in this new environment. Ziker's detailed description of his experiences gives us a sense of how challenging this field site was, and yet how essential it was for him to participate in hunting and trapping as well as observing what others did. Participant observation, the core methodology of cultural anthropology, is often described as a "trial by fire" by novice researchers, whether the field site is a tundra trap line or the ER of an inner-city hospital.

Page 17

Ziker's research plan was to compare two types of households in order to test a new model of change that he called a "survival-economy model." The two household types were those that maintained rights to use state-enterprise hunting land and those, in the minority, that claimed hunting territory as a family/clan holding.

Do you and your friends or relatives participate in sharing networks? What goods and services are shared? Would it change things if everything had a price tag on it, and everyone expected to be paid for services? What are some of the fundamental differences in how people interact when they are functioning in a market economy or in a sharing network?

Page 23

Each chapter begins with a different motif, a design that is both abstract and traditional. Where do you think Ziker found these designs? What might they symbolize? Look ahead in the book to get some clues about who made the designs and how they are displayed. (Hint: try pages 44 and 110.)

Page 24

Tundra and *taiga* are Russian words. Taiga means coniferous forests, and tundra means a flat, boggy, treeless plain typical of the Arctic. As you read, look for other Russian words that have diffused into English. Some may have changed in connotation; for example, *soviet* simply means "council" in Russian, while in English it denotes the hierarchical government structure of the former Soviet Union.

Pages 27–28

Why do you think the Russian government forbids hunting of mountain sheep and musk oxen?

Pages 29–30

Our 12-month calendar, with names of Roman gods, festivals, and emperors, would be meaningless to Arctic hunters and reindeer herders. What are the important seasonal changes by which the Nganasan number their days? Why do you think they observe two years instead of only one in a 12-month span? For Dolgan people, what seasonal elements figure into their names for months?

Page 31

Bear meat is a good source of protein and fat, but neither Dolgan nor Nganasan eat bear. What are the cultural reasons they give for not using bear as a source of food? What might some practical reasons be?

Page 32

Why would Russian city-dwellers want to be flown into the region to hunt caribou? Do you think it is for sport? For needed supplies of meat? For money?

Pages 36–40

As in many subsistence economies, it is not only adult men who work to produce food and other goods, but all age groups. Ziker says that young children are "significant producers of burbot," a freshwater fish caught with bait and hooks. Elderly men also fish, and retired men and women tan animal furs and skins. Children help to gather mushrooms and berries in summer. In your own community, do children have important roles in the economy as producers? Do elders? Or are they mostly consumers?

Pages 43–44

A gendered division of labor, with men hunting and women processing skins and distributing food, is characteristic of most Arctic and subarctic cultures. The people of Ust Avam are no different. When women have a crucial, indispensable role in a society's economic structure, what effect do you think this has on women's status?

Pages 47–53

This section presents data for assessing Ziker's survival-economy model. Judging from the quotes by Sergei, Valery, and others, do you think that people share food just to create reciprocal exchanges? Are there other reasons? The "ethic of sharing" seems to play a role, reinforcing the value of dispersing surplus by giving food to families that cannot reciprocate in the short run.

Pages 54–55

Food has symbolic value as well as practical functions. Oksye's wedding feast was a mix of traditional country food and Russian delicacies. What foods (and drink) do you associate with weddings, holidays, or birthdays?

Page 63

Why is this chapter titled "The Loud Years"? Does it suggest that people protested against colonization and collectivization? Were these protests heard in Moscow?

Page 64

The earliest human activity on the Taimyr Peninsula, found in a Mesolithic or Middle Stone Age site, dates to 7,000 years B.P. (before the present). This date may seem quite recent to students familiar with sites in Africa dating more than a million years ago. Many archaeological sites across Siberia, northern North America, and Greenland are quite recent. Sites in northern Chukotka, not far from the Bering Strait, date around 6,000 B.P.

Further east, the Dorset people occupied a wide area of what is now Canada and Greenland from about 2,500 years B.P. to about 1,000 years B.P., when they were apparently displaced or assimilated by Thule people.

Page 66

Russians moved into the Siberian Arctic in the late sixteenth century, claiming territory in the name of the czar, Ivan IV, also known as Ivan the Terrible. Tribute, a forced payment of goods from the subjugated indigenous people, was taken primarily in furs. Similar encounters occurred in the Aleutian Islands, now part of Alaska, where native peoples were forced to extract resources (principally sea otter and seal furs) to appease invading Russians. In the eastern Arctic, sixteenth-century encounters between Thule people and the crews of British explorer Sir Martin Frobisher were also motivated by a desire to use the northern lands for economic goals, primarily to find and navigate the Northwest Passage and secondarily to bring back gold and other valuable minerals.

To appreciate the magnitude of colonial expansion into Arctic regions between the sixteenth and nineteenth centuries, you could develop, perhaps as a group project, a time-line for European intrusion into the northern regions of Siberia, Alaska, Canada, and Greenland. Two valuable sources for this project are *Crossroads of Continents: Cultures of Siberia and Alaska*, edited by William W. Fitzhugh and Aron Crowell (1988, Smithsonian Institution Press) and *The Handbook of North American Indians*, Volume 5, edited by David Damas (1984, Smithsonian Institution Press).

Page 69

Here we discover that the Dolgan nationality was *created* by colonialism. The ancestors of the Dolgan were bands of herders called Yakut and Evenk who came in the seventeenth century from more southern regions of Siberia to get away from tribute collectors. These herders intermarried with Russians and with other people such as the reindeer-herding Nenets, who spoke Samoyedic languages. Dolgan is actually the name of one of the patrilineal clans of these Yakut-Evenk-Russian populations, but the name has prevailed in ethnographies and in government records. Can you think of other communities, ethnic populations, or even whole nations that were formed artificially through political compromise in the nineteenth and twentieth centuries? (Hint: look at the history of Yugoslavia.)

Page 70

Like other colonial institutions, the "bread-reserve" stores established in 1822 illustrate the mixed benefits and detriments of paternalistic policies. Do you think their benefits to the indigenous people outweighed their negative effects?

Pages 73-76

Paradoxically, the Communist Party of the 1920s found the customs of indigenous Siberians to be "relics of primitive communism," that is, too communistic and not close enough to socialism. The structure superimposed by the party onto the traditional ethic of sharing and mutual aid included "comradeship units" and collective farms. The government provided tools and trade goods, and the people in turn produced commodities from the land such as fish, furs, and caribou meat and skins, a ubiquitous model of change attempted throughout the Siberian Arctic. Did this experiment work? What were some barriers to successful operation? Would you expect resistance among hunters and herders to this program of "collectivization"?

Page 76

Why did the government administrators decide to open a boarding school for indigenous children in the middle of the conflict about forced sale of reindeer to create a reindeer-herding farm? What effect do you think this decision had on people attempting to resist collectivization? Do you think that school attendance was voluntary?

Page 78

If Aksinya "Oksye" Bezrukikh, narrator of "The Loud Year," was a firsthand observer of the rebellion against Russian policies in 1932, how old was she when she told the story to Ziker? How does she recall such vivid detail?

Ziker translates most of Oksye's story, but he keeps an unfamiliar word, *argish*, in the account. We learn later that an argish is a caravan of sleighs of various sizes pulled by reindeer and that the verb "argished" means the movement of entire extended families, with their animals and belongings, north to the tundra or south to grasslands and boreal forest. A model argish is shown on page 117.

Page 79

Arrests and executions of leaders, mostly community elders and shamans, followed the 1932 insurrection. The reindeer belonging to these men were confiscated and transferred to collective farms. What was the impact of these repressive actions on the communities involved?

Pages 86-88

Ziker suggests that unemployment, alcohol abuse, and violent mortality (accidents, homicide, suicide) are correlated problems. He quotes a leader of the Saami (a reindeer-herding people of Arctic Scandinavia as well as of Russia), who believes that unemployment and suicide among the Saami are caused by alcoholism. Have you heard of other indigenous people whose drinking behavior is considered a serious problem by social scientists? Which do you think came first, the unemployment or the alcohol abuse?

Pages 88–89

Through demographic data, Ziker is able to estimate the extent of interethnic marriage in Ust Avam. At the age of 16, when they receive internal passports, children of mixed ancestry are allowed to choose the ethnic identity they prefer. How does this way of designating racial or ethnic identity differ from customary patterns in North America, for example when diversity in schools or employment is being assessed?

Page 90

The population of Ust Avam declined between 1993 and 1997. Before reading the various reasons Ziker gives for this decline, think about how and why any small town in North America might lose population. List three or four of the major factors. Then as you read further, see if the factors you listed are the same as those that Ziker mentions.

Pages 92–95

Ziker makes a convincing case for his claim that fertility is unusually low among women of childbearing age in Ust Avam. Is this an isolated case, or are other regions of eastern Europe experiencing fertility decline? According to the World Health Organization, in the year 2000 the total fertility rate in Belarus was 1.2; in Bulgaria it was 1.1; in Latvia, 1.1; and the Russian Federation, 1.2. The rate in Canada was 1.6 and in the U.S., 2.0. (In contrast, the fertility rate in Rwanda was 6.0 and Afghanistan, 6.9). These figures clarify the situation in Ust Avam. Population decline there is not an anomaly, but part of a current trend in many developed and developing countries.

Page 95

Infant mortality rates are based on deaths of children from birth to 12 months. The 1996 rate of 87 deaths per 1,000 live births in Ust Avam is much higher than in many countries. (Infant mortality in China in 1993 was 35 per 1,000; in India it was 81 per 1,000; in Finland only 4 per 1,000). But when the population is small, it helps to look at the frequency (the actual numbers) of deaths, which in this case are two infants out of 23 born. In the next age group, 5–9, there were no deaths in 116 children, and there was one death among 95 children aged 10 to 14. What additional information would you need to decide whether Ust Avam has un-usually high infant mortality rates, or whether the rates for 1996 were a statistical anomaly?

Page 97

Violent deaths, a category that includes accidents, homicide, and sui-cide, are the highest cause of death in Ust Avam. What categories (age, gender, ethnicity) of people in your society have high death rates due to accidents or other violent causes? If you were not sure, how would you find out? Do you think that drinking alcoholic beverages plays a role in the death rates in Ust Avam? In your own society?

Pages 100–102

Why the violent death rate among Nganasan females is so much higher than among Dolgan females is a mystery. What information do we need to make sense of this difference?

Page 106

The religions and myths of many indigenous peoples contain animistic elements. Animism involves belief in the spirits and souls of both living and non-living things. Not only does an animal (say a bear, a bird, or a fox) have a soul and conscious awareness, just as people do, but in animis-tic thinking, a tree also might have a spirit, as well as a rock, water, the moon, the sky. Both animals and non-living entities can take on human characteristics, act like humans, and affect human destiny. For a look at animism in European culture, consider familiar European folk tales such as "Little Red Riding Hood" or "Goldilocks".

Page 107

The story that Dulsimyaku tells about the baby loon is called a cre-ation myth by anthropologists. Is there a creation story in your family's cultural or religious background?

Pages 107–108

Are you surprised to read that Dulsimyaku and the Ngumtuso ensem-ble allowed a shamanistic performance at the school to be videotaped? What assumptions would lead someone to think that shamanistic rituals would be private and hidden from the camera?

The object Dulsimyaku is holding in Figure 5.1 is an animal skin drum. All across the Arctic, shamans used drums to call their spirit helpers and to help those in the ordinary earth world move into other worlds. On both sides of the Bering Strait, drum dances were central elements of ceremonies honoring the dead. In many northern regions, songs and ceremonies using the drum were suppressed by missionaries and government authorities opposed to shamanism and were almost forgotten by the mid-twentieth century. But in recent years, drum dancing and singing have had an extraordinary rebirth.

Page 109

What does the word "séance" suggest to you? Do you have images of a group of people holding hands in a dark room while a psychic calls up a deceased spirit? Ziker's description here indicates there might be several types of séances.

Pages 111–115

"The Underground Kingdom," *Annyky Doidu*, is a powerful story of a man, a loner who has no interest in other people. One day he falls through a void in his world and ends up in an underground world. People who are living out their lives there, living in tents (*chum*) and herding reindeer, can't see the man who has fallen into their world, but they can sense his presence and are affected by him. Only a shaman can see him and can return him to his home. After returning, the man feels transformed and decides that it is a "sin to live alone."

This mythic odyssey reflects many aspects of Dolgan cosmology and shamanism. Ziker mentions several central themes on page 115. Can you find other themes in the story? What about the man's hunger and his inability to get food? What about the danger he posed to the reindeer and to the young girl who became sick when he touched her? Do the elements of this myth remind you of other stories you know of someone trapped in a strange world, trying to return home, and learning from the experience the value of being at home?

Pages 116–118

Shamans were not priests or healers, strictly speaking, but they were ritual specialists. Anyone who had supernatural powers, both women and men, could be shamans. People either inherited shamanic skills from a relative, learned them by serving as apprentice to a shaman, or acquired these abilities after a near-death experience. People often asked shamans to intercede with the spirit world in times of sickness, poor hunting, and other misfortunes, but it was believed that shamans could also *cause* misfortune. The power to do both good and evil made shamans frightening to many people. If you want to read further, a good source is *Studies in Siberian Shamanism*, edited by Henry N. Michael (U. of Toronto Press, 1963).

Page 119

The Dolgan concept of sin functions much as taboos do: if you behave in a certain way and break the rules, there will be negative consequences. This reasoning is reinforced when a person dies early, miscarries a pregnancy, or becomes sick after having committed the "sin" (the proscribed behavior). There may be no direct cause and effect between a man using a tractor on the delicate tundra ground and dying at the age of 53, but people interpret this outcome as proof that the hunter's behavior had broken "the laws of nature" and led indirectly to misfortune.

Page 121–122

Can you see a connection between animism and the concept of sacred places? Are you surprised that for the Nganasan, graves are among the most sacred places?

Page 123

Syncretism occurs in many religions when people interact and cultures blend. Examples include Umbanda and Macumba, Brazilian possession-trance cults featuring complicated mixtures of Catholic, Indian, and African beliefs and practices.

Page 125

In your society, what legal procedures establish ownership of a parcel of land? In your community, can families or kin groups inherit or purchase land together, or only individuals? What is the situation regarding tribal claims or holdings of land in your province or state?

Pages 126–127

Do you think President Yeltsin's decree of 1992 to establish family/clan holdings in Siberia was a popular or unpopular move? Why do you think so?

Page 128

Why would members of family/clan holdings be called "renters," a derogatory term? What were some of the negative aspects of claiming land through family/clan holdings? What were positive aspects? Which would you choose in that situation?

Page 129

The hunter that Ziker is quoting here is referring to the Russian mafia, an economic class of financiers and entrepreneurs who control and distrib-

ute goods, often through illegal means, in a huge black market and underground (unofficial) economy.

Page 130

Cultural mapping, a useful method for showing economic and social
change, can be done through archived records or through actual maps, on the
ground survey of use patterns of land units. In this case, Ziker uses records.
Do you think this was a more efficient methodology for his purposes?

Pages 131–134

Economic decisions (in this case, whether to claim a family/clan holding) are not necessarily pragmatic, rational, or the result of a formal decision-making process. Ziker's survey shows considerable variation in reasons
hunters claimed or did not claim land holdings. Thinking back on major decisions you and your family have made, how many of them were based on
pragmatic planning? How many were based on other considerations?

Page 135

Given what you have learned about indigenous hunting and trapping
patterns, what is the fundamental problem with the Dudinka government's
expectations that land holdings be used actively year after year?

Page 137

Ziker developed the map in Figure 6.4 using a Garmin GPS instrument.
GPS stands for global positioning system. Originally developed in the 1970s
by the military, GPS uses data communication from global satellites to mobile user terminals. The data allow the user to map geographic locations, in
this case hunting cabins, animal slaughtering stations, and other features
that show use patterns on land holdings and areas held in common.

Page 140–141

In these semi-structured interviews Ziker is attempting to understand
principles of property use. Which properties were considered exclusive
and which were open to others? The answers reflect a general openness to
allowing others to travel through or even to use one's territory. One reason
for this apparent flexibility is that many northern peoples are highly defer-
ent and non-intrusive. This means they don't confront others face to face,
they don't impose themselves on others, and they prefer not to have others
tell them what to do. It is a way of minimizing conflict in a culture where
cooperation is essential that has been described in Athapaskan and Al-
gonkian Indians, in Inuit of Canada, and in Inupiat of Alaska. The answers

to Ziker's questions may have tapped a similar pattern in the personalities of his respondents.

Pages 143–144

Tables 6.4 and 6.5 reflect some remarkable trends: local identity is becoming more important than ethnic identity, and ethnic boundaries are becoming blurred. Most puzzling is the priority given to a "local person" over "relative" and "close relative" in answers to "Who do you prefer to have visit to hunt on your territory?" Something in the wording may give a clue. If the English version is a literal translation of the question, perhaps relatives do not "visit," whereas a local non-relative could be considered a visitor on one's property.

Page 152

If food distribution in your country or region became disrupted and you could not buy meat, vegetables, or dairy products in grocery stores near your home, what would you do? Do you or people in your family know how to get food without purchasing it? Would you share any surplus you had? Why or why not?

Page 153

Ziker suggests that "organized ethnic violence" has not developed in this region because many people with multi-ethnic ancestry can bridge the ethnic groups. Why would one expect ethnic violence in this community? What aspects of eastern European history in the last decade might lead one to expect tensions and violence in a multi-ethnic community?

Pages 154–155

Many Arctic peoples had bilateral kinship systems at the point of contact with Europeans. Bilateral means that kinship and descent are reckoned on both your mother's and father's sides of the family. Unilineal systems (matrilineal or patrilineal) recognize descent only from one side, even though biological relationships on both sides are known. When kinship systems were being categorized and labeled in the nineteenth century, this bilateral pattern was called the "Eskimo" kinship system. The chances are good that you recognize both your mother's side and your father's side as kin, so you probably use an "Eskimo" system.

Page 155

Identities can be known not only through clan names, but also through local group names referring to a place or direction, plus a suffix -alar/-ilar meaning "people of" (such as *Maragilar,* Eastern Dolgan, *Mast-*

agilar, Woods Dolgan, *Uhagilar,* Western Dolgan). This system is also used by Inuit in Canada, where *-miut* means "people of." Thus the full name of the Netsilik Inuit is *Netsilingmiut,* meaning "people of the seal."

Page 156

The *emic* perspective means not only the insider's views or perception, but also the categories and meanings unique to a given cultural system. *Etic* categories are broad units of analysis (e.g., kinship, marriage, property, territory, etc.) into which anthropologists classify the tremendous variety of emic patterns learned in fieldwork. The question Ziker asked to get at these emic variants was what role did relatives play in the lives of the people he interviewed. Ask the same question of your classmates. How much variation in answers do you get? Do some of your answers overlap those given by Ziker's respondents?

Pages 156–158

Try the same experiment that Ziker did in his University of Alaska Fairbanks class: ask your classmates "who has a relative in the class?" Then ask: "who has a relative at this college/university?" Then: "in this town/city?" (You could also try other categories, such as "best friend"). Keep track of the numbers so that you can map the social environment, the kin-based networks, and the density of social ties of students at your campus. Compare what you find to Ziker's findings about the social environment of Dolgan and of Nganasan people.

Page 159–160

Why do you think the end of socialism was mourned in eastern Europe? Why was it viewed as a "golden age"? What has been lost with the dissolution of the Soviet Union? Why didn't the democratic reforms of the early 1990s work better?

Page 161

Ziker writes that remote native communities in the Russian North have become isolated from the national economy. The situation is very different in Alaska and in northern Canada. The Alaskan Lands Settlement Act of 1971 formed native corporations to manage lands and to use compensation monies for community development. Some of the Alaskan corporations, especially the North Slope Borough of the Arctic Slope Regional Corporation, have made large profits through leases to oil companies, and these profits have led to new housing and schools, ownership of radio and television stations, and other investments. In Canada, settlement of land claims and establishment of the Nunavut Territory in 1999 have also led to an enhanced standard of living. Living conditions are also quite good in Kalaallit Nunaat (Greenland), which is now autonomous but is still tightly connected to the Danish economy and politically part of Denmark.

The Russian Association of Indigenous Peoples of the North (RAIPON) is well aware of the successful models of other northern regions and is working to address concerns about the undue poverty and isolation of the Taimyr population. Access the website for RAIPON that Ziker provides (http://www.raipon.org/) to find out what the organization is doing currently.

Page 162

What do you think is the position of the WWF (World Wildlife Fund) regarding animal trapping in the Russian Arctic? How could you find out?

Page 163

To learn more about northern regionalism, look for information on the Inuit Circumpolar Conference (www.inuit.org), the Northern Forum (www.northernforum.org), or the Nunavut Territory (www.gov.nu.ca or www.nunavut.com). Another excellent online source on Arctic history in North America is http://arcticcircle.uconn.edu.